Cost of Capital

Cost of Capital

Estimation and Applications

Shannon P. Pratt, CFA, FASA, CBA

JOHN WILEY & SONS, INC.

New York • Chichester • Weinheim • Brisbane • Singapore • Toronto

Copyright © 1998 by John Wiley & Sons, Inc. All rights reserved.

Published simultaneously in Canada.

Library of Congress Cataloging-in-Publication Data:

Pratt, Shannon P.
    Cost of capital : estimation and applications / Shannon P. Pratt.
      p. cm.
    Includes index.
    ISBN 0-471-19751-3 (cloth : alk. paper)
    1. Capital investments — United States.   2. Business enterprises —
Valuation — United States. I. Title.
HG4028.C4P72   1998
658.15'2 — dc21   97-48814

To my family

Millie

Son Mike Pratt
Daughter-in-law Barbara Brooks
   Randall
   Kenneth
Portland, Oregon

Daughter Georgia Senor
Son-in-law Tom Senor
   Elisa
   Katie
   Graham
Fayetteville, Arkansas

Daughter Susie Wilder
Son-in-law Tim Wilder
   John
   Calvin
Springfield, Virginia

Son Steve Pratt
Daughter-in-law Jenny Pratt
   Adeline
Pasadena, California

and the rest of the grandchildren to come

About the Author

Shannon P. Pratt is a founder and a managing director of Willamette Management Associates, one of the oldest and largest independent valuation consulting, economic analysis, and financial advisory services firms, with offices in principal cities across the United States. He is also a member of the board of directors of Paulson Capital Corp., an investment banking firm.

Over the last 30 years, he has performed valuation engagements for mergers and acquisitions, employee stock ownership plans (ESOPs), fairness opinions, gift and estate taxes, incentive stock options, buy-sell agreements, corporate and partnership dissolutions, dissenting stockholder actions, damages, marital dissolutions, and many other business valuation purposes. He has testified in a wide variety of federal and state courts across the country and frequently participates in arbitration and mediation proceedings.

He holds a doctorate in business administration from Indiana University and is a Chartered Financial Analyst, a Fellow of the American Society of Appraisers, a Certified Business Appraiser, and a Certified Business Counselor. Dr. Pratt's professional recognitions include designation as a Life Member of the Business Valuation Committee of the American Society of Appraisers, past chairman and a Life Member of the ESOP Association Valuation Advisory Committee, and a Life Member of the Institute of Business Appraisers. He currently serves as a Trustee-at-Large of the Appraisal Foundation.

Dr. Pratt is coauthor of *Valuing a Business: The Analysis and Appraisal of Closely Held Companies*, third edition, and *Valuing Small Businesses and Professional Practices*, third edition (both published by McGraw-Hill, Inc.) and *Guide to Business Valuations*, seventh edition (published by Practitioners Publishing Company). He is also editor-in-chief of *Shannon Pratt's Business Valuation Update*, a monthly newsletter on business valuation, and *Pratt's Stats*, a database of privately held business sale transactions. He is a member of the editorial advisory board and a columnist for *Valuation Strategies*, a bimonthly journal.

Dr. Pratt is a course developer and teacher of business valuation courses for the American Society of Appraisers and the American Institute of Certified Public Accountants and a frequent speaker on business valuation at national legal, professional, and trade association meetings. He is currently developing a new course on business valuation for judges and attorneys.

Contents

List of Exhibits

Foreword

Shannon Pratt has been a leader in the valuation field for decades, writing numerous books, operating a consulting and valuation firm, and producing such industry resources as *Shannon Pratt's Business Valuation Update* and *Pratt's Stats*. He has been a collector and provider of data and information on prices, ratios, deals, and sales, as well as legal and tax developments in the industry. He has been a developer and compiler of theoretical approaches and practical procedures. It is now particularly exciting that he has turned his attention to the cost of capital.

The cost of capital is a critical component of both the valuation and the corporate decision-making processes. Yet the theory is much less understood than the theory of forecasting expected cash flows. For example, increasing leverage may increase the cost of equity and the cost of debt without necessarily affecting the weighted average cost of capital. Cost of capital procedures are a frequent source of major logical errors, not just judgment errors. Mistakes of this type can leave the decision maker or appraiser vulnerable, inasmuch as he or she can actually be proven wrong. This is an area where practitioners badly need a guide such as *Cost of Capital*, so that they understand what it is they are doing.

The cost of capital is one of the key components in valuation. But it is rarely observed directly. Instead, it must be estimated. There are numerous models that can be used to estimate the cost of capital, such as build-up models, the Capital Asset Pricing Model, the Discounted Cash Flow Model, and the Arbitrage Pricing Theory. These models may require adjustments for risk, capital structure, size of company, and so forth. There are also many ways to estimate the parameters in these models. All of them may be combined in the weighted average cost of capital. Ibbotson Associates is the provider of many of these estimates. I certainly welcome *Cost of Capital* as a publication that can help to educate practitioners as to what the data mean and how they can use them.

This is a book that is likely to serve as the standard reference on cost of capital. It will join Shannon Pratt's set of valuation books in providing the theoretical foundations and practical procedures in valuation, capital budgeting, and investment decision making. However, cost of capital is the most challenging subject in valuation, with the richest data and most complex issues. I am personally enthusiastic about adding this book to my reference library.

Roger G. Ibbotson
Chairman, Ibbotson Associates
Professor in Practice, Yale School of Management

Preface

Cost of capital estimation is at once the most critical and the most difficult element of most business valuations and capital expenditure decisions. This book provides a primer for both the neophyte and the experienced financial analyst in making or assessing the cost of capital estimate.

This book addresses the following applications:

- Valuation

  Businesses and business interests
  Intangible assets, including intellectual properties
  Other income-generating assets

- Capital budgeting, feasibility studies, and corporate finance decisions

  Capital budgeting and allocation
  Feasibility studies

It includes specific models for applications in each of the aforementioned contexts.

The book is fully indexed and designed to be both a straightforward tutorial and a handy desk reference for:

- Business valuation analysts
- Corporate finance analysts
- CPAs
- Judges and attorneys
- Investment bankers and business sale intermediaries
- Academicians and students

It lays out basic tools that anyone can use immediately either in estimating the cost of capital or in reviewing someone else's cost of capital estimate:

- Basic cost of capital theory

- How cost of capital is used in business and in business asset valuation and capital expenditure decision making

  In the income approach
  In the market approach
  In the excess earnings method

- The basic mathematical formulas used, with clear explanations
- Comprehensive sources of information
- Clear and complete definitions of commonly used terminology
- Common errors — how to identify them in other people's work products and how to avoid them
- A comprehensive bibliography

My goal has been to make this book a state-of-the-art treatise on cost of capital estimation, while still making the treatment understandable to the nonprofessional. To this end, the organization starts with a layperson's understanding of the basic concepts, and then moves from simpler applications to some of the more complex applications that are regularly found in the marketplace. The presentation is generously supplemented with tables, graphical diagrams, and examples.

Cost of capital is dynamic, both in terms of current market statistics and in terms of theoretical development. Readers can keep up to date on both market and theoretical development through the monthly "Cost of Capital Update" section in *Shannon Pratt's Business Valuation Update*. Please contact us with any comments or questions on the book, and/or for a complimentary current issue of the newsletter, at the following address or at (888) BUS-VALU [(888) 287-8258]. Fax (503) 291-7955.

Shannon P. Pratt
4475 S.W. Scholls Ferry Road
Suite 101
Portland, OR 97225

Acknowledgments

This book has benefited immensely from review by many people with a high level of knowledge and experience in cost of capital and valuation. The following people reviewed the entire manuscript, and the book reflects their unstinting efforts and legion constructive suggestions:

Steve Bravo
Apogee Business Valuations, Inc.
Framingham, MA

Jay Fishman
Financial Research, Inc.
Ft. Washington, PA

Jim Hitchner
Phillips Hitchner Group
Atlanta, GA

Roger Ibbotson
Yale University and Ibbotson Associates
New Haven, CT and Chicago, IL

Mike Mattson
The Financial Valuation Group
Chicago, IL

Robert Reilly
Willamette Management Associates
Chicago, IL

Jim Rigby
The Financial Valuation Group
Los Angeles, CA

Chris Rosenthal
Ellin & Tucker
Baltimore, MD

Bob Schweihs
Willamette Management Associates
Chicago, IL

Lee Shepard
Houlihan Lokey Howard & Zukin
San Francisco, CA

Jeff Tarbell
Willamette Management Associates
San Francisco, CA

In addition, I thank Edwin Burmeister of Birr Portfolio Analysis for consultation and review of Chapter 14, "The Arbitrage Pricing Model."

I especially thank Michael Annin and Dominic Falaschetti, both of Ibbotson Associates, for contributing Chapter 13, on using Ibbotson Associates cost of capital data. And I thank Carl R.E. Hoemke of RETS Industrial/Utility Group, Inc., for contributing Chapter 20, on using cost of capital in ad valorem (property tax) valuations. I also thank Chris Mercer of Mercer Capital for Appendix D, on using cost of capital in conjunction with Wiley ValuSource.

Janet Marcley of Business Valuation Resources provided much assistance with this project and was responsible for obtaining permissions to reprint material from other sources. For these permissions, I thank:

    Alcar Group
    BIRR Portfolio Analysis
    Business Appraisal Associates
    Center for Research in Security Prices, University of Chicago
    Ibbotson Associates
    McGraw-Hill Companies
    McKinsey & Company, Inc.
    Peabody Publishing, LP
    Practitioners Publishing Company
    Price Waterhouse, LLP

The bibliography was greatly enhanced by the contributions of Victoria Platt, senior associate, and Charlene Blalock, research associate, both of Willamette Management Associates.

Court case searches for Chapter 19, on cost of capital in the courts, were done by Vanesa Pancic, legal editor of *Shannon Pratt's Business Valuation Update*.

I greatly appreciate the enthusiastic cooperation of the professionals at John Wiley & Sons, John DeRemigis, executive editor; Judy Howarth, associate editor; and Robin Goldstein, associate managing editor.

The entire manuscript was typed by Leslie Slavens, whose accuracy and timeliness were outstanding. I would also like to thank Jennie Spickelmier, a Business Valuation Resources intern, for proofing the manuscript and checking the accuracy of many computations and citations.

Last, but not least, the entire project was coordinated by the assiduous efforts of Charlene Blalock, research associate of Willamette Management Associates, who has successfully persevered in coordinating several books for my colleagues at Willamette, Robert Reilly and Robert Schweihs, and for me.

Shannon Pratt
Portland, Oregon

Introduction

PURPOSE AND OBJECTIVE OF THIS BOOK

The purpose of this book is to present both the theoretical development of cost of capital estimation and its practical application to valuation, capital budgeting, and rate-setting problems encountered in current practice. It is intended both as a learning text for those who want to study the subject and as a handy reference for those who are interested in background or seek direction in some specific aspect of cost of capital.

The objective is to serve two primary categories of users:

1. *The practitioner* who seeks a greater understanding of the latest theory and practice in cost of capital estimation.
2. *The reviewer* who needs to make an informed evaluation of someone else's methodology and data used to produce a cost of capital estimate.

OVERVIEW

The reader can expect the following:

1. *The theory* of what drives the cost of capital
2. *The models* currently in use to estimate cost of capital
3. *The data* available as inputs to the models to estimate cost of capital
4. *How to use the cost of capital estimate* in:
   Valuation
   Feasibility studies
   Corporate finance decisions
5. *How to reflect minority/control and marketability considerations*
6. *Terminology*, with its unfortunately varied and sometimes ambiguous usage in current-day financial analysis

IMPORTANCE OF THE COST OF CAPITAL

The cost of capital estimate is the essential link that enables us to convert a stream of expected income into an estimate of present value. This allows us to make informed pricing decisions for purchases and sales and a comparison of one investment opportunity against another.

COST OF CAPITAL ESSENTIAL IN THE MARKET

In valuation and financial decision making, the cost of capital estimate is just as important as the estimate of the expected amounts of income that will be discounted or capitalized. Yet we continually see income estimates laboriously developed and then converted to estimated value by a cost of capital that is practically pulled out of thin air.

In the marketplace, better-informed cost of capital estimation will improve literally billions of dollars' worth of financial decisions every day.

SOUND SUPPORT ESSENTIAL IN THE COURTROOM

In the courts, billions of dollars turn on experts' disputed cost of capital estimates in many contexts:

- Gift, estate, and income tax disputes
- Dissenting stockholder suits
- Corporate and partnership dissolutions
- Marital property settlements
- Employee stock ownership plans (ESOPs)
- Ad valorem (property) taxes
- Utility rate setting

Fortunately, courts are becoming unwilling to accept "Trust me, I'm a great expert" in these disputes, but are carefully weighing the quality of supporting evidence presented by opposing sides. Because cost of capital is critical to the valuation of any ongoing business, the thorough understanding, analysis, and presentation of cost of capital issues will go a long way toward carrying the day in a battle of experts within a legal setting.

ORGANIZATION OF THIS BOOK

Part I. Cost of Capital Basics

The first chapter defines *cost of capital*. The second chapter describes, in a general sense, how it is used in business valuation and capital budgeting. Chapter 3 defines net cash flow and explains why it is the preferred economic income variable for valuation and capital budgeting. Chapter 4 explains the difference between discounting and capitalizing. Chapter 5 addresses the concept of risk and the impact of risk on the cost of capital. From there we move to the various components of a company's capital structure and the concept of a weighted average of the cost of each component (weighted average cost of capital).

Part II. Estimating the Cost of Equity Capital

The second part explores cost of capital estimation. This includes the build-up model, the Capital Asset Pricing Model (CAPM), Discounted Cash Flow (DCF) models, and Arbitrage Pricing Theory (APT) for estimating the cost of equity.

Part III. Other Topics Related to Cost of Capital

The third part addresses commonly encountered variations in cost of capital application:

- Minority versus controlling interest valuations
- Handling discounts for lack of marketability
- Court case examples of cost of capital issues
- How cost of capital relates to the excess earnings valuation method
- Ad valorem applications
- Common errors

Appendixes

The appendixes provide sources for follow-up to this book, including a detailed bibliography, cost of capital workshops and conferences, sources for the current data needed to implement cost of capital estimation, and a ValuSource PRO software section.

SUMMARY

The book is designed to serve as both a primer and a reference source.

Part I covers cost of capital basics. Part II covers the methods generally used to estimate cost of equity capital. Part III covers a variety of topics commonly encountered in cost of capital applications. The appendixes provide a directory for further study, data sources, and a discussion of using ValuSource PRO software section.

Notation System Used in This Book

A source of confusion for those trying to understand financial theory and methods is the fact that financial writers have not adopted a standard system of notation. The following notation system is taken from the third edition of *Valuing a Business: The Analysis and Appraisal of Closely Held Companies,* by Shannon P. Pratt, Robert F. Reilly, and Robert P. Schweihs.

VALUE AT A POINT IN TIME

PV   = Present value
FV   = Future value
MVIC   = Market value of invested capital

COST OF CAPITAL AND RATE OF RETURN VARIABLES

k = Discount rate (generalized)

k_e = Discount rate for common equity capital (cost of common equity capital). Unless otherwise stated, it generally is assumed that this discount rate is applicable to net cash flow available to common equity.

$k_{e(pt)}$ = Cost of equity prior to tax effect

k_p = Discount rate for preferred equity capital

k_d = Discount rate for debt (net of tax effect, if any)
          (*Note*: for complex capital structures, there could be more than one class of capital in any of the preceding categories, requiring expanded subscripts.)

$k_{d(pt)}$ = Cost of debt prior to tax effect

k_{ni} = Discount rate for equity capital when net income rather than net cash flow is the measure of economic income being discounted

c = Capitalization rate

c_e = Capitalization rate for common equity capital. Unless otherwise stated, it generally is assumed that this capitalization rate is applicable to net cash flow available to common equity.

c_{ni}	= Capitalization rate for net income
c_p	= Capitalization rate for preferred equity capital
c_d	= Capitalization rate for debt
	(*Note*: for complex capital structures, there could be more than one class of capital in any of the preceding categories, requiring expanded subscripts.)
t	= Tax rate (expressed as a percentage of pretax income)
R	= Rate of return
R_f	= Rate of return on a risk-free security
$E(R)$	= Expected rate of return
$E(R_m)$	= Expected rate of return on the "market" (usually used in the context of a market for equity securities, such as the NYSE or S&P 500)
$E(R_i)$	= Expected rate of return on security i
B	= Beta (a coefficient, usually used to modify a rate of return variable)
B_L	= Levered beta
B_U	= Unlevered beta
RP	= Risk premium
RP_m	= Risk premium for the "market" (usually used in the context of a market for equity securities, such as the NYSE or S&P 500)
RP_s	= Risk premium for "small" stocks (usually average size of lowest quintile or decile of NYSE as measured by market value of common equity) over and above RP_m
RP_u	= Risk premium for unsystematic risk attributable to the specific company
RP_i	= Risk premium for the ith security
$K_1 \ldots K_n$	= Risk premium associated with risk factor 1 through n for the average asset in the market (used in conjunction with Arbitrage Pricing Theory)
WACC	= Weighted average cost of capital

INCOME VARIABLES

E	= Expected economic income (in a generalized sense; i.e., could be dividends, any of several possible definitions of cash flows, net income, and so on)
NI	= Net income (after entity-level taxes)
NCF_e	= Net cash flow to equity
NCF_f	= Net cash flow to the firm (to overall invested capital, or entire capital structure, including all equity and long-term debt)
PMT	= Payment (interest and principal payment on debt security)
D	= Dividends
T	= Tax (in dollars)
GCF	= Gross cash flow (usually net income plus non-cash charges)
EBT	= Earnings before taxes

EBIT   = Earnings before interest and taxes
EBDIT   = Earnings before depreciation, interest, and taxes ("Depreciation" in this context usually includes amortization. Some writers use EBITDA to specifically indicate that amortization is included.)

PERIODS OR VARIABLES IN A SERIES

i = The ith period or the ith variable in a series (may be extended to the jth variable, the kth variable, and so on)

n = The number of periods or variables in a series, or the last number in a series

∞ = Infinity

o = Period$_o$, the base period, usually the latest year immediately preceding the valuation date

WEIGHTINGS

W = Weight
W_e = Weight of common equity in capital structure
W_p = Weight of preferred equity in capital structure
W_d = Weight of debt in capital structure
            (*Note*: For purposes of computing a weighted average cost of capital (WACC), it is assumed that preceding weightings are at market value.)

GROWTH

g = Rate of growth in a variable (e.g., net cash flow)

MATHEMATICAL FUNCTIONS

Σ = Sum of (add all the variables that follow)
Π = Product of (multiply together all the variables that follow)
$\bar{x}$ = Mean average (the sum of the values of the variables divided by the number of variables)
G = Geometric mean (the product of the values of the variables taken to the root of the number of variables)

PART I

Cost of Capital Basics

Chapter 1

Defining Cost of Capital

Cost of capital is *the expected rate of return that the market requires in order to attract funds to a particular investment.* In economic terms, the cost of capital for a particular investment is an *opportunity cost*—that is, the cost of foregoing the next best alternative investment. In this sense, it relates to the economic *principle of substitution*—that is, an investor will not invest in a particular asset if there is a more attractive substitute.

The "market" refers to the universe of investors who are reasonable candidates to provide funds for a particular investment. Capital or funds are usually provided in the form of cash, although in some instances, capital may be provided in the form of other assets. The cost of capital is usually expressed in percentage terms, that is, the annual amount of dollars that the investor requires or expects to realize, expressed as a percentage of the dollar amount invested.

Put another way:

> Since the cost of anything can be defined as the price you have to pay to get it, the cost of your capital is the return you must promise in order to get capital from the market, either debt or equity. A company does not set its own cost of capital; it must go to the market to discover it. Yet meeting this cost is the financial market's one basic yardstick for determining whether your performance is adequate.[1]

As the preceding quote suggests, most of the information for estimating the cost of capital for any company, security, or project comes from the investment markets. The cost of capital is always an *expected* return. Thus, analysts and would-be investors never actually observe it. We analyze many types of market data to estimate the cost of capital for a company, security, or project in which we are interested.

As Roger Ibbotson puts it, "The opportunity Cost of Capital is equal to the return that could have been earned on alternative investments at a specific level of risk."[2] In other words, it is the competitive return available in the market on a comparable investment, risk being the most important component of comparability.

COMPONENTS OF A COMPANY'S CAPITAL STRUCTURE

The term *capital* in this context means the components of an entity's capital structure. The primary components of a capital structure include:

- Long-term debt
- Preferred equity (stock or partnership interests with preference features, such as seniority in receipt of dividends or liquidation proceeds)
- Common equity (stock or partnership interests at the lowest or residual level of the capital structure)

There may be more than one subcategory in any or all of the above categories of capital. Also, there may be related forms of capital such as warrants or options. Each component of an entity's capital structure has its unique cost, depending primarily on its respective risk.

Simply and cogently stated, "The cost of equity is the rate of return that investors require to make an equity investment in the firm."[3]

Recognizing that the cost of capital applies to both debt and equity investments, a well-known text states, "Both creditors and shareholders expect to be compensated for the opportunity cost of investing their funds in one particular business instead of others with equivalent risk."[4]

The following quote explains how the cost of capital can be viewed from three different perspectives:

> The cost of capital (sometimes called the expected or required rate of return or the discount rate) can be viewed from three different perspectives. On the asset side of a firm's balance sheet, it is the discount rate that should be used to reduce the future value of cash flows to be derived from the assets to a present value. On the liability side, it is the economic cost to the firm of attracting and retaining capital in a competitive environment where investors (capital providers) carefully analyze and compare all return-generating opportunities. To the investor, it is the return one *expects* and requires from his/her investment in a firm's debt or equity. While each of these perspectives might view the cost of capital differently, they are all viewing *the same number*.[5]

When we talk about the cost of ownership capital (i.e., the expected return to a stock or partnership investor), we usually use the phrase "cost of equity capital." When we talk about the cost of capital to the firm overall (i.e., the average cost of capital for both ownership interests and debt), we usually use the phrase "weighted average cost of capital" (WACC) or "blended cost of capital."

COST OF CAPITAL IS A FUNCTION OF THE INVESTMENT

As Ibbotson puts it, "The cost of capital is a function of the investment, not the investor."[6] The cost of capital comes from the marketplace. The marketplace is the universe of investors for a particular asset.

Brealey and Myers state the same concept: "The true cost of capital depends on the use to which the capital is put."[7] They make the point that it would be an error to evaluate a potential investment on the basis of a company's overall cost of capital if that investment were more or less risky than the company's existing business. "Each project should be evaluated at its *own* opportunity cost of capital."[8]

When a company uses the cost of capital to evaluate a commitment of capital to an investment or project, it often refers to that cost of capital as the "hurdle rate." By the "hurdle rate" they mean the minimum expected rate of return that they would be willing to accept to justify making the investment. As noted in the previous paragraph, the "hurdle rate" for any given prospective investment may be at, above, or below the company's overall cost of capital depending on the degree of risk of the prospective investment compared to the company's overall risk.

The most popular theme of contemporary corporate finance is that companies should be making investments, either capital investments or acquisitions, from which the returns will exceed the cost of capital for that investment. Doing so creates "economic value added," "economic profit," or "shareholder value added."[9]

COST OF CAPITAL IS FORWARD-LOOKING

The cost of capital represents investors' *expectations*. There are several elements to these expectations:

1. The "real" rate of return they expect to obtain in exchange for letting someone else use their money on a riskless basis
2. Expected inflation — the expected depreciation in purchasing power while the money is tied up
3. Risk — the uncertainty as to when and how much cash flow or other economic income will be received

It is the combination of the first two items above which is sometimes referred to as the "time value of money." While these expectations may be different for different investors, the market tends to form a consensus in respect to a particular investment or category of investments. That consensus determines the cost of capital for investments of varying levels of risk.

The cost of capital, derived from investors' expectations and the market's consensus of those expectations, is applied to *expected economic income, usually measured in terms of cash flows,* in order to estimate present values or to compare investment alternatives of similar or differing levels of risk. "Present value," in this context, refers to the dollar amount that a rational and well-informed investor would be willing to pay today for the stream of expected economic income that is being evaluated. In mathematical terms, the cost of capital is the percentage rate of return that equates the stream of expected income with its present cash value.

COST OF CAPITAL IS BASED ON MARKET VALUE, NOT BOOK VALUE

The cost of capital is the expected rate of return on some base value. That base value is measured as the market value of an asset, not it's book value. For example, the yield to maturity shown in the bond quotations in the financial press is based on the closing market price of a bond, not on its face value. Similarly, the implied cost of equity for a company's stock must be (or should be) based on the market price per share at which it trades, not on the company's book value per share of stock. It was noted earlier that the cost of capital is estimated from market data. This data refers to *expected returns relative to market prices*. By applying the cost of capital derived from market expectations to the expected cash flows (or other measure of economic income) from the investment or project under consideration, the market value can be estimated.

COST OF CAPITAL IS USUALLY STATED IN NOMINAL TERMS

Keep in mind that we have talked about expectations including inflation. The return an investor requires includes compensation for reduced purchasing power of the dollar over the life of the investment. Therefore, when the analyst or investor applies the cost of capital to expected returns to estimate value, he or she must also include expected inflation in those expected returns.

This obviously assumes that investors have reasonable consensus expectations regarding inflation. For countries subject to unpredictable hyperinflation, it is sometimes more practical to estimate cost of capital in real terms rather than nominal terms.

COST OF CAPITAL EQUALS DISCOUNT RATE

The essence of the cost of capital is that it is the percentage return that equates expected economic income with present value. The expected rate of return in this context is called a "discount rate." By a *discount rate*, the financial community means an annually compounded rate by which each increment of expected economic income is discounted back to its present value. A discount rate reflects both time value of money and risk, and therefore represents the cost of capital. The sum of the discounted present values of each future period's incremental cash flow or other measure of return equals the present value of the investment, reflecting the expected amounts of return over the life of the investment. The terms "discount rate," "cost of capital," and "required rate of return" are often used interchangeably.

The economic income referenced here represents *total expected returns*. In other words, this economic income includes increments of cash flow realized by the investor while holding the investment, as well as proceeds to the investor on liquidation of the investment. The rate by which these expected future total returns are reduced to present value is the discount rate, which is the *cost of capital* (required rate of return) for a particular investment.

DISCOUNT RATE IS NOT THE SAME AS CAPITALIZATION RATE

Discount rate and capitalization rate are two distinctly different concepts. As noted in the previous section, discount rate equates to cost of capital. It is a rate applied to *all* expected incremental returns to convert the expected return stream to a present value.

A capitalization rate, however, is merely a divisor applied to *one single* element of return to estimate a present value. The only instance in which the discount rate is equal to the capitalization rate is when each future increment of expected return is equal, and the expected returns are in perpetuity. One of the few examples would be a preferred stock paying a fixed amount of dividend per share in perpetuity.

In the unique case, where an amount of return is expected to grow at a constant rate in perpetuity, the capitalization rate applicable to that expected return is equal to the discount rate less the expected rate of growth. There is more on the relationship between discount and capitalization rates in future chapters.

SUMMARY

As stated in the Introduction, "The cost of capital estimate is the essential link that enables us to convert a stream of expected income into an estimate of present value."

Cost of capital has several key characteristics:

- It is *market driven*. It is the expected rate of return that the market requires to commit capital to an investment.
- It is a function of the *investment*, not the *investor.*
- It is *forward-looking*, based on *expected* returns.
- The base against which cost of capital is measured is *market value*, not book value.
- It is usually measured in *nominal terms*, that is, including expected inflation.
- It is the link, called a *discount rate*, that equates expected future returns for the life of the investment with the present value of the investment at a given date.

Notes

1. Mike Kaufman "Determining the Cost of Capital," in *Handbook of Budgeting*, 3d ed., Robert Rachlin, ed. (New York: John Wiley & Sons, 1993), 11–3.
2. Ibbotson Associates, *Cost of Capital Workshop* (Chicago: Ibbotson Associates, 1998), Chapter 1, p.2.
3. Aswath Damodaran, *Investment Valuation* (New York: John Wiley & Sons, 1996), 49.
4. Tom Copeland, Tim Koller, and Jack Murren, *Valuation: Measuring and Managing the Value of Companies* (New York: John Wiley & Sons, 1996), 171.
5. *Stocks, Bonds, Bills and Inflation 1997 Yearbook* (Chicago: Ibbotson Associates, 1997), 143.
6. Ibbotson Associates, *Cost of Capital Workshop*, Chapter 1, p.7.
7. Richard A. Brealey and Stewart S. Myers, *Principles of Corporate Finance*, 5th ed. (New York: McGraw-Hill, 1996), 205.
8. Ibid.
9. See, for example, Copeland et al., *Valuation*, and Alfred Rapport, *Creating Shareholder Value*, Revised Edition (New York: The Free Press, 1998).

Chapter 2

Introduction to Cost of Capital Applications: Valuation and Project Selection

Cost of capital has many applications, the two most common being valuation and capital investment project selection. These two applications are very closely related. This chapter discusses these two applications in very general terms, so that the reader can quickly understand the concept as to how the cost of capital is used every day in valuations and financial decisions worth billions of dollars. Later chapters discuss these applications in more detail.

NET CASH FLOW IS THE PREFERRED ECONOMIC INCOME MEASURE

For the purpose of this chapter we will assume that the measure of economic income to which cost of capital will be applied is *net cash flow* (sometimes called *free cash flow*). The concept of net cash flow is that it is discretionary cash available to be paid out to capital stakeholders (e.g., dividends, withdrawals, discretionary bonuses) without jeopardizing the projected ongoing operations of the business. We will provide a more exact definition of net cash flow in Chapter 3.

Net cash flow is the measure of economic income on which most financial analysts today prefer to focus for both valuation and capital investment project selection. We explain the reasons for this preference in more detail in Chapter 3. Obviously, the fact that net cash flow represents money available for disposal to capital stakeholders at the owner's discretion is one of the major reasons for preferring this measure of economic income. Although the contemporary literature of corporate finance widely embraces a preference for net cash flow as the relevant economic income variable to which to apply cost of capital for valuation and decision making, I should point out that there is still a contingent of folks who like to focus on accounting income.[1]

COST OF CAPITAL IS THE PROPER DISCOUNT RATE

At the end of Chapter 1, I said that the cost of capital is customarily used as a discount rate in order to convert expected future returns to a present value. This concept is summarized succinctly by Brealey and Myers: "Value today always equals future cash flow discounted at the opportunity cost of capital."[2]

In this context, let's keep in mind the following two critical characteristics of a discount rate:

1. Definition: A *discount rate* is a yield rate used to convert anticipated future payments or receipts into present value (i.e., a cash value as of today, or as of a specified valuation date).
2. The discount rate represents the *total rate of return* that the investor expects to realize on the amount invested.

The use of the cost of capital to estimate present value thus requires two sets of estimates:

1. The *numerator*: The expected amount of return on the investment in each future period over the life of the investment
2. The *denominator:* The discount rate, which is the cost of capital

Usually, analysts and investors make the simplifying assumption that the cost of capital is constant over the life of the investment and use the same cost of capital to apply to each increment of expected future return. There are, however, special cases in which analysts may estimate a discrete cost of capital to apply to the expected return in each future period. (An example is where the analyst anticipates a changing weighted average cost of capital because of a changing capital structure.) However, well-known author, professor, and consultant Dr. Alfred Rappaport espouses a constant cost of capital in his 1998 edition of *Creating Shareholder Value:*

> The appropriate rate for discounting the company's cash flow stream is the weighted average of the costs of debt and equity capital. . . . It is important to emphasize that the relative weights attached to debt and equity, respectively, are neither predicated on dollars the firm has raised in the past, nor do they constitute the relative proportions of dollars the firm plans to raise in the current year. Instead, the relevant weights should

be based on the proportions of debt and equity that the firm targets for its capital structure over the long-term planning period.[3]

THE PRESENT VALUE FORMULA

Putting what has been said in terms of a mathematical formula, we have the following, which is the essence of using cost of capital to estimate present value:

Formula 2.1

$$PV = \frac{NCF_1}{(1 + k)} + \frac{NCF_2}{(1 + k)^2} + \cdots + \frac{NCF_n}{(1 + k)^n}$$

where:

PV = Present value
$NCF_1 \ldots NCF_n$ = Net cash flow (or other measure of economic income) expected in each of the periods 1 through n, n being the final cash flow in the life of the investment
k = Cost of capital applicable to the defined stream of net cash flow

The critical job for the analyst is to match the cost of capital estimate to the definition of the economic income stream being discounted. This is largely a function of reflecting in the cost of capital estimate the degree of risk that is inherent in the expected cash flows being discounted. The relationship between risk and the cost of capital is the subject of Chapter 5.

AN EXAMPLE: VALUING A BOND

A simple example of the use of Formula 2.1 is valuing a bond for which a risk rating has been estimated. Let's make the following assumptions:

1. The bond has a face value of $1,000.
2. It pays 8% interest on its face value.
3. The bond pays interest once a year, at the end of the year. (This, of course, is a simplifying assumption. Some bonds and notes pay only annually, but most publicly traded bonds pay interest semiannually.)
4. The bond matures exactly three years from the valuation date.
5. As of the valuation date, the market yield to maturity (total rate of return, including interest payments and price appreciation) for bonds of the same risk grade as the subject bond is 10%.

Note the important implications of this scenario:

1. The issuing company's *imbedded cost of capital* for this bond is only 8%, although the *market cost of capital* at the valuation date is 10%. This may be because the general level of interest rates was lower at the time of issuance of this particular bond, or because the market's rating of the risk associated with this bond increased between the date of issuance and the valuation date.

2. If the issuing company wished to issue new debt on comparable terms as of the valuation date, it presumably would have to offer investors a 10% yield, the current market-driven cost of capital for bonds of that risk grade, in order to induce investors to purchase the bonds.

3. For purposes of valuation and capital budgeting decisions, when we refer to cost of capital, we mean market cost of capital, not imbedded cost of capital. (Imbedded cost of capital is sometimes used in utility rate making, but this chapter focuses only on valuation and capital budgeting applications of cost of capital.)

Substituting numbers derived from the preceding assumptions into Formula 2.1 gives us the following:

Formula 2.2

$$
\begin{aligned}
PV &= \frac{\$80}{(1+.10)} + \frac{\$80}{(1+.10)^2} + \frac{\$80}{(1+.10)^3} + \frac{\$1,000}{(1+.10)^3} \\
&= \frac{\$80}{1.10} + \frac{\$80}{1.21} + \frac{\$80}{1.331} + \frac{\$1,000}{1.331} \\
&= \$72.73 + \$66.12 + \$60.10 + \$751.32 \\
&= \underline{\underline{\$950.27}}
\end{aligned}
$$

In this example, the fair market value of the subject bond as of the valuation date was $950.27. That is the amount that a willing buyer would expect to pay and a willing seller would expect to receive (before taking into consideration any transaction costs).

RELATIONSHIP OF DISCOUNT RATE TO CAPITALIZATION RATE

It is important to distinguish between a discount rate and a capitalization rate, and to understand the relationship between the two. The following are critical characteristics of a capitalization rate:

1. Definition: *A capitalization rate* is a yield rate used to convert a single payment or measure of economic income into present value (as opposed to a dis-

count rate, which is used to convert *all* expected future payments to a present value).

2. The capitalization rate represents only the *current rate of return* (as opposed to a discount rate, which represents the *total rate of return*).

APPLICATIONS TO BUSINESSES, BUSINESS INTERESTS, PROJECTS, AND DIVISIONS

The same construct can be used to value an equity interest in a company or a company's entire invested capital. One projects the cash flows available to the interest to be valued, and discounts those cash flows at a cost of capital discount rate that reflects the risk associated with achieving the particular cash flows. Details of this procedure for valuing entire companies or interests in companies are presented in later chapters.

Similarly, the same construct can be applied to evaluating a capital budgeting decision, such as building a plant or buying equipment. In that case, the cash flows to be discounted are *incremental* cash flows, that is, cash flows resulting from the decision that would not occur absent the decision. The early portions of the cash flow stream may be negative, while funds are being invested in the project.

The primary relationship to remember is that cost of capital is a function of the investment, not the investor. Therefore, the analyst must evaluate the risk of each project under consideration. If the risk of the project is greater or less than the company's overall risk, then the cost of capital by which that project is evaluated should be commensurately higher or lower than the company's overall cost of capital.

Although some companies apply a single "hurdle rate" to all proposed projects or investments, the consensus as I read it in the literature of corporate finance is that the rate to apply to evaluate any investment should be based on the risk of that investment, not the company's overall risk, which drives the company's cost of capital. I agree with this consensus position. If the company invests in something more risky than its normal operations, this will marginally increase the company's risk. When this is recognized and reflected in the market it will thus raise the company's cost of capital. If the returns on the riskier new investment are not great enough to allow the company to achieve higher returns commensurate with this higher cost of capital, the result will be a lowering of the stock price and a loss of shareholder value.

Somewhere between estimating cost of capital for an entire company and cost of capital for a specific project is the matter of divisional cost of capital, or estimating cost of capital for a division of a company. In many respects, estimating cost of capital for a division is akin to estimating cost of capital for an entire privately held company.

SUMMARY

The most common cost of capital applications are valuation of an investment or prospective investment and project selection decisions (the core component of capital budgeting). In both applications, returns expected from the capital outlay are discounted to a present value by a discount rate, which should be the cost of capital applicable to the specific investment or project. The measure of returns generally preferred today is *net cash flow*, as discussed in the next chapter.

Notes

1. See, for example, Chris Mercer, *Valuing Financial Institutions* (Burr Ridge, IL: McGraw-Hill, 1992), Chapter 13; and his article "The Adjusted Capital Asset Pricing Model for Developing Capitalization Rates," *Business Valuation Review*, December 1989, 147 et. seq.
2. Richard A. Brealey and Stewart C. Myers, *Principles of Corporate Finance*, 5th ed. (New York: McGraw-Hill, 1996), 73.
3. Alfred Rappaport, *Creating Shareholder Value* (New York: The Free Press, 1998), 37.

Chapter 3

Net Cash Flow: The Preferred Measure of Return

Cost of capital is a meaningless concept until we define the measure of economic income to which it is to be applied. The variable of choice for most financial decision making based on the tools of modern finance is *net cash flow*. This, obviously, poses two critical questions:

1. How do we define net cash flow?
2. Why is it considered the best economic income variable to use in net present value analysis?

DEFINING NET CASH FLOW

Net cash flow is cash that a business or project does not have to retain and reinvest in itself in order to sustain the projected levels of cash flows in future years. In other words, it is cash that is available to be paid out in any year to the owners of capital without jeopardizing the company's expected cash flow generating capability in future years. (*Net cash flow* is sometimes called *free cash flow*. It is also sometimes called *net free cash flow*, although this phrase seems redundant. Finance terminology being as ambiguous as it is, we occasionally find minor variations in the definitions of these terms.)

Net Cash Flow to Equity

In valuing *equity* by discounting or capitalizing expected cash flows (keeping in mind the important difference between discounting and capitalizing, as discussed in both earlier and later chapters), *net cash flow to equity* (NCF_e in our notation system) is defined as follows:

Net income (after tax)

+ Noncash charges (e.g., depreciation, amortization, deferred revenue, deferred taxes)
− Capital expenditures*
− Additions to net working capital*
± Changes in long-term debt (add cash from borrowing, subtract repayments)*
= Net cash flow to equity

*Only amounts necessary to support projected operations

Net Cash Flow to Invested Capital

In valuing the entire *invested capital* of a company or project by discounting or capitalizing expected cash flows, *net cash flow to invested capital* (NCF_f in our notation system) is defined as follows:

Net income (after tax)

+ Noncash charges (e.g., depreciation, amortization, deferred revenue, deferred taxes)
− Capital expenditures*
− Additions to net working capital*
+ Interest expense (net of the tax deduction resulting from interest as a tax-deductible expense)
= Net cash flow to invested capital

*Only amounts necessary to support projected operations

Occasionally, we find an analyst treating earnings before interest, taxes, depreciation, and amortization (EBITDA) as if it were free cash flow. This error is not a minor matter, since the analyst has added back the noncash charges without deducting the capital expenditure investments, not to mention additions to working capital, necessary to keep the operation functioning as expected.

When we discount net cash flow to equity, the appropriate discount rate is the cost of equity capital. When we discount net cash flow to all invested capital, the appropriate discount rate is the weighted average cost of capital (WACC).

NET CASH FLOWS SHOULD BE PROBABILITY-WEIGHTED EXPECTED VALUES

Net cash flows to be discounted or capitalized should be *expected values,* that is, *probability-weighted* cash flows.

If the distribution of possible cash flows in each period is symmetrical above and below the most likely cash flow in that period, then the most likely cash flow is equal to the probability-weighted cash flow (the mathematical expected value of the distribution). However, many distributions of possible cash flows are skewed. This is where probability weighting comes into play. Exhibit 3.1 tabulates the probability-weighted expected values of projected cash flows under a symmetrically distributed scenario and a skewed distribution scenario. Exhibit 3.2 portrays the information in Exhibit 3.1 graphically.

Exhibit 3.1

Scenario A — Symmetrical Cash Flow Expectation

Midpoint of Range	Probability of Occurrence	Weighted Value
$1,600	.01	$ 16
1,500	.09	135
1,300	.20	260
1,000	.40	400
700	.20	140
500	.09	45
400	.01	4
	1.00	$1,000

Scenario B — Skewed Cash Flow Expectation

Midpoint of Range	Probability of Occurrence	Weighted Value
$1,600	.01	$ 16
1,500	.04	60
1,300	.20	260
1,000	.35	350
700	.25	175
500	.10	50
(100)	.04	(4)
(600)	.01	(6)
	1.00	$901

Exhibit 3.2

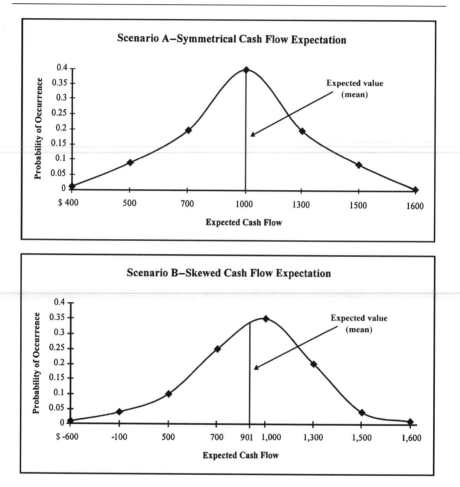

In both scenario A and scenario B, the most likely cash flow is $1,000. In scenario A, the expected value (probability weighted) is also $1,000. But in scenario B, the expected value is only $901. In scenario B, the $901 is the figure that should appear in the numerator of the discounted cash flow formula, not $1,000. Most analysts do not have the luxury of a probability distribution for each expected cash flow, but should be aware of the concept when deciding on the amount of each expected cash flow to be discounted.

WHY NET CASH FLOW IS THE PREFERRED MEASURE OF ECONOMIC INCOME

There are two reasons that the financial community tends to focus on net cash flow as the preferred measure of economic income to be discounted by the opportunity cost of capital to estimate the net present value of an investment opportunity:

1. *Conceptual:* It's what you really get (what an investor actually expects to receive).
2. *Empirical:* It's the economic income measure for which we have the best historical data available to estimate a discount rate.

Conceptual Reason for Preferring Net Cash Flow

Net cash flow, as defined earlier, is that portion of the cash flow over which the control owner has total discretion as to its disposition. It is not necessary to retain net cash flow in order to sustain the business; rather, it is available to be paid out to owners or used for any other desired purpose. This is the measure of economic income of greatest interest to most investors.

Empirical Reason for Preferring Net Cash Flow

If the Ibbotson Associates' data are used to develop an equity discount rate — using either the build-up model or the Capital Asset Pricing Model (CAPM) — the discount rate is applicable to net cash flow available to the equity investor. This is because the Ibbotson return data have two components:

1. Dividends
2. Change in stock price

The investor receives the dividends, so their utilization is entirely discretionary to the investor. The realization of the change in stock price by the investor is equally discretionary, because the stocks are highly liquid (i.e., they can be sold at their market price at any time, with the seller receiving the proceeds in cash within three business days).

The fact that the net cash flows are measured after tax seems to cause a great deal of confusion among some people. The phrase "after tax" means after corporate taxes, but the cash flows are still before any personal taxes that may be incurred as a result of receipt of the cash flows.

SUMMARY

Net cash flow is the measure of economic income that most financial analysts prefer to use today when using the cost of capital for valuation or project selection. If valuing cash flows to equity, the discount rate should be the cost of equity capital. If valuing cash flows to debt, the discount rate should be the cost of the debt capital. If valuing cash flows available for all invested capital, the discount rate should be the weighted average cost of capital (WACC).

There are two good reasons that financial analysts lean toward using net cash flow as the preferred measure of economic income when using cost of capital for valuation or project selection:

1. *Conceptually*, it is the amount of discretionary money available to be distributed without disrupting the projected ongoing operations of the enterprise.
2. *Empirically*, it is the economic income measure for which we have the best historical data available for estimating cost of equity capital.

Net cash flows should be measured as the mathematical expected value of the probability-weighted distribution of expected outcomes for each projected period of returns, not the most likely value. In Chapter 5, on risk, we define risk in terms of uncertainty of possible outcomes, a definition intended to encompass the entire range of possible returns for each future period.

Discounting Versus Capitalizing

In the context of cost of capital applications, there is a very clear distinction between a discount rate and a capitalization rate. The first two chapters explained that the cost of capital is used as a discount rate to discount a stream of future returns to a present value. This process is called *discounting*.

In the process called discounting, we project *all* expected returns from the subject investment to the respective class or classes of capital over the life of the investment. Thus, the percentage return that we call the discount rate represents the total compound rate of return that an investor in that class of investment expects to achieve over the life of the investment.

There is a related process for estimating present value, which we call *capitalizing*. In capitalizing, instead of projecting all future returns on the investment to the respective class(es) of capital, we focus on the return of just one single period, usually the return expected in the first year immediately following the valuation date. We then divide that single number by a divisor called the *capitalization rate*. This process is called *capitalizing*.

As we will see, the process of capitalizing is really just a shorthand form of discounting, and the capitalization rate is actually a derivative of the discount rate. That is, the capitalization rate, as used in the income approach to valuation or project selection, is formed by derivation from the discount rate. (This differs from the market approach to valuation, where capitalization rates for various economic income measures are observed directly in the marketplace.)

THE CAPITALIZATION FORMULA

Putting what we have just said in terms of a formula, we have the following:

Formula 4.1

$$PV = \frac{NCF_1}{c}$$

where:

   PV = Present value
   NCF_1 = Net cash flow expected in the first period immediately following
          the valuation date
   c = Capitalization rate

AN EXAMPLE: VALUING A PREFERRED STOCK

A simple example of applying Formula 4.1 uses a preferred stock for which a risk rating has been estimated. Let's make the following assumptions:

1. The preferred stock pays dividends of $5 per share per year.
2. The preferred stock is issued in perpetuity and is not callable.
3. It pays dividends once a year, at the end of the year. (This, of course, is a simplifying assumption. Some privately owned preferred stocks pay only annually, but most publicly traded preferred stocks pay dividends quarterly.)
4. As of the valuation date, the market yield for preferred stocks of the same risk grade as the subject preferred stock is 10%. (We also must assume comparable rights, such as voting, liquidation preference, redemption, conversion, participation, cumulative dividends, and so on.)
5. There is no prospect of liquidation.

Note that it makes no difference whatsoever what the par value of the preferred stock is, since it is issued in perpetuity and there is no prospect of a liquidation. The entire cash flow that an investor can expect to receive over the life of the investment (perpetuity in this case) is the $5 per year per share dividend.

Substituting numbers derived from the preceding assumptions into Formula 4.1 produces the following:

Formula 4.2

$$PV = \frac{\$5.00}{.10}$$

$$= \$50.00$$

In this example, the estimated fair market value of the subject preferred stock is $50 per share. That is the amount that a willing buyer would expect to pay and a willing seller would expect to receive (before taking into consideration any transaction costs).

FUNCTIONAL RELATIONSHIP BETWEEN DISCOUNT RATE AND CAPITALIZATION RATE

The preceding example presented the simplest possible scenario in which to apply the cost of capital through the capitalization method: a fixed cash flow stream in perpetuity. This is the one unique situation in which the discount rate (cost of capital) equals the capitalization rate. The discount rate equals the capitalization rate because no growth or decline in the investor's cash flow is expected. But most real-world investments aren't quite that simple.

In the case of an investment in common stock, a partnership interest, or a capital budgeting project in an operating company, investors often are expecting some level of growth over time in the cash flows available to pay dividends or partnership withdrawals. Even if unit volume is expected to remain constant (that is, no real growth), investors still might expect cash flows to grow at a rate approximating expected inflation. If the expected annually compounded rate of growth is stable and sustainable over a long period of time, then the discount rate (cost of capital) can be converted to a capitalization rate.

As stated earlier, the capitalization rate is a function of the discount rate. This obviously raises the question, What is the functional relationship between the discount rate and the capitalization rate?

Assuming stable long-term growth in the cash flows available to the investment being valued, the capitalization rate equals the discount rate minus the expected long-term growth rate. In terms of a formula, this functional relationship can be stated as follows:

Formula 4.3

$$c = k - g$$

where:

c = Capitalization rate

k = Discount rate (cost of capital) for the subject investment

g = Expected long-term sustainable growth rate in the cash flow available to the subject investment

The critical assumption in this formula is that the growth in the return available to the capital is relatively constant over the long term (technically in perpetuity).

Caveat: Note carefully the phrase "return available to the capital." This does not include growth in overall company cash flows that are dependent on future capital investment. A common error is to use a rate of growth that could not be achieved without additional capital investment. The only growth that counts is in returns to the *existing* capital, or the capital investment being evaluated.

Now we know two essential things about using the cost of capital to estimate present value using the capitalization method, assuming relatively stable, long-term growth in the return available to the investor:

1. Present value equals the next period's expected cash flow divided by the capitalization rate.

2. The capitalization rate is the discount rate (cost of capital) less the sustainable expected long-term rate of growth in the cash flow. (Technically, sustainable growth in this context means in perpetuity. However, after 15 or 20 years, the remaining rate of growth has minimal impact on the present value.)

We can combine these two relationships into a single formula as follows:

Formula 4.4

$$PV = \frac{NCF_1}{k - g}$$

where:

PV = Present value

NCF_1 = Net cash flow expected in period 1, the period immediately following the valuation date

k = Discount rate (cost of capital)

g = Expected long-term sustainable growth rate in net cash flow to investor

A simple example of substituting numbers into Formula 4.4 is an equity investment with a constant expected growth in net cash flow. Let's make the following assumptions:

1. The net cash flow in period 1 is expected to be $100.

2. The cost of capital (market required total return, the discount rate) for this investment is estimated to be 13%.
3. The sustainable rate of growth in net cash flow from year 1 to perpetuity is expected to be 3%.

Substituting numbers from the preceding assumptions into Formula 4.4 gives us the following:

Formula 4.5

$$PV = \frac{\$100}{.13 - .03}$$

$$= \frac{\$100}{.10}$$

$$= \underline{\underline{\$1,000}}$$

In this example, the estimated fair market value of the investment is $1,000. That is the amount a willing buyer would expect to pay and a willing seller would expect to receive (before taking into consideration any transaction costs).

THE MAJOR DIFFERENCE BETWEEN DISCOUNTING AND CAPITALIZING

From the foregoing, we can now deduce the following critical insight: *The difference between discounting and capitalizing is in how we reflect changes over time in expected future cash flows.*

In *discounting*: Each future increment of return is estimated specifically and put in the numerator.

In *capitalizing*: Estimates of changes in future returns are lumped into one annually compounded growth rate, which is then subtracted from the discount rate in the denominator.

If we assume that there really is a constant compounded growth rate in net cash flow to the investor in perpetuity, then it is a mathematical truism that the discounting method and the capitalizing method will produce identical values. (See the later section in this chapter titled "Equivalency of Discounting and Capitalizing Models" for an illustration of how this truism works.)

THE GORDON GROWTH MODEL

One frequently encountered minor modification to Formulas 4.4 and 4.5 is to start with the "base period" being the period just completed prior to the valuation date instead of starting with the next period's estimate. The assumption is that cash flows will grow evenly in perpetuity from the period immediately preceding the valuation date. This scenario is stated in a formula known as the "Gordon Growth Model."

Formula 4.6

$$PV = \frac{NCF_0(1+g)}{k-g}$$

where:

PV = Present value

NCF_0 = Net cash flow in period 0, the period immediately preceding the valuation date

k = Discount rate (cost of capital)

g = Expected long-term sustainable growth rate in net cash flow to investor

Note that in order for this model to make economic sense, NCF_0 must represent a normalized amount of cash flow from the investment for the previous year, from which a steady rate of growth is expected to proceed. Therefore, NCF_0 need not be the actual cash flow for period 0, but may be the result of certain normalization adjustments, such as elimination of the effect of one or more nonrecurring factors.

In fact, if NCF_0 *is* the actual net cash flow for period 0, it is incumbent on the valuation analyst to take reasonable steps to be satisfied that NCF_0 is indeed the most reasonable base from which to start the expected growth impounded in the growth rate. Furthermore, the valuation report should state the steps taken and the assumptions made in concluding that last year's actual results are the most realistic base for expected growth. Mechanistic acceptance of recent results as being representative of future expectations is one of the most common errors in implementing the capitalization method of valuation.

For a simple example of using numbers in Formula 4.6, accept all assumptions in the previous example, with the exception that the $100 net cash flow expected in period 1 is instead the normalized base cash flow for period 0. (The $100 is for the period just ended, rather than the expectation for the period just starting.) Substituting the numbers with these assumptions into Formula 4.6 produces the following:

Formula 4.7

$$PV = \frac{\$100\,(1+.03)}{.13-.03}$$

$$= \frac{\$103}{.10}$$

$$= \underline{\underline{\$1,030}}$$

In this example, the estimated fair market value of the investment is $1,030. That is the amount that a willing buyer would expect to pay and a willing seller would expect to receive (before taking into consideration any transaction costs).

Note that the relationship between this and the previous example is simple and straightforward. We backed up the receipt of the $100 by one period, and the value of the investment was higher by 3%, the growth rate. In a constant growth model, assuming that all of the available cash flows are distributed, the value of the investment grows at the same rate as the rate of growth of the cash flows. This is because, in defining net cash flow (as we did in the previous chapter), we have already subtracted the amount of reinvestment necessary to support the projected growth.

The investor in the above example thus earns a *total* rate of return of 13%, comprised of 10% current return (the capitalization rate) plus 3% annually compounded growth in the value of the investment.

COMBINING DISCOUNTING AND CAPITALIZING (TWO-STAGE MODEL)

For many investments, even given an accurate estimate of the cost of capital, there are practical problems with either a pure discounting or a pure capitalizing method of valuation.

Problem with discounting: There are few equity investments for which returns for each specific incremental period can be projected with accuracy many years into the future.

Problem with capitalizing: For most equity investments, it is not reasonable to expect a constant growth rate in perpetuity from either the year preceding or the year following the valuation date.

This dilemma is typically dealt with by combining the discounting method and the capitalizing method into a *two-stage model*. The idea is to project discrete cash flows for some number of periods into the future and then to project a steady growth model starting at the end of the discrete projection period. Each period's discrete cash flow is discounted to a present value, and the capitalized value of the projected cash flows following the end of the discrete projection period is also discounted back to a present value. The sum of the present values is the total present value. The capitalized value of the projected cash flows following the discrete projection period is called the *terminal value* or *residual value*.

The preceding narrative explanation of a "two-stage model" is summarized in the following steps:

1. Decide on the reasonable length of time for which discrete projections can be made.
2. Estimate specific amounts of expected cash flow for each of the discrete projection periods.
3. Estimate a long-term sustainable rate of growth in cash flows from the end of the discrete projection period forward.

4. Use the Gordon Growth Model (Formulas 4.6 and 4.7) to estimate value as of the end of the discrete projection period.
5. Discount each of the increments of cash flow back to a present value at the discount rate (cost of capital) for the number of periods until it is received.
6. Discount the "terminal value" (estimated in step 4) back to a present value for the number of periods in the discrete projection period (the same number of periods as the last increment of cash flow).
7. Sum the values derived from steps 5 and 6. These steps can be summarized in the following formula:

Formula 4.8

$$PV = \frac{NCF_1}{(1 + k)} + \frac{NCF_2}{(1 + k)^2} + \cdots + \frac{NCF_n}{(1 + k)^n} + \frac{\dfrac{NCF_n(1 + g)}{k - g}}{(1 + k)^n}$$

where:

$NCF_1 \ldots NCF_n$ = Net cash flow expected in each of the periods 1 through n, n being the last period of the discrete cash flow projections

k = Discount rate (cost of capital)

g = Expected long-term sustainable growth rate in net cash flow, starting with the last period of the discrete projection as the base year

The discrete projection period in the two-stage model is typically between five and ten years. However, for simplicity in applying Formula 4.8, we'll just use a three-year discrete projection period. Let's make the following assumptions:

1. Expected net cash flows for years 1, 2, and 3 are $100, $120, and $140, respectively.
2. Beyond year 3, cash flow is expected to grow fairly evenly at a rate of about 5% in perpetuity.
3. The cost of capital for this investment is estimated to be 12%.

Substituting numbers derived from these assumptions into Formula 4.8 produces the following:

Formula 4.9

$$PV = \frac{\$100}{(1+.12)} + \frac{\$120}{(1+.12)^2} + \frac{\$140}{(1+.12)^3} + \frac{\dfrac{\$140\,(1+.05)}{.12-.05}}{(1+.12)^3}$$

$$= \frac{\$100}{1.12} + \frac{\$120}{1.2544} + \frac{\$140}{1.4049} + \frac{\dfrac{\$147}{.07}}{1.4049}$$

$$= \$89.29 + \$95.66 + \$99.65 + \frac{\$2,100}{1.4049}$$

$$= \$89.29 + \$95.66 + \$99.65 + \$1,494.77$$

$$= \underline{\underline{\$1,779.37}}$$

Thus, the estimated fair market value of this investment is $1,779.37. This is the amount that a willing buyer would expect to pay and a willing seller would expect to receive (before consideration of any transaction costs).

A common error is to discount the terminal value for $n + 1$ periods instead of n periods. The assumption we have made is that the nth period cash flow is received at the end of the nth period, and the terminal value is the amount for which we estimate we could sell the investment as of the end of the nth period. The end of one period and the beginning of the next period are the same moment in time, so they must be discounted for the same number of periods.

Note that in the preceding example, the "terminal value" represents 83% of the total present value ($1,494.77 ÷ $1,779.37 = .83). At this point it is wise to note a couple of relationships that the analyst should always keep in mind when using cost of capital in a two-stage model for valuation:

1. The shorter the projection period, the greater the impact of the terminal value on the total present value.
2. The closer the estimated growth rate is to the cost of capital, the more sensitive the model is to changes in assumptions regarding the growth rate (this is true for the straight capitalization model as well as the two-stage model). Of course, if the growth rate exceeds the cost of capital, the model implodes and is useless.

In some cases, the terminal value may not be a perpetuity model. For example, one might assume liquidation at that point, and the terminal value could be a salvage value.

EQUIVALENCY OF DISCOUNTING AND CAPITALIZING MODELS

As stated earlier, if all assumptions are met, the discounting and capitalizing methods of using the cost of capital will produce identical estimates of present value. Let's test this on the example we used in Formula 4.5. Recall that we assumed cash flow in period 1 of $100, growing in perpetuity at 3%. The cost of capital (the discount rate) was 13%, so we subtracted the growth rate of 3% to get a capitalization rate of 10%. Capitalizing the $100 period 1 expected cash flow at 10% gave us an estimated present value of $1,000 ($100 ÷ .10 = $1,000).

Let's take these same assumptions and put them into a discounting model. For simplicity, we will only use three periods for the discrete projection period, but it would not make any difference how many discrete projection periods we used.

Formula 4.10

$$PV = \frac{\$100}{(1 + .13)} + \frac{\$100\,(1 + .03)}{(1 + .13)^2} + \frac{\$100\,(1.03)^2}{(1 + .13)^3} + \frac{\dfrac{\$100\,(1.03)^3}{.13 - .03}}{(1.13)^3}$$

$$= \frac{\$100}{1.13} + \frac{\$103}{1.2769} + \frac{\$106.09}{1.4429} + \frac{\dfrac{\$109.27}{.10}}{1.4429}$$

$$= \$88.496 + \$80.664 + \$73.526 + \frac{\$1092.70}{1.4429}$$

$$= \$88.50 + \$80.67 + \$73.53 + \$757.30$$

$$= \underline{\underline{\$1,000}}$$

This example, showing the equivalency of using cost of capital in either the discounting or the capitalizing model, when all assumptions are met, demonstrates the point that capitalizing is really just a shorthand form of discounting. When using a capitalizing model, the analyst should think about whether the answer would work out the same if it were expanded to a full discounting model. If not, it may be propitious to review and possibly adjust certain assumptions. If the discounting and capitalization models produce different answers using the same cost of capital, there may be some kind of internal inconsistency.

THE MID-YEAR CONVENTION

In all of our examples, we have assumed that cash flows are received at the end of each year. Even if a company realizes cash flows throughout the year, payouts to the investors may be made only at the end of the year when the managers have seen how the full year has turned out and have an idea about what the next year looks like.

For some companies or investments, however, it may be more reasonable to assume that the cash flows are distributed more or less evenly throughout the year. To accommodate this latter assumption, we can modify our formulas for what we call the *mid-year convention*. The mid-year convention always results in a higher value, because the discount or capitalization rate remains the same and the assumption is that the investor does not have to wait quite as long to receive returns.

The Mid-Year Discounting Convention

We can make a simple modification to Formula 2.1 (discounting) to what we call the *mid-year discounting convention*. To do this, we merely subtract a half year from the exponent in the denominator of the equation.

Formula 2.1, the discounting equation, now becomes:

Formula 4.11

$$PV = \frac{NCF_1}{(1 + k)^{.5}} + \frac{NCF_2}{(1 + k)^{1.5}} + \cdots + \frac{NCF_n}{(1 + k)^{n - .5}}$$

The Mid-Year Capitalization Convention

Similarly, we can make a modification to the capitalization formula to reflect the receipt of cash flows throughout the year. The modification to Formula 4.4, the capitalization equation, is handled by accelerating the returns by a half year in the numerator:[1]

Formula 4.12

$$PV = \frac{NCF_1(1 + k)^{.5}}{k - g}$$

The Mid-Year Convention in the Two-Stage Model

Combining discrete period discounting and capitalized terminal value into a two-stage model as shown in Formula 4.8, the mid-year convention two-stage equation becomes the following:

Formula 4.13

$$PV = \frac{NCF_1}{(1 + k)^{.5}} + \frac{NCF_2}{(1 + k)^{1.5}} + \cdots + \frac{NCF_n}{(1 + k)^{n-.5}} + \frac{\dfrac{NCF_n(1 + g)(1 + k)^{.5}}{k - g}}{(1 + k)^n}$$

Using the same assumptions as in Formula 4.9 (where the value was $1,779.37) produces the following:

Formula 4.14

$$PV = \frac{\$100}{(1 + .12)^{.5}} + \frac{\$120}{(1 + .12)^{1.5}} + \frac{\$140}{(1 + .12)^{2.5}} + \frac{\dfrac{\$140(1+.05)(1 + .12)^{.5}}{.12 - .05}}{(1 + .12)^3}$$

$$= \frac{\$100}{1.058} + \frac{\$120}{1.185} + \frac{\$140}{1.328} + \frac{\dfrac{\$155.526}{.07}}{1.4049}$$

$$= \$94.52 + \$101.27 + \$105.42 + \frac{\$2,221.80}{1.4049}$$

$$= \$94.52 + \$101.27 + \$105.42 + \$1,581.46$$

$$= \underline{\$1,882.67}$$

In this case, using the mid-year convention increased the value by $103.30 ($1,882.67 − $1,779.37 = $103.30) or 5.8% ($103.30 ÷ $1,779.37 = .058).

The reader should also be aware that there is an alternative version of the terminal value factor in the two-stage model that actually is equivalent to that used in the preceding formula. Instead of using the modified capitalization equation in the numerator of the terminal value factor, the normal terminal value capitalization equation is used, and the terminal value is discounted by $n - .5$ years instead of n years.

This equation reads as follows:

Formula 4.15

$$PV = \frac{NCF_1}{(1 + k)^{.5}} + \frac{NCF_2}{(1 + k)^{1.5}} + \cdots + \frac{NCF_n}{(1 + k)^{n-.5}} + \frac{\dfrac{NCF_n(1 + g)}{k - g}}{(1 + k)^{n-.5}}$$

Using the same numbers as in Formula 4.14, this works out to:

$$PV = \frac{\$100}{(1+.12)^{.5}} + \frac{\$120}{(1+.12)^{1.5}} + \frac{\$140}{(1+.12)^{2.5}} + \frac{\dfrac{\$140(1+.05)}{.12-.05}}{(1+.12)^{2.5}}$$

$$= \frac{\$100}{1.058} + \frac{\$120}{1.185} + \frac{\$140}{1.328} + \frac{\dfrac{\$147}{.07}}{1.328}$$

$$= \$94.52 + \$101.27 + \$105.42 + \frac{\$2,100}{1.328}$$

$$= \$94.52 + \$101.27 + \$105.42 + \$1,581.32$$

$$= \underline{\underline{\$1,882.53}}$$

(The $.14 difference is a matter of rounding.)

SUMMARY

This chapter has shown the mechanics of *discounting* and *capitalizing,* and has defined the difference between a *discount rate* and a *capitalization rate.*

It has shown that capitalizing is merely a short-form version of discounting. The essential difference between the discounting method and the capitalizing method is how changes in expected cash flows over time are reflected in the respective formulas. All things being equal, the discounting method and the capitalizing method will yield identical results. However, the validity of the capitalizing method in the income approach to valuation is dependent on the assumption that the difference between the discount rate and the capitalization rate represents a long-term average rate of growth in the income variable being capitalized.

Because many companies are likely to expect near-term changes in levels of their returns that are not expected to be representative of longer-term expectations, many analysts use a combination of discounting and capitalizing for valuation. To accomplish this, they implement the following steps:

1. Project discrete amounts of return for some period of years until the company is expected to reach a stabilized level from which relatively constant growth may be expected to proceed.

2. Use the Gordon Growth Model to estimate a "terminal value" as of the end of the discrete projection period.

3. Discount each discrete projected cash flow to a present value at the cost of capital for the number of periods until it is expected to be received.

4. Discount the terminal value to a present value at the cost of capital for the number of periods in the discrete projection period (the *beginning* of the assumed stable growth period.)

5. Add the values from steps 3 and 4.

Most discounting and capitalization formulas reflect the implicit assumption that investors will realize their cash flows at the end of each year. If it is assumed that they will receive cash flows more or less evenly throughout the year, the formulas can be modified by the mid-year convention.

Note

1. Proof of the accuracy of this method was presented in "Capitalization Using a Mid-Year Convention," by Todd A. Kaltman, *Business Valuation Review* (December 1995), 178–182.

Chapter 5

Relationship Between Risk and the Cost of Capital

The cost of capital for any given investment is a combination of two basic factors:[1]

1. A *risk-free rate*. By a risk-free rate we mean a rate of return that is available in the market on an investment that is free of default risk, usually the yield to maturity on a U.S. government security.

2. A *premium for risk*. An expected amount of return over and above the risk-free rate to compensate the investor for accepting risk.

Quantifying the amount by which risk affects the cost of capital for any particular company or investment is arguably one of the most difficult analyses in the field of corporate finance, including valuation and capital budgeting.

DEFINING RISK

Probably the most widely accepted definition of risk in the context of business valuation is *the degree of certainty or uncertainty as to the realization of expected returns*.[2] This means uncertainty as to both the amounts and the timing of expected returns. Note that the definition incorporates as the reference point *expected returns*. By expected returns, in a technical sense, we mean the expected value (mean average) of the probability distribution of possible returns for each forecast period. This concept was explained in Chapter 3 in the discussion of net cash flow. The point here is to understand that the uncertainty encompasses the full distribution of possible returns for each period both above and below the expected value.

Inasmuch as uncertainty is within the mind of each individual investor, we cannot measure the risk directly. Consequently, participants in the financial markets have developed ways of measuring factors that investors normally would take into consideration in their effort to incorporate risk into their required rate of return.

TYPES OF RISK

Although risk arises from many sources, this chapter addresses risk in the economic sense, as used in the conventional methods of estimating cost of capital. In this context, capital market theory divides risk into three components:

1. *Maturity risk* (also called *horizon risk* or *interest rate risk*)
2. *Systematic risk* (also called *market risk*)
3. *Unsystematic risk* (sometimes called *company risk, specific risk,* or *residual risk*)

Maturity Risk

Maturity risk (also called horizon risk or interest rate risk) is the risk that the value of the investment may go up or down because of changes in the general level of interest rates. The longer the term of an investment, the greater the maturity risk. For example, market prices of long-term bonds fluctuate much more in response to changes in levels of interest rates than do short-term bonds or notes. When we refer to the yields of U.S. government bonds as *riskless rates*, we mean that we regard them as free from the prospect of default, but we recognize that they do incorporate maturity risk: the longer the maturity, the greater the susceptibility to change in market price in response to changes in market rates of interest. In regard to interest rates, much of the uncertainty derives from the uncertainty of future inflation levels.

Systematic Risk

Systematic risk (also called market risk) is the uncertainty of future returns because of the sensitivity of the return on a subject investment to movements in return for the investment market as a whole. Although this is a broad conceptual definition, in practical application the investment market as a whole is generally limited to the U.S. equity markets and is typically measured by returns on either the New York Stock Exchange index or the Standard & Poor's 500 index.

Some theoreticians say that the only risk that the capital markets reward with an expected premium rate of return is systematic risk, because *unsystematic risk* can be eliminated by holding a well-diversified portfolio of investments. Although this may be true for active publicly traded securities, it generally is not practical to hold a portfolio of closely held companies that is well enough diversified to eliminate all risk except that of the market itself.

As we get into the chapters on the various methods of estimating the cost of capital, we will see that systematic risk is a factor specifically measured for a particular company or industry in some methods, but not at all or not necessarily in others. Systematic risk is taken into consideration in the capital asset pricing model (CAPM), which is the subject of Chapter 9. It is commonly measured by a factor called *beta*, which attempts to measure the sensitivity of the returns realized by a company or an industry to movements in returns of "the market," usually defined as either the New York Stock Exchange or the Standard & Poor's 500 Stock composite.

Unsystematic Risk

Unsystematic risk (also called specific risk or residual risk) is the uncertainty of expected returns arising from factors other than the market itself. These factors typically include characteristics of the industry and the individual company. In international investing, they can also include characteristics of a particular country.

Much of the unsystematic risk of an investment may be captured in the *size premium*, which is the subject of Chapter 11. Fully capturing unsystematic risk in the discount rate requires analysis of the company, in comparison with other companies, which is also discussed in Chapter 5.

HOW RISK IMPACTS THE COST OF CAPITAL

As noted at the beginning of this chapter, the cost of capital (the expected rate of return that the market requires to attract money to the subject investment) has two components:[3]

1. A riskless rate
2. A risk premium

As the market's perception of the degree of risk of an investment goes up, the rate of return that the market requires (the discount rate) goes up. The higher the market's required rate of return, the lower the present value of the investment.

Risk is the ultimate concern to investors. The riskless rate compensates investors for renting out their money, so to speak; that is, delaying consumption over some future time period and receiving back dollars with less purchasing power. This component of the cost of capital is readily observable in the marketplace, and generally differs from one investment to another only to the extent of the time horizon (maturity) selected for measurement of the riskless rate.

The risk premium, however, is due to the uncertainty of expected returns, and is much harder to estimate and also varies widely from one prospective capital investment to another. One could say that the market abhors uncertainty, and consequently demands a high price (in terms of required rate of return or cost of capital) to accept uncertainty. Since uncertainty as to timing and amounts of future receipts is greatest for equity investors, the high risk forces equity as a class to have the highest cost of capital. The risk premium varies greatly from one company or project to another, but for most smaller companies the risk premium component of the cost of capital is greater than the riskless rate component.

COST OF EQUITY CAPITAL

When using either the build-up method (Chapter 8) or the Capital Asset Pricing Model (Chapter 9), we estimate one or more components of a risk premium and add the total risk premium to the riskless rate in order to estimate the cost of equity capital.

When using publicly traded stock data to estimate the cost of equity capital — the discounted cash flow (DCF) method (Chapter 12) — we get a total cost of equity capital without any explicit breakdown as to how much of it is attributable to a riskless rate and how much is attributable to the risk premium.

COST OF CONVENTIONAL DEBT AND PREFERRED EQUITY CAPITAL

The cost of debt and preferred stock capital generally depends on risk factors identified by fixed income rating services such as Standard & Poor's and Moody's. The rates of return for securities with comparable risk factors generally can be observed in the market.[4]

COST OF OVERALL INVESTED CAPITAL (WACC)

The cost of total invested capital is a blending of the costs of each component, called the *weighted average cost of capital* (WACC). Chapter 6 discusses each component in the capital structure, and Chapter 7 addresses the weighted average cost of capital.

SUMMARY

The cost of capital is a function of the market's risk-free rate plus a premium for the risk associated with the investment. *Risk* is the degree of certainty or uncertainty as to the realization of the expected returns from the investment.

Most analysts choose to use a long-term government security as a proxy for the "risk-free" rate. It is assumed that this rate is free of default risk, but it is recognized that it includes interest rate risk; that is, the market value of the principal will change with changes in the general level of interest rates.

In an economic sense, the market distinguishes between *systematic risk* and *unsystematic risk*. Systematic risk is the sensitivity of returns on the subject investment to returns on the overall market. Unsystematic risk is risk unique to the subject company or industry as opposed to the market as a whole.

Risk impacts the cost of each of the components of capital, that is, debt, senior equity, and common equity. Since risk has an impact on each capital component, it also has an impact on the weighted average cost of capital.

As risk goes up, the cost of capital goes up, and value goes down. Because risk cannot be observed directly in the market, it must be estimated. The impact of risk on the cost of capital is at once one of the most essential and one of the most difficult analyses in corporate finance and investments.

Notes

1. A third factor is liquidity, but that is usually treated as a separate adjustment, as discussed in Chapter 16.
2. Shannon P. Pratt, Robert F. Reilly, and Robert P. Schweihs, *Valuing a Business: The Analysis and Appraisal of Closely Held Companies*, 3d ed. (Burr Ridge, IL: McGraw-Hill, 1996), 40.
3. As noted in note 1, a third element — lack of marketability or liquidity — may be impounded into the discount rate, but more often it is treated as a separate adjustment to value. This is covered in Chapter 16.
4. This text deals primarily with the cost of equity and the weighted average cost of capital. For detailed discussions on cost of debt and cost of preferred equity, see Chapter 20 and 21 respectively, in Pratt, Reilly, and Schweihs, *Valuing a Business*.

Chapter 6

Cost Components of a Company's Capital Structure

Debt
    Tax Effect Lowers Cost of Debt
    Personal Guarantees
Preferred Equity
Convertible Debt or Preferred Stock
Common Stock or Partnership Interests
Summary

The capital structure of many companies includes two or more components, each of which has its own cost of capital. Such companies may be said to have a complex capital structure. The major components commonly found are:

- Debt
- Preferred stock
- Common stock or partnership interests

Similarly, a project being considered in a capital budgeting decision may be financed by multiple components of capital.

In a complex capital structure, each of these general components may have subcomponents, and each subcomponent may have a different cost of capital. In addition, there may be hybrid or special securities, such as convertible debt or preferred stock, warrants, options, or leases.

Ultimately, a company's or project's overall cost of capital is a result of the blending of the individual costs of each of these components. This chapter briefly discusses each of the capital structure components, and Chapter 7 shows the process of blending them into a company's or project's overall cost of capital, which is called the weighted average cost of capital (WACC).

Estimation of the costs of conventional fixed-income components of the capital structure, that is, straight debt and preferred stock, is relatively straightforward, because costs of capital for securities of comparable risk usually are directly observable in the market and the company's actual imbedded cost is often at or very close to current market rates. Although there can be many controversies surrounding costs of fixed income capital, especially if unusual provisions exist, we discuss these components only briefly here, and the rest of this book deals primarily with the critically important but highly elusive and controversial issue of the cost of equity.

DEBT

Conceptually, only long-term liabilities are included in a capital structure. However, many closely held companies, especially smaller ones, use what is technically short-term interest-bearing debt as if it were long-term debt. In these cases, it becomes a matter of the analyst's judgment as to whether or not to reclassify the short-term debt as long-term debt and include it in the capital structure for the purpose of estimating the company's overall cost of capital (weighted average cost of capital).

Usually, the cost of debt is equivalent to the company's interest expense (after tax effects) and is readily ascertainable from the footnotes to the company's financial statements (if the company has either audited or reviewed statements, or compiled statements with footnote information). If the rate the company is paying is not a current market rate (e.g., long-term debt issued at a time that market rates were significantly different), then the analyst should estimate what a current market rate would be for that component of the company's capital structure.

Standard & Poor's publishes debt rating criteria along with the *Standard & Poor's Bond Guide.* The analyst can see how the investment would fit into the bond rating system, then check the financial press to see what the yields are for the estimated rating.[1] Some companies have more than one class of debt, each with its own cost of debt capital.

The relevant market "yield" is either the *yield to maturity* or the *yield to call date.* This is the total return that the debt holder expects to receive over the life of the debt instrument, including current yield and any appreciation or depreciation from the market price, to the redemption of the debt at either its maturity or call date, if callable. If the stated interest rate is above current market rates, the bond would be expected to sell at a premium, and the yield to call date would usually be the appropriate yield, because it probably would be in the issuer's best interest to call it (redeem it) as soon as possible and refinance it at a lower interest cost. If the stated interest rate is below current market rates, then it usually would not be attractive to the company to call it, and the yield to maturity would be the most appropriate rate.

Tax Effect Lowers Cost of Debt

Because interest expense on debt is a tax-deductible expense to a company, the net cost of debt to the company is the interest paid less the tax saving resulting from the deductible interest payment. This cost of debt can be expressed by the following formula:

Formula 6.1

$$k_{dt} = k_d (1 - t)$$

where:

k_d = Rate of interest on debt
k_{dt} = Discount rate for debt (the company's after-tax cost of debt capital)
t = Tax rate (expressed as a percentage of pretax income)

For decision-making purposes, most corporate finance theoreticians recommend using the marginal tax rate if that differs from the company's effective tax rate.[2] That makes sense, since the marginal rate will be the cost incurred as a result of the investment. However, the focus should be on the marginal rate over the life of the investment if that is different from the marginal cost incurred initially.

Personal Guarantees

When estimating the cost of private company debt, the analyst should ascertain whether the debt is secured by personal guarantees. If so, this is an additional cost of debt that is not reflected directly in the financial statements (or in some cases, may not even be disclosed). Such guarantees would justify an upward adjustment in the company's cost of debt. The author is not aware of any published studies to help quantify this factor. Therefore, it becomes a subjective adjustment on the part of the valuer.[3]

PREFERRED EQUITY

If the capital structure includes preferred equity, the yield rate can be used as the cost of that component. If the dividend is at or close to the current market rate for preferred stocks of comparable features and risk, then the stated rate can be a proxy for market yield. If the rate is not close to a current market yield rate, then the analyst should estimate what a current market yield rate would be for that component of the company's capital structure.

Standard & Poor's publishes preferred stock rating criteria along with the *Standard & Poor's Stock Guide*. The analyst can see how the company's preferred stock would fit into the preferred stock rating system, then check the financial press to see what the yields are for preferred stocks with similar features and estimated rating.[4] The analyst must be conscious to adjust for any differences in features often found in privately issued preferred equity, such as special voting or liquidation rights. If the preferred stock is callable, the same analysis of the market rate of dividend compared to the dividend relative to call price as discussed with respect to debt applies to the preferred stock.

CONVERTIBLE DEBT OR PREFERRED STOCK

Convertible debt or convertible preferred stock is essentially two securities combined into one: a straight debt or preferred stock element plus a warrant. The cost of capital for the convertible instrument is the sum of the costs of these two elements.

A *warrant* is a long-term call option issued by a company on a specific class of its own common equity, usually at a fixed price. Understanding convertibles is easiest if you analyze them first as debt or nonconvertible preferred stocks and then as warrants (long-term call options).[5]

COMMON STOCK OR PARTNERSHIP INTERESTS

Part II of this book is devoted to estimating the cost of common equity. Unlike yields to maturity on debt or yields on preferred stock, the cost of common equity for specific companies or risk categories cannot be directly observed in the market.

The cost of equity capital is the expected rate of return that is needed in order to induce investors to place funds in a particular equity investment. As with the returns on bonds or preferred stock, the returns on common equity have two components:

1. Dividends or distributions
2. Changes in market value (capital gains or losses)

Because the cost of capital is a forward-looking concept, and these expectations as to amounts of return cannot be directly observed, they must be estimated from current and past market evidence. Analysts primarily use two methods of estimating the cost of equity capital from market data, each with variations:

1. Single or multifactor approaches:
   a. Build-up models (Chapter 8)
   b. Capital Asset Pricing Model (CAPM) (Chapters 9 and 10)
2. Discounted cash flow (DCF) approach (Chapter 12)
   a. Single-stage DCF model
   b. Multistage DCF models

Another multifactor method gaining acceptance in some circles, primarily oriented to larger companies, is called Arbitrage Pricing Theory (Chapter 14). Each of these methods of estimating the cost of equity capital is described in detail in their respective subsequent chapters.

SUMMARY

The typical components of a company's capital structure are summarized in Exhibit 6.1. In addition to the straight debt, preferred equity, and common equity shown in Exhibit 6.1, some companies have hybrid securities such as convertible debt or preferred stock and options or warrants.

Exhibit 6.1   Capital Structure Components

Short-term notes	Not technically part of the capital structure, but may be included in many cases, especially if being used as if long-term (e.g., officer loans)
Long-term debt	YES
Capital leases	Normally YES
Preferred stock	YES
Common stock Additional paid-in capital Retained earnings	YES — all part of common equity
Off-balance sheet options or warrants	Normally YES

The next chapter explains how to put the costs of each of these components together to get a company's overall cost of capital, called the weighted average cost of capital (WACC). Whereas this chapter has addressed briefly the cost of each component, the rest of the book will focus primarily on the many ways to estimate the cost of equity capital.

Notes

1. A detailed description of estimating the cost of debt is found in Chapter 20, "Debt Securities" in Shannon P. Pratt, Robert F. Reilly, and Robert P. Schweihs, *Valuing a Business: The Analysis and Appraisal of Closely Held Companies*, 3d ed. (Burr Ridge, IL: McGraw-Hill, 1996), 479–91.
2. See, for example, Richard A. Brealey and Stewart C. Myers, *Principles of Corporate Finance*, 5th ed. (New York: McGraw-Hill, 1996), 475.
3. If any reader can shed light on quantifying the cost of personal guarantees as a part of the cost of the company's debt capital, please contact the author at the address shown in the Preface, and it will be published in *Shannon Pratt's Business Valuation Update*.
4. A detailed description of estimating the cost of preferred stock is found in Chapter 21, "Preferred Stock," in Pratt, Reilly, and Schweihs, *Valuing a Business*, 492–513.
5. Valuing warrants and options is beyond the scope of this book. For an extensive treatment of this topic, see Chapters 20–22 in Brealey and Myers, *Principles of Corporate Finance*.

Weighted Average Cost of Capital

In the previous chapter we identified components of a company's capital structure. In this chapter we blend their costs together to estimate the company's overall cost of capital. In other words, we want to estimate the weighted cost for all of the company's invested capital or the capital to be committed to a specific project.

WHEN TO USE WEIGHTED AVERAGE COST OF CAPITAL (WACC)

The most obvious instance in which to use WACC is when the objective is to value the entire capital structure of a company. An example would be when considering an acquisition and the buyer expects to pay off all equity and debt holders and refinance the whole thing in a different way that better suits the buyer. Sometimes WACC is used even when the objective is ultimately to value only the equity. One would value the entire capital structure and then subtract the market value of the debt to estimate the value of the equity. This procedure frequently is used in highly leveraged situations.

WACC is especially appropriate for project selection in capital budgeting. The proportions of debt and equity that could be available to finance different kinds of projects could be different (e.g., asset-intensive projects may be financed with more debt), and the cost of capital should be based on the specific investment.

This, obviously, introduces the idea that we have to compute or estimate the weight (percentage of the total) for each component of the capital structure. The critical point is that *the relative weightings of debt and equity or other capital components are based on the market values of each component, not on the book values.*

WEIGHTED AVERAGE COST OF CAPITAL (WACC) FORMULA

As noted in the discussion of debt in Chapter 6, the weighted average cost of capital (WACC) is based on the cost of each component net of any corporate level tax effect of that component. We noted that in the return to the debt component, interest is a tax-deductible expense to a corporate taxpayer. Whatever taxes *are* paid are an actual cash expense to the company, and the returns available to equity holders is *after* the payment of corporate-level taxes.

Because we are interested in cash flows after entity-level taxes, literature and practitioners sometime refer to the WACC as an "after-tax WACC." The basic formula for computing the after-tax WACC for an entity with three capital structure components is as follows:

Formula 7.1

$$WACC = (k_e \times W_e) + (k_p \times W_p) + (k_{d(pt)}[1 - t] \times W_d)$$

where:

$WACC$ = Weighted average cost of capital
k_e = Cost of common equity capital
W_e = Percentage of common equity in the capital structure, at market value
k_p = Cost of preferred equity
W_p = Percentage of preferred equity in the capital structure, at market value
$k_{d(pt)}$ = Cost of debt (pretax)
t = Tax rate
W_d = Percentage of debt in the capital structure, at market value

COMPUTING WACC FOR A PUBLIC COMPANY

For active publicly traded securities, one can compute the weights for each capital component by multiplying the amount of each component outstanding by the market price of each, and then computing the percentage that each component represents out of the total market value. The steps for this procedure are as follows:

1. Identify the number of shares or units of each component of the capital structure.
2. Determine the market price per unit of each component of the capital structure as of the valuation date.
3. Multiply the number of units of each component by the market price per unit. This gives the total market value for each capital structure component.

4. Sum the total market values of each component, from Step 3. This gives the market value of invested capital (MVIC).

5. Divide the total market value of each component (from Step 3) by the total MVIC (from Step 4). This gives the percentage weight to be accorded to each component of the capital structure.

To illustrate the process of computing weights for each capital structure component, let us make the following assumptions for American Brainstorming Company (ABC):

1. 5 million shares of common stock issued and outstanding
2. Closing common stock price per share: $8.00
3. 1 million shares of preferred stock issued and outstanding
4. Closing preferred stock price per share: $20.00
5. $10 million face value of bonds issued and outstanding
6. Closing bond price: 90 (This means 90% of face value. Because bonds usually have $1,000 face value, this would be $900 per bond.)

From the preceding information, the capital structure weights can be computed as follows:

Component	Amount	Price	Component Total	Weight
Common stock	5,000,000	$ 8.00	$40,000,000	58%
Preferred stock	1,000,000	$20.00	20,000,000	29%
Bonds	$10,000,000	$90.00	9,000,000	13%
	Market value of invested capital		$69,000,000	100%

We still need a few more pieces of information before we can work out the weighted average cost of capital:

1. *Cost of common equity.* Because we have not yet given the reader any information as to how to estimate cost of common equity (i.e., the subject of Part II), we will *assume* that ABC's cost of common equity is 20%.

2. *Cost of preferred equity.* The cumulative, nonparticipating dividend on the preferred stock is $2.50 per share per year. Since its market price is $20, the cost of preferred equity is 12.5% ($2.50 ÷ $20.00 = .125).

3. *Cost of debt* (before tax effect). The bonds pay a 9% interest rate on their face value, or $90 per bond per year. Therefore, the current yield is 10% ($90 ÷ $900 = .10). However, remember that the cost of debt is the *yield to maturity*, not the current yield. We make the simplifying assumptions that the bonds mature three years from the valuation date and that the interest is paid only at the end

of each year. Our problem here is very much like that addressed in Formulas 2.1 and 2.2, except that we know the present value (PV), but what we have to solve for is the cost of debt capital (k_d) before tax effect. Putting it in the same form as Formulas 2.1 and 2.2 would look like this:

Formula 7.2

$$\$900 = \frac{\$90}{\left(1 + k_d\right)} + \frac{\$90}{\left(1 + k_d\right)^2} + \frac{\$90}{\left(1 + k_d\right)^3} + \frac{\$1,000}{\left(1 + k_d\right)^3}$$

Without going through the gyrations of transforming this formula to show the independent variable as k_d, we'll simply work it out on our trusty pocket financial calculator and find that $k_d \cong 13\%$. [Some readers may find it surprising that the example shows the pretax cost of the debt a half point (.5%) higher than the cost of preferred stock, which is in a lower position of claims on the balance sheet. This sometimes happens when the preferred stock is attractive for taxable corporations to hold, because only a small portion of the dividends paid are taxable income to the receiving corporation.]

4. *Tax rate*. The combined federal and state income tax rate for ABC is 40%.

Now we are prepared to substitute all of these numbers into Formula 7.1 to compute a weighted average cost of capital for ABC:

Formula 7.3

$$WACC = (.20 \times .58) + (.125 \times .29) + (.13 \,[1 - .40] \times .13)$$
$$= .116 + .036 + (.078 \times .13)$$
$$= .116 + .036 + .010$$
$$= .162 \text{ or } 16.2\%$$

Many people prefer to set up this formula in tabular form:

Component	Cost		Weight		Weighted Cost
Common stock	.20	×	.58	=	.116
Preferred stock	.125	×	.29	=	.036
Debt (after tax)	.078	×	.13	=	.010
		Weighted average cost of capital			.162

COMPUTING WACC FOR A PRIVATE COMPANY

In computing WACC for a closely held company project, or proposed project, we have one important additional problem to cope with: Because there is no market for the securities, we have to *estimate* market values in order to compute the capital structure weightings. As we will see, the estimated weightings for each component of the capital structure becomes an *iterative process*. Fortunately, computers do this exercise very quickly. (To "iterate" means to repeat. An "iterative process" is one that is repetitious. In this case, we estimate market value weights because the actual market values are unknown. We may re-estimate weights several times until the computed market value weights come fairly close to the weights used in estimating the WACC.)

The steps in the iterative process for estimating capital structure component weights for a closely held company can be summarized as follows:

1. Estimate the market value of senior securities (debt and preferred equity), and hold that dollar amount fixed throughout the process.
2. Make a first estimate of the market value weights of the senior securities and the common equity. (As a generality, the farther above book value you expect the equity market value to be, the greater the first estimate of the equity percentage compared with its percentage at book value.)
3. Using the first approximation weights, make a first approximation computation of the WACC, using Formula 7.1.
4. Project (1) the net cash flows available to all invested capital, and (2) the projected growth rate necessary for either a discounting valuation model (Formula 2.1) or a capitalizing valuation model (Formula 4.4).
5. Using the first approximation WACC from Step 3 and the projected cash flows from Step 4, compute a first approximation market value of invested capital (MVIC).
6. Subtract from the MVIC from Step 4 the value of the senior securities from Step 1. This gives the first approximation value of the common equity.
7. Compute the capital structure weights using the equity value from Step 6.
8. Repeat the process, starting with Step 3, until the computed market value weights come reasonably close to the weights used in computing the WACC.

For simplicity, we will demonstrate this process using only a two-component capital structure, common equity and debt. To further simplify it, we will use the capitalization model. (The iterative process works just as well with a discounting model, but a few more figures are involved.)

We will carry out the example based on the following assumptions for the Donald E. Frump company (DEF):

1. The *balance sheet* shows *book values* as follows:
Long-term debt	$400,000	(40%)
Common equity	$600,000	(60%)
2. *Interest rate* on the debt is 10%, and that approximates DEF's current cost of borrowing.

3. DEF's *cost of equity* has been estimated to be 25%.
4. DEF's *tax rate* is 40%.
5. NCF_{f1} = $250,000 (*Estimated net cash flow* to all invested capital for the 12 months immediately following the valuation date).
6. *Growth: NCF_f* (net cash flow available to all invested capital) is expected to grow fairly evenly following the first year at 5% per year.

If we start with the balance sheet book values as a first approximation of capital structure weightings, putting the assumed DEF balance sheet numbers into Formula 7.1, the first approximation of the capital structure weightings is as follows:

Formula 7.4

$$WACC = (.25 \times .60) + (.10[1 - .40] \times .40)$$
$$= .15 + (.06 \times .40)$$
$$= .15 + .024$$
$$= .174$$

This implies an overall cost of capital (WACC) of 17.4%.

The next step in the iteration process is to compute what the market value of all the invested capital would be at this WACC. Substituting numbers from the preceding information in the basic constant growth capitalization formula (Formula 4.4), we get the following:

Formula 7.5

$$PV_f = \frac{\$250,000}{.174 - .05}$$
$$= \frac{\$250,000}{.124}$$
$$= \$2,016,219$$

Subtracting the debt of $400,000 implies a market value of equity of $1,616,129 ($2,016,129 − $400,000 = $1,616,129). That is not even close to the book value of equity of $600,000. In fact, on this basis, the proportions of the market values of the components of the capital structure would be as follows:

Component	Value	Weight
Common stock	$1,616,129	80%
Debt	400,000	20%
Market value of invested capital	$2,016,129	100%

This certainly sends us back to the drawing board to try again, because our first approximation was 60/40, and this calculation produced a significantly different (80/20) result. This time, let's try the following weights:

$$
\begin{array}{ll}
\text{Common stock} & 75\% \\
\text{Debt} & 25\%
\end{array}
$$

Substituting these weights in the formula for WACC produces the following:

Formula 7.6

$$
\begin{aligned}
WACC &= (.25 \times .75) + (.10[1 - .40] \times .25) \\
&= .1875 + (.06 \times .25) \\
&= .1875 + .015 \\
&= .2025
\end{aligned}
$$

This implies an overall cost of capital (WACC) of 20.25%, significantly higher than the 17.4% in our first approximation.

Taking the next step, substituting this new estimate of WACC in the constant growth capitalization formula, we get the following:

$$
\begin{aligned}
PV_f &= \frac{\$250,000}{.2025 - .05} \\
&= \frac{\$250,000}{.1525} \\
&= \$1,639,344
\end{aligned}
$$

Subtracting the debt of $400,000 implies a market value of equity of $1,239,344 ($1,639,344 − $400,000 = $1,239,344). On this basis, the proportions of the market values of the components of the capital structure are as follows:

Component	Value	Weight
Common stock	$1,239,344	75.6%
Debt	400,000	24.4%
Market value of invested capital	$1,639,344	100.0%

This is close enough for most applications. After all, this isn't an exact science. This WACC of 20.25% is much more reasonable for this company than our first approximation of 17.4%. But it could be made exactly precise with further iterations.

The point to note is that the first approximation of the capital structure weighting led to a 30% overvaluation of DEF's stock. This certainly demonstrates the importance of using capital structure component weightings at market value, not at book value, for the purpose of estimating a company's WACC. The iterative process is necessary to develop a good estimate of the WACC, and therefore a sound and defensible estimate of the value of the overall capital, whether the valuation is using the WACC as a discount rate in the discounting method or a base rate from which to subtract growth when applying the capitalization method.

SHOULD AN ACTUAL OR HYPOTHETICAL CAPITAL STRUCTURE BE USED?

If a company or an interest in a company is to be valued as it is, assuming the capital structure will remain intact, then the amount of debt in the company's actual capital structure should be used. If a minority interest is to be valued by a procedure involving (first) valuing overall capital and (then) subtracting debt, the company's actual amount of debt in its capital structure may be appropriate. This is because it would be beyond the power of a minority stockholder to change the capital structure.

If a controlling interest is to be valued and the standard of value is *fair market value*, an argument can be made that an industry-average capital structure should be used, inasmuch as a control buyer would have the power to change the capital structure and the industry average could represent the most likely result. However, it would be important to understand how the industry-average capital structure is derived and whether or not it is reasonable to expect the subject company to achieve it, given current conditions of the company itself as well as financial market conditions. If the "industry average" capital structure is comprised of public companies and the subject is private, the subject may not be able to achieve the public company average, because public companies often have greater access to lower-cost senior capital than do private companies.

If a controlling interest is to be valued under the standard of *investment value* (value to a particular buyer or seller rather than the hypothetical buyer or seller that is asssumed under the fair market value standard), then the buyer's or owner's actual or desired capital structure could be used.

Note that when using an industry-average capital structure, it must be at market value, not book value. Most composite industry statistics sources (e.g., *Robert Morris Associates Annual Statement Studies* and all the various services based on federal income tax return data) report balance sheet figures and ratios at book value. Industry average capital structures at market value can be computed using data from selected guideline public companies in the industry, or from sources such as Ibbotson Associates' *Cost of Capital Quarterly* (see Data Resources in Appendix C), noting the caveat against assuming that private companies can achieve public company capital structures.

SUMMARY

We have outlined the process of computing a WACC for both public and private companies and for proposed capital projects. Because the weights of the capital structure components must be at market value, and private company stocks do not have market values, the process of computing the WACC for a private company is an iterative one, starting with approximations of market value weights of capital structure components.

Under some circumstances (e.g., a minority interest valuation) we may use a company's actual (currently existing) capital structure to estimate the WACC. If a controlling interest valuation is sought where it is reasonable to alter the company's capital structure, a hypothetical capital structure may be used to estimate the WACC.

There is much controversy about the potential impact on the WACC as a result of altering the capital structure.

PART II

Estimating the Cost of Equity Capital

Build-up Models

In previous chapters we have discussed the cost of capital in terms of its two major components, a *risk-free rate* and a *risk premium*. This chapter examines these components in general, dividing the equity risk premium into its three principal subcomponents.

Accordingly, the typical "build-up model" for estimating the cost of common equity capital consists of the following components:

1. A "risk-free" rate
2. A premium for risk, including any or all of the following subcomponents
   a. A general equity risk premium
   b. A size premium
   c. A specific company risk premium

In international investing, there may also be a country risk premium, reflecting uncertainties owing to economic and political instability in the particular country. With respect to using WACC in other countries, you should consider what the risk-free rate is in the foreign country (e.g., interest rate on that country's government debt) and the risk premium in that country as measured by stock market returns in excess of return on the foreign government bonds. The risk-free rate and foreign equity risk premium are likely to incorporate the foreign country risk premium, including any currency-related risk. In some countries, there might be a risk discount as compared to the United States.

It is probably a mistake to use the U.S. risk-free rate in determining foreign country cost of capital. In the event that a foreign risk premium is not available, which can often be the case, especially with smaller countries, you can use the U.S. risk premium applied to the foreign risk-free rate. (Bloomberg is an excellent source of foreign country government bond rates.)

FORMULA FOR THE EQUITY COST OF CAPITAL BUILD-UP MODEL

Stating the preceding information in terms of a formula, the formula for the equity cost of capital build-up model is as follows:

Formula 8.1

$$E(R_i) = R_f + RP_m + RP_s + RP_u$$

where:

$E(R_i)$ = Expected (market required) rate of return on security i
R_f = The rate of return available on a risk-free security as of the valuation date
RP_m = The general equity risk premium for the "market"
RP_s = Risk premium for small size
RP_u = Risk premium attributable to the specific company (the u stands for unsystematic risk, as defined in Chapter 5).

After a discussion of how to develop each of these four components, we will substitute some numbers into the formula in order to reach an estimated cost of equity capital for a sample company.

THE RISK-FREE RATE

The general notion of a "risk-free rate" is the return available as of the valuation date on a security that the market generally regards as being free of the risk of default.

Risk-Free Rate Represented by U.S. Treasury Securities

In the build-up model (as well as in other models) analysts typically use the yield to maturity on U.S. government securities, as of the effective valuation date, as the risk-free rate. They generally choose U.S. Treasury obligations of one of the following three maturities:

- 30-day
- 5-year
- 20-year

Sources for yields to maturity for maturities of any length as of any valuation date can be found in the daily financial press.

Components of the Risk-Free Rate

The so-called risk-free rate reflects the following three components:

1. *Rental Rate*: A real return for lending out the funds over the investment period, thus forgoing consumption for which the funds otherwise could be used
2. *Inflation*: The expected rate of inflation over the term of the risk-free investment
3. *Maturity risk or investment rate risk*: As discussed in Chapter 5, the risk that the principal's market value will rise or fall during the period to maturity as a function of changes in the general level of interest rates

All three of these economic factors are impounded into the yield to maturity for any given maturity length. However, it is not possible to observe the market consensus as to how much of the yield for any given maturity is attributable to each of these factors.

It is very important to note that this basic risk-free rate *does include inflation*. Therefore, when it is used to estimate a cost of capital to be used to discount expected future cash flows, those future cash flows should also reflect the effect of inflation. In the economic sense of nominal versus real dollars, we are building a cost of capital in nominal terms, and it should be used to discount expected returns which are also expressed in nominal terms.

Why Only Three Specific Maturities?

The reason the risk-free rate is typically chosen from one of only three specific maturities is that the build-up model incorporates a general equity risk premium that often is based on historical data developed by Ibbotson Associates.

- Ibbotson data provide short-term, intermediate-term, and long-term equity risk premium series, based on data corresponding to the aforementioned three maturities.
- The reason that 20 years is the longest maturity is that the Ibbotson data go all the way back to 1926, and 20 years was the longest U.S. Treasury obligation issued during the earlier years of that time period.

Selecting the Best Risk-Free Maturity

The consensus of financial analysts today is to use the 20-year U.S. Treasury yield to maturity as of the effective date of valuation for the following reasons:

- It most closely matches the often-assumed perpetual lifetime horizon of an equity investment.
- The longest-term yields to maturity fluctuate considerably less than short-term rates and thus are less likely to introduce unwarranted short-term distortions into the actual cost of capital.
- People generally are willing to recognize and accept the fact that the maturity risk is impounded into this base, or otherwise risk-free, rate.
- It matches the longest-term bond over which the equity risk premium is measured in the Ibbotson Associates data series.

Many analysts use a 30-year yield, but as a practical matter it usually is not greatly different than the 20-year yield.

Sometimes analysts select a 5-year rate to match the perceived investment horizon for the subject equity investment. The 30-day rate is the purest risk-free base rate, in that it contains virtually no maturity risk. If inflation is high, it does reflect the inflation component, but it contains little compensation for inflation uncertainty.

THE EQUITY RISK PREMIUM

On an equity investment, the return on investment that the investor will (or has the opportunity to) realize usually has two components:

1. Distributions during the holding period (e.g., dividends or withdrawals)
2. The capital gain or loss in the value of the investment. (For an active public security, it is considered part of the return whether or not the investor chooses to realize it, because the investor has that choice at any time.)

Obviously, these expected amounts of returns on equities are much less certain (or more risky) than the interest and maturity payments on U.S. Treasury obligations. This difference in riskiness is well documented by much higher standard deviations (year-to-year volatility) in returns on the stock market, as compared with the standard deviation of year-to-year returns on U.S. Treasury obligations.

To accept this greater risk, investors demand higher expected returns for investing in equities than for investing in U.S. Treasury obligations. This differential in expected return on the broad stock market over U.S. Treasury obligations (sometimes referred to as the *excess return*, but not to be confused with the *excess earnings method*) is called the *equity risk premium.*

In practice, a common method of estimating this expected equity risk premium is to use historical data. It is common to compute it as the average excess return (broad stock market over U.S. Treasuries) over some historical period of time. Since cost of capital is a forward-looking concept, a key assumption being implied when using historical data is that the amount of excess return that investors expect for investing in stocks, over the amount expected from Treasuries, for their future time horizon is approximately equal to the excess returns that have actually been achieved in the broad stock market in the historical period for which the equity risk premium was computed.

Ibbotson Associates Is the Primary Source of Historical Risk Premium Data

Ibbotson Associates publishes historical risk premium data in its annually updated *Stocks, Bonds, Bills & Inflation.* This publication is described in some detail in Chapter 13, on using Ibbotson data, and ordering information is included in Appendix C, "Data Resources." This source is a core part of any corporate finance data library, especially for a practitioner of business valuations.

Arithmetic or Geometric Mean Historical Average Equity Risk Premium?

Ibbotson publishes both an arithmetic and a geometric mean equity risk premium series. In the arithmetic mean series, the procedure is to add up all the excess returns over the periods and divide by the number of periods.

The formula for the familiar arithmetic mean is as follows:

Formula 8.2

$$\overline{X} = \frac{\sum_{n}^{1} R_i}{n}$$

where:

$\bar{X}$ = Mean average

R_i = Return for the ith period (the returns measured for each period are actually excess returns, that is, the difference between the equity market return and the Treasury obligation income return for the period)

n = Number of observation periods

In the geometric mean series, the procedure is to add 1 to the excess return for each period, multiply these all together, take the root of the number of periods, and subtract 1 at the end. The geometric mean result is the *annually compounded* rate of excess return.

The formula for the less familiar geometric mean is as follows:

Formula 8.3

$$G = \left[\prod_n (1 + R_i) \right]^{\frac{1}{n}} - 1$$

Sometimes also written as:

$$G = \sqrt[n]{\prod_n (1 + R_i)} - 1$$

where:

G = Geometric average

R_i = Return for the ith period (the returns measured for each period are actually excess returns, that is, the difference between the equity market return and the Treasury obligation income return for the period)

n = Number of observation periods

Mathematically, the geometric mean is always lower than the arithmetic mean unless all observations are equal, in which case the arithmetic and geometric means are equal.

Ibbotson's position is that, for valuation purposes, the historical equity risk premium should be the arithmetic mean applied to the expected value of the probability distribution of the expected return for each period. This is discussed further in Chapter 13, on using Ibbotson data.

The Ibbotson position that the long-term arithmetic average equity risk premium is the best proxy for today's equity risk premium has wide acceptance. For example, the view is supported by one of the leading corporate finance texts, Brealey and Myers's *Principles of Corporate Finance*, where they state, "If the cost of capital is estimated from historic returns or risk premiums, use arithmetic averages, not compound rates of return."[1] However, this view is not universally held. For a contrary view (i.e., that the geometric mean differences more closely approximate the market's required return), see Tom Copeland, Tim Koller, and Jack Murrin's *Valuation: Measuring and Managing the Value of Companies*.[2] There have also been articles on this controversy in *Business Valuation Review*, the quarterly journal of the Business Valuation Committee of the American Society of Appraisers. The arithmetic means is technically correct when applied to the expected value of the cash flows. However, since it takes a long time period to develop a statistically valid historical risk premium, it could produce a high indicated cost of capital relative to any specific date's current market conditions.

Over What Historical Time Period Should the Equity Risk Premium Be Calculated?

In regard to the historical time period over which equity risk should be calculated, Ibbotson offers the following observations:

- Reasons to focus on recent history:
   The recent past may be most relevant to an investor.
   Return patterns may change over time.
   The longer period includes "major events" (e.g., WWI, WWII, The Depression) which have not repeated in some time.
- Reasons to focus on long-term history:
   Long-term historical returns have shown surprising stability.
   Short-term observations may lead to illogical forecasts.
   Focusing on the recent past ignores dramatic historical events and their impact on market returns. We don't know what major events lie ahead.
   Law of large numbers: more observations lead to a more accurate estimate.

Exhibit 8.1 shows the arithmetic average equity risk premiums over various time periods as calculated by Ibbotson.

It should be noted that as the length of the measurement period shortens, the standard error of the estimate widens substantially. This is one of the reasons why Ibbotson advocates using the full historical period covered by the data, 1926 through the present, as discussed more fully in Chapter 13.

Estimating Equity Risk Premiums by the DCF Method

An alternative to using the historical average equity risk premium data to estimate the current equity risk premium is called the discounted cash flow (DCF) method. The DCF method uses market prices and analysts' growth estimates as of the effective date for individual companies and industries to estimate the market's implied expected rate of return.

Exhibit 8.1   Equity Risk Premium Measured for Various Time Periods

Period Length	Period	Large Cap Stocks Arithmetic Mean Total Return	Equity Risk Premium over Bonds
71 years	1926–1996	12.7%	7.5%
70 years	1927–1996	12.7%	7.5%
60 years	1937–1996	12.6%	7.1%
50 years	1947–1996	13.8%	7.6%
40 years	1957–1996	12.4%	5.3%
30 years	1967–1996	13.0%	4.9%
20 years	1977–1996	15.3%	6.4%
15 years	1982–1996	17.4%	8.6%
10 years	1987–1996	16.0%	8.3%
5 years	1992–1996	15.9%	8.9%

Source: Ibbotson Associates Cost of Capital Workshop (May 1997). Used with permission. All rights reserved.

The general idea of the DCF Model is quite simple: Rearrange a capitalization model (e.g., the Gordon Growth Model) or a discounting model to make the present value (the market price of the stock) a known quantity and solve the equation for k, the implied cost of the equity capital. The difference between k (the implied cost of equity capital for the company or industry) and R_f (the risk-free rate as of the same time) is the implied equity risk premium.

The DCF method is widely used among investment bankers and portfolio managers. During the mid-1990s the method consistently yielded lower equity risk premiums than the historical average equity risk premium method.

Data to implement the DCF method are included in Ibbotson's *Cost of Capital Quarterly* as well as in other sources included in Appendix C, "Data Resources." Chapter 12 is devoted to further implementation of the DCF method.

THE SMALL STOCK PREMIUM

Recent studies have provided strong evidence that the degree of risk and corresponding cost of capital increase with the decreasing size of the company. The studies show that this addition to the equity risk premium is over and above the amount that would be warranted just as a result of the companies' systematic risk. Following the next two chapters, which explain the Capital Asset Pricing Model (CAPM) and the proper use of beta, Chapter 11 discusses the results of research on this phenomenon, as well as the sources.

THE SPECIFIC COMPANY RISK PREMIUM

To the extent that the subject company's risk characteristics may be greater or less than the typical risk characteristics of the companies from which the equity risk premium and the size premium were drawn, a further adjustment may be necessary to estimate the cost of capital for the specific company. Such adjustment may be based on (but not necessarily limited to) analysis of the following factors:

1. Size smaller than the smallest size premium group
2. Industry risk
3. Volatility of returns
4. Leverage
5. Other company-specific factors

Size Smaller Than the Smallest Size Premium Group

As will be seen in Exhibit 11.4, the smallest size group for which we have specific size premium data averages $30 million in market value of equity, $37 million in sales, and so forth. If the subject company is somewhat smaller than this cutoff, most observers believe that a further size premium adjustment is warranted, but there have not yet been adequate empirical studies to quantify this amount. Accordingly, a conservative approach may be appropriate, perhaps adding a point or two to the discount rate for a significantly smaller company and leaving any greater adjustments to be attributed to other specifically identifiable risk factors. (The author plans to research this issue over the next year, using the *Pratt's Stats* private company transaction database, and will report the result in *Shannon Pratt's Business Valuation Update*.)

Industry Risk

The industry in which the company operates may have more or less risk than the average of other companies in the same size category. This differential is very hard to quantify in the build-up model. However, if the company is obviously in a very low-risk industry (e.g., water distribution) or a very high-risk industry (e.g., airlines), a point or two adjustment, either downward or upward, for this factor may be warranted.

Volatility of Returns

High volatility of return (usually measured by the standard deviation of historical returns over some period) is another risk factor. However, without comparable data for the average of the other companies in the size category and/or industry, it is

not possible to make a quantified comparison. If the analyst perceives that the subject company returns are either unusually stable or unusually volatile as compared
with others in the size category and/or industry, some adjustment for this factor may
be warranted.

Leverage

Leverage is clearly a factor that can be compared between the subject company
and its size peers. Exhibit 11.4 gives both the market value of equity and the market
value of invested capital for each size category.

For example, the smallest size category averages $30 million in market value of
equity and $41 million in market value of invested capital, or a capital structure of
roughly 25% debt and 75% equity, at market value. Size breakdowns in terms of
other size measures show generally similar capital structures. If the subject company's capital structure significantly departs from this average, some upward or downward adjustment to the cost of equity relative to the average company in the size
category would seem warranted. For example, highly levered companies should have
higher equity costs of capital when compared to companies with lower debt levels,
all else being equal. Of course, a decrease in the required equity return might be
warranted if the subject's capital structure has little or no debt.

Other Company-Specific Factors

Other factors specific to a particular company that affect risk could include, for
example:

1. Concentration of customer base
2. Key person dependence
3. Key supplier dependence
4. Abnormal present or pending competition
5. Pending regulatory changes
6. Pending lawsuits
7. A wide variety of other possible specific factors

Since the size premium tends to reflect some factors of this type, the analyst should
adjust further only for specific items that are truly unique to the subject company.
Unfortunately, despite the widespread use by analysts and appraisers of a company-
specific and/or industry-specific risk premium in a build-up (or CAPM) model, I am
not aware of any academic research into the subject, and it remains in the realm of
the analyst's judgment.[3]

AN EXAMPLE OF A BUILD-UP MODEL

Now that we've discussed the factors in the build-up model, we can substitute some numbers into Formula 8.1. We start with the following assumptions about Shannon's Bull Market (SBM), a regional steak house chain with excellent food and friendly service:

1. *Risk-free rate.* We will use the 20-year Treasury bond, for which the yield to maturity at the valuation date was 6.5%.
2. *Equity risk premium.* We will use the Ibbotson Associates' arithmetic average equity risk premium. The *SBBI 1997 Yearbook* shows that to be 7.5%.
3. *Size premium.* The *SBBI 1997 Yearbook* shows that the size premium for the 10th decile—smallest 10% of New York Stock Exchange (NYSE) stocks—over and above the general equity risk premium is 9.3% in excess of a CAPM equity risk premium that does not reflect size.[4]
4. *Company-specific risk premium.* SBM is considerably smaller than the average of the smallest 10% of NYSE stocks, and our analyst perceives that the restaurant industry is more risky than the average for those companies. Although the assessment is somewhat subjective, our analyst recommends adding a company-specific risk factor of 3.0% because of risk factors that he has identified as unique to this company.

Substituting the preceding information in Formula 8.1, we have the following:

Formula 8.2

$$E(R_i) = 6.5 + 7.5 + 9.3 + 3.0$$
$$= 26.5$$

So the estimated cost of capital for SBM is approximately 26.5%.

Some analysts prefer to present these calculations in tabular form, such as the following:

Build-up Cost of Equity Capital for SBM

Risk-free rate	6.5%
Equity risk premium	7.5%
Size premium	9.3%
Company-specific risk premium	3.0%
SBM cost of equity capital	26.3%

If we were using the Capital Asset Pricing Model (CAPM) (the subject of the next chapter), a portion of the size premium and, probably, all of the industry portion of the specific risk premium would be captured in the "beta" factor, which is the difference between CAPM and the straight build-up model. Of course, if these build-up model figures were being presented in a formal valuation report, each of the numbers in the calculation would be footnoted as to its source, and each would be supported by a narrative explanation.

SUMMARY

The build-up model for estimating the cost of equity capital has four components:

1. A risk-free rate
2. A general equity risk premium
3. A size premium
4. A specific company risk adjustment (which can be either positive or negative, depending on the risk comparisons between the subject company and others from which the size premium was derived).

These factors are summarized schematically in Exhibit 8.2. In a sense, the build-up method is a version of the Capital Asset Pricing Model (CAPM), the subject of the next chapter, without specifically incorporating systematic risk.

Exhibit 8.2   Summary of Development of Equity Discount Rate

Risk-free rate*	20-year, 5-year, or 30-day Treasury yield as of valuation date
+ Equity risk premium	Long-, intermediate-, or short-horizon equity risk premium (corresponding to risk-free yield above)**
+ Size premium	Small stock premium
± Specific risk	Specific risk difference in subject company relative to companies from which above data drawn

* The "risk-free" rate actually has one element of risk: *maturity risk* (sometimes called *interest rate risk* or *horizon risk*) — the risk that the value of the bond will fluctuate with changes in the general level of interest rates.
** Corresponding to Ibbotson's historical risk premium studies, as found in *Stocks, Bonds, Bills, and Inflation* yearbooks.

Notes

1. Richard A. Brealey and Stewart C. Myers, *Principles of Corporate Finance*, 5th ed. (New York: McGraw-Hill, 1996), 146–147.
2. Tom Copeland, Tim Koller, and Jack Murrin, *Valuation: Measuring and Managing the Value of Companies*, 2d ed. (New York: John Wiley & Sons, 1996), 261–263.

3. If readers are aware of any statistical material available to help quantify a company- or industry-specific portion of an equity risk premium, please contact the author at the address shown in the Preface, and the author will publish it in *Shannon Pratt's Business Valuation Update*.

4. The *SBBI 1997 Yearbook* shows the tenth decile actual return in excess of the riskless rate of 16.75% (p.138). Subtracting this from the long-horizon equity risk premium of 7.5% (p. 161) implies a size premium of approximately 9.3% if you assume that beta equals 1.0. In the build-up method, it would not be necessary to break down the general equity risk premium from the size component; one could simply use the total return in excess of the 20-year bond rate, that is, the 16.75%.

Chapter 9

The Capital Asset Pricing Model (CAPM)[1]

THE CONCEPT OF SYSTEMATIC RISK

For more than 30 years financial theorists have generally favored the notion that using the Capital Asset Pricing Model (CAPM) is the preferred method to estimate the cost of equity capital. In spite of many criticisms, it still is the most widely used model for estimating the cost of equity capital, especially for larger companies.

The only difference between the CAPM and the build-up model presented in the preceding chapter is the introduction of *systematic risk* as a modifier to the general equity risk premium. Systematic risk is measured by a factor called *beta*. Beta measures the sensitivity of excess total returns (total returns over the risk-free rate returns) on any individual security or portfolio of securities to the total excess returns on some measure of the market, such as the New York Stock Exchange (NYSE) or Standard & Poor's 500 Stock Composite Index.

The following chapter discusses the specific measurements of beta. Note at this point, however, that beta is based on total returns, which have two components:

1. Dividends
2. Change in market price

Inasmuch as privately held companies have no market price, their betas cannot be measured directly. Thus, to use the CAPM to estimate the cost of capital for a private company, it is necessary to estimate a proxy beta for that company. This is usually accomplished by using an average beta for the industry group or by selecting specific guideline public companies and using some composite, such as the average or median, of their betas.

BACKGROUND OF THE CAPITAL ASSET PRICING MODEL

The Capital Asset Pricing Model (CAPM) is part of a larger body of economic theory known as *capital market theory* (CMT). CMT also includes *security analysis* and *portfolio management theory*, a normative theory that describes how investors *should* behave in selecting common stocks for their portfolios, under a given set of assumptions. In contrast, the CAPM is a *positive* theory, meaning it describes the market relationships that *will* result if investors behave in the manner prescribed by portfolio theory.

The CAPM is a conceptual cornerstone of modern capital market theory. Its relevance to business valuations and capital budgeting is that businesses, business interests, and business investments are a subset of the investment opportunities available in the total capital market; thus, the determination of the prices of businesses theoretically should be subject to the same economic forces and relationships that determine the prices of other investment assets.

SYSTEMATIC AND UNSYSTEMATIC RISK

In Chapter 5 we defined risk conceptually as the degree of uncertainty or uncertainty as to the realization of expected future returns. Capital market theory divides risk into two components (other than maturity risk), systematic risk and unsystematic risk. Stated in nontechnical terms, *systematic risk* is the uncertainty of future returns owing to the sensitivity of the return on the subject investment to movements in the returns for a composite measure of marketable investments. *Unsystematic risk* is a function of the characteristics of the industry, the individual company, and the type of investment interest. To the extent that the industry as a whole is sensitive to market movements, that portion of the industry's risk would be captured in beta, the measure of systematic risk. Company-specific characteristics may include, for example, management's ability to weather changing economic conditions, relations between labor and management, the possibility of strikes, the success or failure of a particular marketing program, or any other factor specific to the company. Total risk depends on both systematic and unsystematic factors.

A fundamental assumption of the CAPM is that the risk premium portion of a security's expected return is a function of that security's systematic risk. This is because capital market theory assumes that investors hold, or have the ability to hold, common stocks in large, well-diversified portfolios. Under that assumption, investors will not require compensation (i.e., a higher return) for the unsystematic risk because they can easily diversify it away. Therefore, the only risk pertinent to a study of capital asset pricing theory is systematic risk. As one well-known corporate fi-nance text put it:

> The crucial distinction between diversifiable and nondiversifiable risks is the main idea underlying the capital asset pricing model.[2]

USING BETA TO ESTIMATE EXPECTED RATE OF RETURN

The CAPM leads to the conclusion that the equity risk premium (the required excess rate of return for a security over and above the risk-free rate) is a linear func-tion of the security's beta. This linear function is described in the following univari-ate linear regression formula:

Formula 9.1

$$E(R_i) = R_f + B(RP_m)$$

where:

$E(R_i)$ = Expected return (cost of capital) for an individual security
R_f = Rate of return available on a risk-free security (as of the valuation date)
B = Beta
RP_m = Equity risk premium for the market as a whole (or, by definition, the equity risk premium for a security with a beta of 1.0)

The preceding linear relationship is shown schematically in Exhibit 9.1, which presents the security market line (SML).

According to capital asset pricing theory, if the combination of an analyst's ex-pected rate of return on a given security and its risk, as measured by beta, places it below the security market line, such as security X in Exhibit 9.1, the analyst would consider that security (e.g., common stock) mispriced. It would be mispriced in the sense that the analyst's expected return on that security is less than it would be if the security were correctly priced, assuming fully efficient capital markets.

To put the security in equilibrium according to that analyst's expectations, the price of the security must decline, allowing the rate of return to increase until it is just sufficient to compensate the investor for bearing the security's risk. In theory, all common stocks in the market, in equilibrium, adjust in price until the consensus ex-pected rate of return on each is sufficient to compensate investors for holding them. In that situation the systematic risk/expected rate of return characteristics of all those securities will place them on the security market line.

Exhibit 9.1   Security Market Line

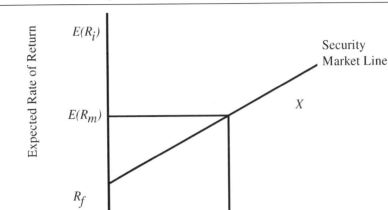

In this diagram

$E(R_i)$ = Expected return for the individual security
$E(R_m)$ = Expected return on the market
R_f = Risk-free rate available as of the valuation date
X = The risk and return profile for a particular company

In a market in perfect equilibrium, all securities would fall on the security market line. If security X has a high beta (as shown in the diagram) and a security analyst expects the returns for that security to be as shown, the analyst would consider the security overpriced.

Source: Adapted from Shannon P. Pratt, Robert F. Reilly, and Robert P. Schweihs, *Valuing a Business: The Analysis and Appraisal of Closely Held Companies*, 3d ed. (Burr Ridge, IL: McGraw-Hill, 1996), 169. Reprinted with permission of The McGraw-Hill Companies.

As Exhibit 9.1 shows, the beta for the market as a whole is 1.0. Therefore, from a numerical standpoint, the beta has the following interpretations:

Beta > 1.0   When market rates of return move up or down, the rates of return for the subject tend to move in the same direction and with greater magnitude. For example, for a stock with no dividend, if the market is up 10%, the price of a stock with a beta of 1.2 would be expected to be up 12%. If the market is down 10%, the price of the same stock would be expected to be down 12%. Many high tech companies are good examples of stocks with high betas.

Beta = 1.0   Fluctuations in rates of return for the subject tend to equal fluctuations in rates of return for the market.

Beta < 1.0   When market rates of return move up or down, rates of return for the subject tend to move up or down, but to a lesser extent. For example, for a stock with no dividend, if the market is up 10%, the price of a stock with a beta of .8 would be expected to be up 8%. The classic example of a low beta stock would be a utility that has not diversified into more risky activities.

Negative beta   Rates of return for the subject tend to move in the opposite
(rare)   direction from changes in rates of return for the market. Stocks with negative betas are rare. A few gold mining companies have had negative betas in the past.

To illustrate, using the preceding formula as part of the process of estimating a company's cost of equity capital, consider stocks of average size, publicly traded companies i, j, and k, with betas of 0.8, 1.0, and 1.2, respectively, a risk-free rate in the market of 7% (.07) at the valuation date, and a market equity risk premium of 8% (.08).

For company i, which is less sensitive to market movements than the average company, we can substitute in Formula 9.1 as follows:

Formula 9.2

$$E(R_i) = 0.07 + 0.8(0.08)$$
$$= 0.07 + 0.064$$
$$= 0.134$$

Thus, the cost of equity capital for company i is estimated to be 13.4% because it is less risky, in terms of systematic risk, than the average stock on the market.

For company j, which has average sensitivity to market movements, we can substitute in Formula 9.1 as follows:

Formula 9.3

$$E(R_j) = 0.07 + 1.0(0.08)$$
$$= 0.07 + 0.08$$
$$= 0.15$$

So the cost of equity capital for company j is estimated to be 15%, the estimated cost of capital for the average stock, because its systematic risk is equal to the average of the market as a whole.

For company k, which has greater than average sensitivity to market movements, we can substitute in Formula 9.1 as follows:

Formula 9.4

$$E(R_k) = 0.07 + 1.2(0.08)$$
$$= 0.07 + 0.096$$
$$= 0.166$$

Thus, the cost of equity capital for company k is estimated to be 16.6% because it is more risky, in terms of systematic risk, than the average stock on the market.

Note that in the preceding *pure* formulation of the CAPM, the required rate of return is composed of only two factors:

1. The risk-free rate
2. The market's general equity risk premium, as modified by the beta for the subject security

EXPANDING CAPM TO INCORPORATE SIZE PREMIUM AND SPECIFIC RISK

The Firm Size Phenomenon

Many empirical studies performed since CAPM was originally developed have indicated that the realized total returns on smaller companies have been substantially greater over a long period of time than the original formulation of the CAPM (as given in Formula 9.1) would have predicted. Ibbotson Associates comments on this phenomenon as follows:

> One of the most remarkable discoveries of modern finance is the finding of a relationship between firm size and return. On average, small companies have higher returns than large ones. . . .
>
> The firm size phenomenon is remarkable in several ways. First, the greater risk of small stocks does not, in the context of the capital asset pricing model, fully account for their higher returns over the long term. In the CAPM, only systematic or beta risk is rewarded. Small company stocks have had returns in excess of those implied by the betas of small stocks. Secondly, the calendar annual return differences between small and large companies are serially correlated. This suggests that past annual returns may be serially correlated. This suggests that past annual returns may be of some value in predicting future annual returns. Such serial correlation, or auto-correlation, is practically unknown in the market for large stocks and in most other capital markets.[3]

The size effect is the subject of Chapter 11.

The Specific Risk Factor

The notion that the only component of risk that investors care about is the systematic risk component is based on the assumption that all unsystematic risk can be eliminated by holding a perfectly diversified portfolio of risky assets that will, by definition, have a beta of 1.0.

Without addressing the validity of that assumption for the public markets (for the purpose of this book), it is obviously not feasible for investors in privately held companies to hold such a perfectly diversified portfolio that would eliminate all unsystematic risk. Therefore, for the cost of capital for privately held companies, even when using the CAPM, we have to consider whether there may be other risk elements that neither the beta factor (systematic risk) nor the size premium fully accounts for. If so, an adjustment to the discount rate for unsystematic risk would be appropriate.

Just as in the build-up model, the "specific risk" factor could be negative if the analyst were to conclude that the subject company was less risky than the average of the other companies from which the proxy estimates for the other elements of the cost of equity capital were drawn. For example, a company could have a well-protected, above-average price for its products as a result of a strong trademark, resulting in significantly less earnings volatility than experienced by its competitors.

EXPANDED CAPM COST OF CAPITAL FORMULA

If we expand CAPM to also reflect the size effect and specific risk, we can expand the cost of equity capital formula to add these two factors as follows:

Formula 9.5

$$E(R_i) = R_f + B(RP_m) + RP_s + RP_u$$

where:

$E(R_i)$ = Expected rate of return on security i
R_f = Rate of return available on a risk-free security as of the valuation date
RP_m = General equity risk premium for the market
RP_s = Risk premium for small size
RP_u = Risk premium attributable to the specific company (u stands for unsystematic risk)
B = Beta

Note that the *only* difference between this formula and the build-up model formula (Formula 8.1) is the addition of the beta coefficient. The values of the size and company-specific risk premium, however, are likely to differ from those used in the build-up model, because some portion of those risks may have been captured in beta.

To put some numbers into Formula 9.5, we will make some assumptions about Lazard, Hazard, and Zipp (LHZ), a fictional investment banking firm with publicly traded stock:

1. *Risk-free rate.* As of the valuation date, the yield to maturity on 20-year U.S. government bonds is 7.0%.
2. *Beta.* The LHZ beta is 1.3.
3. *Equity risk premium.* The general equity risk premium is 8.0%.
4. *Size premium.* The size premium for this size firm in excess of the risk captured in CAPM through beta is 3.5%. (We will assume here that is on the borderline between Ibbotson's ninth and tenth size deciles.)
5. *Company-specific risk factor.* Because of special risk factors, the analyst has estimated that there should be an additional specific risk factor of 1.0%.

Substituting this information in Formula 9.5, we have the following:

Formula 9.6

$$E(R_i) = 7.0 + 1.3(8.0) + 3.5 + 1.0$$
$$= 7.0 + 10.4 + 3.5 + 1.0$$
$$= 21.9$$

Thus, the estimated cost of equity capital for LHZ is 21.9%.

Some analysts prefer to present the preceding calculations in tabular form, which may look like the following:

CAPM Cost of Equity Capital for LHZ

Risk-free rate		7.0%
Equity risk premium:		
General equity risk premium	8.0	
Beta	× 1.3	
	10.4	
Small stock size premium		3.5
Specific risk premium		1.0
LHZ cost of equity capital		21.9%

Of course, if this information were being presented in a formal valuation report, each of the numbers would be footnoted as to its source and each would be supported by narrative explanation.

One other difference between CAPM and the build-up model is the amount of the small stock size premium. In CAPM, only the size premium in excess of CAPM is added, thus avoiding double-counting any portion of the size premium that was already captured by beta. On average, smaller companies do have higher betas than larger companies. The average beta for companies of this size is 1.38, as shown later in Exhibit 13.2. The CAPM return in excess of the riskless rate for companies of this size was 10.37% (as shown in Exhibit 13.2), or 2.37% greater than the general equity risk premium. Therefore, if using a straight build-up model instead of CAPM, one might consider using a small stock premium of about 5.9% $(3.5 + 2.37 \cong 5.9)$.

ASSUMPTIONS UNDERLYING THE CAPITAL ASSET PRICING MODEL

The assumptions underlying the CAPM are as follows:

1. Investors are risk averse.
2. Rational investors seek to hold efficient portfolios, that is, portfolios that are fully diversified.
3. All investors have identical investment time horizons (i.e., expected holding periods).
4. All investors have identical expectations about such variables as expected rates of return and how capitalization rates are generated.
5. There are no transaction costs.
6. There are no investment-related taxes (however, there may be corporate income taxes).
7. The rate received from lending money is the same as the cost of borrowing money.
8. The market has perfect divisibility and liquidity (i.e., investors can readily buy or sell any desired fractional interest).

Obviously, the extent to which these assumptions are or are not met in the real world will have a bearing on the application of the CAPM for the valuation of closely held businesses, business interests, or investment projects. For example, while the perfect divisibility and liquidity assumption approximates reality for publicly traded stocks, this is not so for privately held companies. This is one reason that the company-specific, nonsystematic risk factor may be rewarded in expected returns for closely held companies even if it is not for public companies.

The CAPM, like most economic models, offers a theoretical framework for how certain relationships would exist subject to certain assumptions. While not all assumptions are met in the real world, it provides a reasonable economic model for estimation of the cost of capital. Other models are discussed in future chapters.

SUMMARY

The Capital Asset Pricing Model (CAPM) expands on the build-up model by introducing the beta coefficient, an estimate of *systematic risk*, the sensitivity of returns for the subject to returns for the market. The CAPM has several underlying assumptions, which may be met to a greater or lesser extent for the market as a whole or for any particular company or investment.

Exhibit 9.2 is a schematic summary of using the CAPM to estimate the cost of equity capital.

Exhibit 9.2   Capital Asset Pricing Model Method of Estimating Equity Discount Rate

Risk-free rate*	20-year, 5-year, or 30-day Treasury yield as of valuation date
+ Equity risk premium**	Long-, intermediate-, or short-horizon equity risk premium (corresponding to risk-free yield above) } In CAPM, multiply the general equity risk premium by beta.
+ Size premium	Small stock premium
± Specific risk	Specific risk difference in subject company relative to companies from which above data are drawn

 * The "risk-free" rate actually has one element of risk: *maturity risk* (sometimes called *interest risk* or *horizon risk*) — the risk that the value of the bond will fluctuate with changes in the general level of interest rates.
** This assumes that the equity risk premium will be based on Ibbotson's historical data. The equity risk premium could also be estimated from DCF model data, as discussed in Chapter 12.

Notes

1. Chapter 9 draws heavily on Shannon P. Pratt, Robert F. Reilly, and Robert P. Schweihs, *Valuing a Business: The Analysis and Appraisal of Closely Held Companies*, 3d ed. (Burr Ridge, IL: McGraw-Hill, 1996).
2. Richard A. Brealey and Stewart C. Myers, *Principles of Corporate Finance,* 5th ed. (New York: McGraw-Hill, 1996), 990.
3. Ibbotson Associates, *Stocks, Bonds, Bills and Inflation, 1997 Yearbook* (Chicago: Ibbotson Associates, 1997), 125–126.

Chapter 10

Proper Use of Betas

As discussed in the previous chapter, the beta is used as a modifier to the equity risk premium in the context of the Capital Asset Pricing Model (CAPM). The purpose of this chapter is to explore some widely used variations in the construction and application of betas.

ESTIMATION OF BETA

Systematic risk is measured in the Capital Asset Pricing Model by a factor called *beta*. Beta is a function of the relationship between the return on an individual security and the return on the market as measured by a broad market index such as the Standard & Poor's 500 Stock Composite Index.

Beta is often measured by comparing the excess return on an individual security relative to the excess return on the market index. By *excess return*, we mean the total return (which includes both dividends and capital gains and losses) over and above the return available on a risk-free investment (e.g., U.S. Treasuries).

Theorists prefer to measure beta on the basis of excess returns rather than total returns. However, a comparison of measurements by the two choices show that, as a practical matter, it makes little difference. Ibbotson Associates uses excess returns in all its computations.

A common method of calculating beta is to compute the slope of the best-fit line between the (excess) return on the individual security and the (excess) return on the market. An example of this is shown in Exhibit 10.1.

Exhibit 10.1 Computation of Beta

Month End, t^a	Return on Security A[b]	Return on S&P Index[c]
1/78	(0.038)	(0.080)
2/78	0.076	0.048
3/78	0.062	0.008
—		
—		
—		
9/87	(0.004)	0.040
10/87	0.091	0.016
11/87	0.174	0.109
12/87	0.083	(0.030)
Sum	1.800	0.840
Average	0.015	0.007

$$\text{Beta} = \frac{\text{Covariance (Security A, S\&P Index)}}{\text{Variance of S\&P Index}} = \frac{0.00175}{.00194} = 0.90$$

a. 10 years or 120 months
b. Returns based on end-of-month prices and dividend payments
c. Returns based on end-of-month S&P Index

Source: Shannon P. Pratt, Robert F. Reilly, and Robert P. Schweihs, *Valuing a Business: The Analysis and Appraisal of Closely Held Companies*, 3d ed. (Burr Ridge, IL: McGraw-Hill, 1996), 167. Reprinted with permission.

Because, as noted in the previous chapter, we cannot compute a beta directly for a privately held company, we go to reference sources to obtain betas for guideline public companies or industries so as to determine a proxy beta to use for our private company. Details on these sources are to be found in Appendix C, Data Resources.

DIFFERENCES IN ESTIMATION OF BETA

It is important to understand that there are significant differences between betas for the same stock published by different financial reporting services. One of the implications is that betas for guideline companies used in a valuation should all come from the same source. If all betas for guideline companies are not available from a single source, the best solution is probably to use the source providing betas for the greatest number of guideline companies, and not use betas given for the others. Otherwise an "apples and oranges" mixture will result.

Differences in the beta measurement derive from choices within the following four variables:

1. The length of the total time period over which the returns are measured
2. The periodicity (frequency) of measurement within that time period
3. The choice of an index to use as a market proxy
4. The risk-free rate above which the excess returns should be measured

In addition to how these four variables are treated, there are adjustments that can be made to recognize the beta's tendency to adjust toward 1.0. These adjustments are discussed later in the chapter.

Length of the Measurement Period

Most services that calculate beta use a two- to five-year measurement period, with five years being the most common. The Ibbotson Associates' *Beta Book* uses 60 months for most stocks, but includes a beta based on as few as 36 months if data are available for only this length of time.

Frequency of Data Measurement

Data may be measured daily, weekly, monthly, quarterly, or annually. Monthly is the most common frequency, although *Value Line* uses five years of weekly data.

Choice of Market Index

The market index used in calculating beta could be any of the following or, in some cases, another index:

- Standard & Poor's 500
- NYSE
- NYSE and ASE
- NYSE, ASE, and OTC
- Value Line Index

In order for an index to be representative of the market, it must be market capitalization weighted. That is, the weight for each company in the index is determined by the market value of its equity. The sizes of the companies in the Standard & Poor's 500 are so great that the Standard & Poor's 500 comprises about 70% of the total capitalization of all of the stock constituting the combined indexes listed here.

Furthermore, the broader market indices shown above correlate almost perfectly with the S&P 500 index.

As a result, it does not make a great deal of difference which index is used. Ibbotson uses the NYSE in its calculations for the *Cost of Capital Quarterly* and the *Beta Book*.

Choice of Risk-Free Rate

To avoid the maturity risk (interest rate risk) inherent in long-term bonds, the risk-free rate used to compute excess returns is generally either the Treasury bill rate or the income return only from Treasury bonds. Ibbotson uses the 30-day T-bill in its calculations for the *Cost of Capital Quarterly* and the *Beta Book*.

A list of sources for betas is included in Appendix C, "Data Resources."

LEVERED AND UNLEVERED BETAS

Published betas for publicly traded stocks typically reflect the capital structure of each respective company. These betas are sometimes referred to as *levered betas*, betas reflecting the leverage in the company's capital structure. If the leverage of the company subject to appraisal differs significantly from the leverage of the guideline companies selected for analysis, or if the debt levels of the guideline companies differ significantly from one another, it may be desirable to remove the effect that leverage has on the betas before using them as a proxy to estimate the beta of the subject.

When the firm's beta is measured based on observed historical total returns (as most betas are), its measurement necessarily includes volatility related to the company's financial risk. In particular, the equity of companies that have higher levels of debt is more risky than the equity of companies that have less leverage (all else being equal). In other words, levered betas incorporate two risk factors that bear on systematic risk: business risk and financial (or capital structure) risk.

This adjustment for leverage differences is performed by first computing unlevered betas for the guideline companies. An *unlevered beta* is the beta a company would have if it had no debt. The second step is to decide where the subject company's risk would fall on an unlevered basis relative to the guideline companies. The third and final step is to relever the beta for the subject company on the basis of one or more assumed capital structures. The result will be a market-derived beta that has been specifically adjusted for the degree of financial leverage of the subject company.

To summarize, the steps are as follows:

1. Compute an unlevered beta for each of the guideline companies.
2. Decide where the risk would fall for the subject company relative to the guideline companies, assuming all had 100% equity capital structures.

3. Relever the beta for the subject company based on one or more assumed capital structures.

The formulas and an example for carrying out this process are shown in Exhibit 10.2. Of course, this leverage adjustment procedure takes as given all the assumptions of the Capital Asset Pricing Model.

With respect to levered versus unlevered betas, it is important to note that the capital structure of companies can often change significantly over the measurement period of the beta. For example, a beta could be measured during a five-year period in which, for the majority of time, a company was unleveraged. If at the end of the five-year measurement period the company has become highly leveraged, the levered betas computed would incorporate very little leverage. Yet, in unlevering the beta, the analyst would incorporate the current level of leverage, which is high. Thus the unlevered beta could be highly underestimated. The reverse effect applies for a company that deleverages during the beta measurement period. There is not a specific method of correcting for this other than being sure to take capital structure changes into consideration when unlevering the beta. It could be a reasonable approach to determine the average leverage for the company during the beta measurement period rather than the leverage at the end of the measurement period.

Keep in mind that capital structures for both the guideline companies and the subject companies are assumed to be based on market values in this process. If the relevered beta is used to estimate the market value of a company on a controlling basis, and if it is anticipated that the actual capital structure will be adjusted to the proportions of debt and equity in the assumed capital structure, then only one assumed capital structure is necessary. However, if the amount of debt in the subject capital structure will *not* be adjusted, an iterative process may be required. The initial assumed capital structure for the subject will influence the cost of equity, which will, in turn, influence the relative proportions of debt and equity at market value. It may be necessary to try several assumed capital structures until one of them produces an estimate of equity value that actually results in the assumed capital structure.

Exhibit 10.2   Computing Unlevered and Relevered Betas

The following is the formula for computing an unlevered beta (a beta assuming 100% equity in the capital structure).

$$B_u = \frac{B_L}{1 + (1 - t)W_d/W_e}$$

where:

B_u = Beta unlevered
B_L = Beta levered
t = Tax rate for the company
W_d = Percent debt in the capital structure
W_e = Percent equity in the capital structure

(continued)

Exhibit 10.2 *(continued)*

Example

Assume that for guideline company A:
   Levered (published) beta: 1.2
   Tax rate: .40
   Capital structure: 30% debt, 70% equity

$$B_u = \frac{1.2}{1 + (1 - .40).30/.70}$$

$$= \frac{1.2}{1 + .60(.429)}$$

$$= \frac{1.2}{1.257}$$

$$= .95$$

Assume you made the previous calculation for all the guideline companies, the average unlevered beta was .90, and you believe the riskiness of your subject company, on an unlevered basis, is about equal to the average for the guideline companies. The next step is to relever the beta for your subject company based on its tax rate and one or more assumed capital structures. The formula to adjust an unlevered beta to a levered beta is as follows:

$$B_L = B_u\left(1 + (1 - t)W_d/W_e\right)$$

where the definitions of the variables are the same as in the formula for computing unlevered betas.

Example

Assume for the subject company:
   Unlevered beta: .90
   Tax rate: .30
   Capital structure: 60% debt, 40% equity

$$B_L = .90(1 + (1 - .30).60/.40)$$
$$= .90(1 + .70(1.5))$$
$$= .90(2.05)$$
$$= 1.85$$

Source: Shannon P. Pratt, Robert F. Reilly, and Robert P. Schweihs, *Valuing a Business: The Analysis and Appraisal of Closely Held Companies*, 3d ed. (Burr Ridge, IL: McGraw-Hill, 1996), 170. Reprinted with permission.

This process of unlevering and relevering betas to an assumed capital structure is based on the assumption that the subject business interest has the ability to change the capital structure of the subject company. In the case of the valuation of a minority ownership interest, for example, the subject business interest may not have that ability.[1]

MODIFIED BETAS: SHRUNK AND LAGGED

Several recent research studies have provided significant support for two interesting hypotheses regarding betas:

- *Tendency toward industry average.* Over time, a company's beta tends toward its industry's average beta. The higher the standard error in the regression used to calculate the beta, the greater the tendency to move toward the industry average.
- *The lag effect.* For all but the largest companies, the prices of individual stocks tend to react in part to movements in the overall market with a lag. The smaller the company, the greater is the lag in the price reaction. Recognizing these phenomena, Ibbotson Associates vice president and economist Paul D. Kaplan, himself a participant in some of the relevant studies, introduced new methodologies in the first 1997 *Beta Book* to reflect this latest research.

Adjusted Beta Incorporates Industry Norm (Shrunk Beta)

The adjusted beta is computed by a rather sophisticated technique called *Vasicek Shrinkage*.[2] Without getting overly technical, the general idea is that betas with the highest statistical standard errors are adjusted toward the industry average more than betas with lower standard errors. Because high-beta stocks also tend to have the highest standard errors in their betas, they tend to be subject to the most adjustment toward their industry average.

"Sum Beta" Incorporates Lag Effect

Because of the lag in all but the largest companies' sensitivity to movements in the overall market, traditional betas tend to understate systematic risk. As the first edition (1997) of the *Beta Book* explains it, "Because of nonsynchronous price reactions, the traditional betas estimated by ordinary least squares are biased down for all but the largest companies."[3]

The research suggests that this understatement of systematic risk by the traditional beta measurements accounts in part, but certainly not wholly, for the fact that

Exhibit 10.3 Excerpt From First 1997 *Beta Book*

		CAPM: Ordinary Least Squares					CAPM: Sum Beta (Including Lag)				
Ticker	Company	OLS Beta	t-Stat	R-Sqr	Pr Grp Beta	Adj Beta	Sum Beta	t-Stat	R-Sqr	Pr Grp Beta	Adj Beta
ARX	Aeroflex Inc.	-0.48	-0.63	0.01	1.18	0.80	2.25	2.13	0.18	1.63	1.80
AIM	Aerosonic Corp.	1.06	1.62	0.04	1.03	1.04	2.84	3.01	0.14	1.17	1.72
ARVX	Aerovox Inc.	1.67	2.05	0.07	1.29	1.36	1.61	1.30	0.07	1.83	1.78
AES	AES Corp.	0.69	1.39	0.03	0.74	0.71	1.12	1.51	0.04	0.64	0.85
AET	Aetna Inc.	1.28	4.09	0.22	1.08	1.21	1.21	2.55	0.22	1.04	1.15
ATRM	Aetrium Inc.*	1.11	1.22	0.04	1.06	1.06	2.87	2.21	0.12	1.20	1.54
AFCX	AFC Cable Systems Inc.*	0.53	0.73	0.02	1.14	0.99	1.29	1.20	0.04	1.18	1.21
AFCB	Affiliated Community Bancorp*	0.56	1.45	0.06	1.00	0.76	-0.44	-0.83	0.22	1.33	0.26
AFL	AFLAC Inc.	0.61	2.10	0.07	1.08	0.76	0.64	1.46	0.07	1.04	0.76
AFPC	AFP Imaging Corp.	0.28	0.24	0.00	1.06	0.97	2.34	1.37	0.04	1.20	1.35
ASV	AG Services of America	0.23	0.41	0.00	0.88	0.65	1.75	2.14	0.10	0.89	1.23
AGBG	AG-BAG Intl. Ltd.	-0.24	-0.27	0.00	1.25	0.97	1.03	0.79	0.03	1.47	1.38
AG	AGCO Corp.*	3.05	3.49	0.18	1.25	1.58	3.85	2.83	0.19	1.47	1.93
AHSI	Ages Health Services Inc.*	2.84	0.37	0.00	1.06	1.07	NMF	NMF	NMF	1.27	NMF
ATG	AGL Resources Inc.	0.50	1.86	0.06	0.74	0.57	0.30	0.73	0.06	0.64	0.39

* Company with less than 60 months' data (minimum 36 months).
Source: *Ibbotson Associates' Beta Book*, first 1997 edition (Chicago: Ibbotson Associates, 1997), 3. Used with permission. All rights reserved.

small stocks achieve excess returns over and above their apparent capital asset pricing model required returns (where the market equity risk premium is adjusted for beta).

A new *sum beta* consists of a multiple regression of a stock's current month's excess returns over the 30-day T-bill rate on the market's current month's excess returns and on the market's previous month's excess returns, and then a summing of the coefficients. This helps to capture more fully the lagged effect of comovement in a company's returns with returns on the market (systematic risk).[4]

Exhibit 10.3 is an excerpt from Ibbotson's first 1997 *Beta Book* (which is published twice annually). Note that it includes a traditional least squares regression beta, an adjusted beta, a sum beta, and an adjusted sum beta. Although betas for individual stocks all have notoriously low R-squareds (proportion of total variance of individual stock returns that can be explained by market movements), it can be noted in Exhibit 10.3 that sum betas clearly have a tendency toward higher R-squareds than ordinary least squares (OLS) betas.

Chapter 13, on using Ibbotson data, shows an entire sample page from the *Beta Book*.

SUMMARY

A *beta* is a measure of the sensitivity of the movement in returns on a particular stock to movements in returns on some measure of the market. As such, beta measures systematic risk. In cost of capital estimation, beta is used as a modifier to the general equity risk premium in using the Capital Asset Pricing Model.

There are many variations on the way betas are measured by different sources of published betas. Thus, a beta for a stock computed by one source may be very different from a beta computed for the same stock by another source.

Modern research is attempting to improve betas. Two such improvements implemented recently are the "shrunk beta," which blends the individual stock beta with the industry beta, and the "lagged beta," which blends the beta for the stock and the market during a concurrent time period, with a beta regressed on the market's previous period returns. These two adjustments both help to reduce "outliers," thus perhaps making the betas based on observed historical data a little more representative of what one might expect in the future.

Notes

1. This section has assumed beta of debt is zero. Actually, debt tends to have betas of about .2 to .3, slightly alleviating the unlevered/beta differential.
2. The formula, used in the Ibbotson *Beta Book*, was first suggested by Oldrich A. Vasicek, "A Note on Using Cross-Sectional Information in Bayesian Estimation of Security Prices," *The Journal of Finance*, 1973. The company beta and the peer group (industry) beta are weighted. The greater the statistical confidence in the company beta, the greater the weight on the company beta relative to the peer group beta.
3. Ibbotson Associates, *Beta Book* (Chicago: Ibbotson Associates, 1997).
4. The sum beta estimates conform with the expectation that betas are higher for lower capitalization stocks. Research also shows that sum betas are positively related to subsequent realized returns over a long period of time (see Roger G. Ibbotson, Paul D. Kaplan, and James D. Peterson, "Estimates of Small-Stock Betas Are Much Too Low," *Journal of Portfolio Management*, summer 1997).

Chapter 11

The Size Effect

Ibbotson Associates Studies
Price Waterhouse Studies
Possible Extensions of Size Effect Studies
Summary

In the chapters on the build-up and the Capital Asset Pricing Model (CAPM) cost of equity estimation models, we have made reference to "the size effect," the general idea that smaller size is associated with higher risk and, therefore, higher cost of capital. To help quantify the size effect in terms of its impact on cost of equity capital, this chapter presents empirical data from two independent sets of studies:

1. Ibbotson Associates studies
2. Price Waterhouse studies

Both of these sets of studies use rate of return data developed at the University of Chicago Center for Research in Security Prices (CRSP).

IBBOTSON ASSOCIATES STUDIES

For many years, Ibbotson Associates has broken down NYSE stock returns into quintiles by size, as measured by the aggregate market value of the common equity. In recent years Ibbotson has further refined the breakdowns into decile groups. The excess returns over the basic general equity risk premium increase dramatically with decreasing size, as shown in Exhibit 11.1. This excess return is especially noticeable for the smallest 10% of the companies. Exhibit 11.2 shows the market capitalization of the respective decile groups.

From 1926 through 1981, Ibbotson's "small stock" group was composed of stocks making up the fifth quintile (i.e., ninth and tenth deciles) of the New York Stock Exchange (NYSE), ranked by capitalization (price times number of shares outstanding). From 1982 forward, the small stock return series is the total return achieved by the Dimensional Fund Advisors (DFA) Small Company 9/10 (for ninth and tenth deciles) Fund. The Fund is a market-value-weighted index of the ninth and

Estimating the Cost of Equity Capital

Exhibit 11.1   Size-Decile Portfolios of the NYSE, Long-Term Returns in Excess
of CAPM from 1926 to 1996

Decile	Beta*	Arithmetic Mean Return	Actual Return in Excess of Riskless Rate**	CAPM Return in Excess of Riskless Rate**	Size Premium (Return in Excess of CAPM)
1	0.90	11.56%	6.38%	6.75%	−0.36%
2	1.04	13.45	8.28	7.82	0.47
3	1.09	14.14	8.96	8.19	0.77
4	1.13	14.80	9.62	8.50	1.13
5	1.16	15.62	10.45	8.73	1.72
6	1.19	15.60	10.42	8.91	1.52
7	1.24	16.13	10.96	9.31	1.65
8	1.28	17.27	12.10	9.62	2.47
9	1.35	17.98	12.81	10.16	2.65
10	1.46	21.92	16.75	10.97	5.78
Mid-Cap, 3–5	1.12	14.60	9.42	8.38	1.04
Low-Cap, 6–8	1.22	16.10	10.92	9.18	1.75
Micro-Cap, 9–10	1.38	19.02	13.85	10.37	3.47

* Betas are estimated from monthly returns in excess of the 30-day U.S. Treasury bill total return,
  January 1926–December 1996.
** Historical riskless rate measured by the 71-year arithmetic mean income return component of
   20-year government bonds (5.17%).

Source: *Stocks, Bonds, Bills & Inflation*, 1997 Yearbook (Chicago: Ibbotson Associates, 1997), 138.
Annual updates work by Roger G. Ibbotson and Rex A. Sinquefield. Used with permission. All
rights reserved.

Exhibit 11.2   Size-Deciles of the NYSE: Bounds, Size, and Composition

Decile	Historical Average Percentage of Total Capitalization	Recent Number of Companies	Recent Decile Market Capitalization (in thousands)	Recent Percentage of Total Capitalization
				From 1926 to 1996
1–Largest	65.05%	178	$3,829,530,148	65.89%
2	14.50	178	841,759,402	14.48
3	7.66	179	439,282,816	7.56
4	4.62	178	264,606,408	4.55
5	3.03	178	166,637,798	2.87
6	2.04	178	112,512,008	1.94
7	1.38	179	75,609,047	1.30
8	0.91	178	46,449,037	0.80
9	0.56	178	25,984,075	0.45
10–Smallest	0.25	179	9,332,089	0.16
Mid-Cap, 3–5	15.31	535	870,527,022	14.98
Low-Cap, 6–8	4.33	535	234,570,092	4.04
Micro-Cap, 9–10	0.81	357	35,316,164	0.61

Exhibit 11.2 *(continued)*

Historical average percentage of total capitalization shows the average, over the last 71 years, of the decile market values as a percentage of the total NYSE calculated each year. Number of companies in deciles, recent market capitalization of deciles, and recent percentage of total capitalization are as of September 30, 1996.

Decile	Recent Market Capitalization (in thousands)	Company Name
1–Largest	$150,264,205	General Electric Co.
2	6,956,744	Federated Dept. Stores Inc.
3	3,241,700	First of America Bank Corp.
4	1,889,744	Union Texas Petroleum Holdings Inc.
5	1,151,137	LaFarge Corp.
6	755,312	Flores & Rucks Inc.
7	521,465	America West Airlines Inc.
8	336,403	Cabot Oil & Gas Corp.
9	197,375	Owen Healthcare Inc.
10–Smallest	93,979	IMO Industries Inc.

Market capitalization and name of largest company in each decile as of September 30, 1996.

Source: *Stocks, Bonds, Bills & Inflation*, 1997 Yearbook (Chicago: Ibbotson Associates, 1997), 136. Annual updates work by Roger G. Ibbotson and Rex A. Sinquefield. Used with permission. All rights reserved. Data compiled by Center for Research in Security Prices (CRSP), © CRSP University of Chicago. Used with permission. All rights reserved.

tenth deciles of the NYSE, plus stock listed on the American Stock Exchange and over-the-counter with the same or less capitalization than the upper bound of the NYSE ninth decile.

At year-end 1996, the DFA Small Company Fund contained approximately 2,635 stocks, with a weighted average market capitalization of $163 million. The unweighted average market capitalization was $101 million, while the median was $67 million.[1] These numbers change every year, with a sizable upward trend in recent years. Those using the data should reference numbers that are as current as possible.

The Ibbotson data in the *Stocks, Bonds, Bills, and Inflation* (SBBI) *Yearbooks* show both total size effect above the general market equity risk premium and the size effect over and above CAPM (the latter having already accounted for beta, which tends to be higher for smaller stocks), so the data can be used either with a straight build-up model or with a CAPM model. If using the data with a straight build-up model, one would use the total size effect above the general market equity risk premium. If using the data with a CAPM model, one would use the size effect over and above the CAPM indicated equity risk premium, where the beta would have captured some of the size effect.

Further discussion of the use of the Ibbotson small stock data is included in Chapter 13, on using Ibbotson Associates data.

PRICE WATERHOUSE STUDIES

Roger Grabowski and David King of Price Waterhouse have extended the study of the small stock phenomenon to encompass additional detail. In particular:

1. They have studied more size categories. They have broken down the stocks into 25 size groups, each representing 4% of the stocks by size included in the NYSE, instead of the 10 groupings used by Ibbotson Associates.
2. They have introduced seven additional size criteria, in addition to market value of equity. These size criteria are:
   a. Market value of equity
   b. Book value of equity
   c. Five-year average net income
   d. Market value of invested capital
   e. Book value of invested capital
   f. Five-year average EBITDA (earnings before interest, taxes, depreciation, and amortization)
   g. Sales
   h. Number of employees

The Price Waterhouse (PW) data cover the years 1963 (the first year of Compustat data) through the present, as compared with 1926 through the present for the Ibbotson data. Two results of the PW studies seem strikingly significant:

1. In spite of the different time period, the average results are very close to the Ibbotson results.
2. The results are significantly similar for all eight measures of company size.

Although the market value of common equity has both the highest degree of statistical significance and the steepest slope when regressing average returns against size, all size measures show a high degree of statistical significance. This is quite convenient in the context of valuation of private companies, since it enables one to start with a known size measure rather than estimated market value of equity, which is the value being sought.

A summary of the results of the PW studies is shown in Exhibit 11.3. PW has also compiled data for a separate set of financially distressed companies, that is, any company with one or more of the following characteristics:

- In bankruptcy or liquidation
- Negative five-year average net income
- Negative book value of equity
- Debt to total capital > 80% (debt measured at book value, equity at market value)

Returns for these companies with high financial risk are shown at the bottom of the tables in Exhibit 11.3.

Exhibit 11.3 shows both the actual premium for each size group and the smoothed premium. The smoothed premium is based on regression analysis. In most parts of the size range, the smoothed premium is probably most appropriate to use.

It is important to note, however, that we find a pronounced jump in the premium in the smallest 4% of companies. This is of interest to many business valuators, since this jump occurs in a size category in which, as a practical matter, many

Exhibit 11.3 Summary Results of Price Waterhouse Size Effect Studies

Historical Equity Risk Premiums: Averages Since 1963
Data for Year Ending December 31, 1996

Portfolio Rank by Size	Market Value of Equity			Book Value of Equity			5-Year Average Net Income			Market Value of Invested Capital		
	Average ($ mils.)	Arithmetic Average Premium	Smoothed Average Premium	Average ($ mils.)	Arithmetic Average Premium	Smoothed Average Premium	Average ($ mils.)	Arithmetic Average Premium	Smoothed Average Premium	Average ($ mils.)	Arithmetic Average Premium	Smoothed Average Premium
1	40,860	5.21%	2.29%	10,225	5.43%	3.75%	1,572	5.62%	3.90%	52,246	5.02%	2.51%
2	12,776	3.94%	4.17%	4,664	5.01%	4.94%	575	5.81%	5.24%	17,601	3.49%	4.25%
3	7,619	3.53%	5.00%	2,866	5.80%	5.68%	367	5.19%	5.84%	10,828	4.48%	5.03%
4	5,069	6.16%	5.66%	2,104	5.24%	6.14%	238	5.15%	6.41%	6,883	4.54%	5.75%
5	4,280	4.20%	5.93%	1,575	6.52%	6.58%	188	5.78%	6.73%	5,608	5.37%	6.08%
6	3,288	6.26%	6.36%	1,335	7.50%	6.83%	141	8.57%	7.11%	4,532	8.36%	6.42%
7	2,502	6.74%	6.80%	1,087	6.82%	7.14%	110	6.74%	7.44%	3,733	7.12%	6.73%
8	2,156	7.52%	7.04%	893	6.31%	7.44%	95	7.61%	7.65%	2,958	6.21%	7.10%
9	1,957	6.16%	7.19%	752	6.02%	7.70%	76	7.05%	7.93%	2,483	6.44%	7.38%
10	1,610	7.94%	7.51%	652	7.62%	7.91%	67	6.44%	8.11%	2,124	7.47%	7.63%
11	1,368	8.01%	7.77%	577	9.39%	8.10%	55	9.72%	8.36%	1,896	6.47%	7.81%
12	1,181	8.55%	8.01%	472	9.50%	8.40%	46	8.12%	8.60%	1,676	8.37%	8.01%
13	1,017	7.53%	8.25%	415	7.61%	8.59%	37	9.14%	8.88%	1,438	8.81%	8.25%
14	864	8.79%	8.51%	363	8.68%	8.80%	33	7.90%	9.06%	1,188	8.73%	8.56%
15	710	8.60%	8.83%	314	9.00%	9.02%	28	9.46%	9.27%	996	9.64%	8.84%
16	586	9.25%	9.14%	281	9.89%	9.18%	24	9.21%	9.46%	832	9.53%	9.13%
17	496	8.07%	9.41%	237	8.83%	9.44%	20	10.99%	9.70%	673	8.91%	9.46%
18	408	10.56%	9.72%	208	8.48%	9.64%	16	10.44%	9.98%	572	7.57%	9.72%
19	344	9.21%	10.00%	174	9.52%	9.91%	14	9.22%	10.22%	494	10.20%	9.96%
20	285	9.21%	10.30%	146	10.70%	10.17%	11	10.72%	10.47%	396	11.14%	10.31%
21	225	11.32%	10.68%	125	10.00%	10.41%	9	11.45%	10.81%	316	10.34%	10.67%
22	170	10.34%	11.14%	100	11.62%	10.74%	7	12.13%	11.19%	237	11.71%	11.13%
23	130	12.10%	11.56%	84	10.72%	11.00%	5	11.52%	11.63%	186	10.43%	11.52%
24	85	12.45%	12.26%	60	11.52%	11.50%	3	12.11%	12.20%	126	12.25%	12.14%
25	30	15.83%	13.92%	24	14.17%	12.91%	1	13.67%	13.58%	46	15.55%	13.77%
High financial risk		14.63%			14.09%			14.63%			14.63%	
Constant			19.42%			17.70%			13.71%			19.86%
Slope			−3.71%			−3.48%			−3.07%			−3.68%

Exhibit 11.3   *(continued)*

Portfolio Rank by Size	Book Value of Invested Capital			5-Year Average EBITDA			Sales			Number of Employees		
	Average ($ mils.)	Arithmetic Average Premium	Smoothed Average Premium	Average ($ mils.)	Arithmetic Average Premium	Smoothed Average Premium	Average ($ mils.)	Arithmetic Average Premium	Smoothed Average Premium	Average ($ mils.)	Arithmetic Average Premium	Smoothed Average Premium
1	22,397	4.64%	3.36%	4,860	5.92%	4.21%	33,180	6.43%	5.29%	181,966	5.98%	5.81%
2	9,282	4.43%	4.69%	1,856	5.29%	5.48%	11,821	5.37%	6.41%	59,133	6.66%	6.86%
3	5,790	5.10%	5.40%	1,213	5.84%	6.04%	8,159	7.14%	6.82%	40,819	7.17%	7.20%
4	4,173	6.28%	5.89%	788	5.61%	6.62%	5,673	7.58%	7.22%	31,672	7.93%	7.43%
5	2,978	6.58%	6.39%	603	6.76%	6.97%	4,174	8.69%	7.55%	24,425	8.52%	7.67%
6	2,323	7.72%	6.77%	472	8.31%	7.29%	3,344	7.85%	7.79%	17,962	8.43%	7.96%
7	1,896	6.81%	7.07%	361	7.76%	7.65%	2,776	7.74%	8.00%	15,419	7.42%	8.10%
8	1,646	5.56%	7.28%	318	6.42%	7.81%	2,332	7.06%	8.19%	12,828	7.68%	8.27%
9	1,383	6.16%	7.55%	264	6.47%	8.06%	2,007	6.77%	8.35%	10,385	8.98%	8.47%
10	1,241	7.40%	7.71%	226	7.48%	8.27%	1,596	7.94%	8.60%	8,437	9.04%	8.66%
11	1,018	7.70%	8.01%	189	8.68%	8.51%	1,345	8.87%	8.79%	6,863	9.01%	8.85%
12	815	8.13%	8.34%	157	9.55%	8.75%	1,128	11.00%	8.98%	6,260	8.95%	8.93%
13	741	8.07%	8.48%	141	10.46%	8.89%	1,003	11.77%	9.11%	5,417	9.31%	9.07%
14	630	10.54%	8.73%	112	8.52%	9.20%	892	7.84%	9.23%	4,655	8.61%	9.21%
15	526	8.87%	9.00%	92	8.27%	9.45%	753	9.00%	9.42%	3,938	9.98%	9.36%
16	469	8.78%	9.17%	84	10.49%	9.57%	678	8.37%	9.53%	3,520	9.60%	9.47%
17	407	9.55%	9.38%	69	10.01%	9.83%	583	10.45%	9.70%	2,928	8.63%	9.64%
18	342	10.91%	9.64%	59	10.21%	10.05%	521	8.99%	9.82%	2,438	8.63%	9.81%
19	285	10.39%	9.92%	50	10.55%	10.25%	420	9.46%	10.05%	2,173	7.92%	9.91%
20	243	10.14%	10.16%	40	8.84%	10.56%	336	9.85%	10.30%	1,787	11.21%	10.10%
21	198	8.86%	10.47%	33	10.52%	10.81%	279	9.21%	10.50%	1,446	9.91%	10.29%
22	152	10.27%	10.86%	27	11.68%	11.10%	235	9.75%	10.69%	1,101	10.75%	10.54%
23	121	11.03%	11.21%	20	12.80%	11.50%	177	13.09%	11.00%	875	10.98%	10.76%
24	88	12.24%	11.68%	13	12.82%	12.08%	123	11.38%	11.39%	595	10.65%	11.11%
25	36	14.03%	13.05%	5	13.09%	13.40%	47	13.55%	12.44%	223	13.55%	12.02%
High financial risk		14.27%			14.86%			14.64%			15.22%	
Constant			18.41%			15.44%			16.65%			17.03%
Slope			−3.46%			−3.05%			−2.51%			−2.13%

Used with permission of Price Waterhouse LLP

Source: Data originally presented by David King of Price Waterhouse at the American Society of Appraisers Annual International Conference in Houston, Texas, June 1997. Table compiled by and published in *Shannon Pratt's Business Valuation Update* (August 1997), 3.

more valuation assignments are performed. For seven of the eight size measures, the actual premium for the smallest group was greater than the "smoothed" premium, generally by a considerable margin.

As a point of reference, the arithmetic risk premium from Ibbotson *SBBI* data, calculated since 1963, as in the PW study, comes to 5.07% for large stocks and 10.73% for small stocks (9th and 10th deciles combined), which would lead one to conclude that the data are quite compatible.[2]

Note that the PW data shown in Exhibit 11.3 do not show small stock returns in excess of CAPM. Therefore, the data as shown in Exhibit 11.3 are suitable to use with a straight build-up model, but not with a CAPM model. The returns shown in Exhibit 11.3 include the general equity risk premium. Therefore, analysts can approximate an equity cost of capital reflecting various size measures (before any company-specific adjustment) by adding the appropriate equity risk premium from Exhibit 11.3 to the 20-year Treasury bond rate. Full background on the details of the PW studies and information on how to use the data along with a beta in the context of CAPM are contained in the background studies, which are shown in full on *Business Valuation Update Online* (see the Bibliography in Appendix A and Data Resources in Appendix C).

POSSIBLE EXTENSIONS OF SIZE EFFECT STUDIES

The size effect studies presented in this chapter are based entirely on transactions in the public stock markets. The smallest 4% of the stocks in the PW study have an average market value of $30 million. There are literally hundreds of thousands of companies smaller than this for which cost of capital estimation is relevant, both for valuation and for potential project assessment purposes.

Where the data leave off seems to raise the question, "Is it valid to extrapolate these results beyond the observed population to infer even higher costs of capital for smaller companies?" From purely a statistician's viewpoint, the answer would be "no". We can't know with certainty whether the population beyond the observed range would continue the trend. But most corporate finance practitioners and academicians with whom the author has discussed this question, as well as most business brokers and merger and acquisition intermediaries, conclude that the answer is "yes".

One of our goals over the next year or two is to study this issue further, which will be facilitated by the new database being developed, *Pratt's Stats*, covering business sale transactions all the way from $100,000 to $100 million in value. In the meantime, if readers have any insights to offer, please contact the author at the address or telephone number shown in the Preface.

SUMMARY

Two independent sets of empirical studies provide strong support for the proposition that cost of capital tends to increase with decreasing company size. Users of cost of capital data should make themselves aware of updates of these and possibly other similar studies in order to incorporate the latest current size effect data in cost of capital estimates, whether using build-up models, CAPM, or other cost of equity models. The data currently available provide empirical evidence to help quantify the cost of capital for smaller companies, and the subject presently is attracting considerable new research interest.

Notes

1. *Stocks, Bonds, Bills & Inflation 1997 Yearbook* (Chicago: Ibbotson Associates, 1997), 51, 53.
2. "New Studies Quantifying Size Premiums Offer Strong Cost of Capital Support," Shannon Pratt's *Business Valuation Update*, August 1997, p.3.

Chapter 12

The DCF Method of Estimating Cost of Capital

Theory of the DCF Method
Single-Stage DCF Model
Multistage DCF Models
Sources of Information
Summary

As discussed earlier in this book, there are several ways to estimate the cost of equity capital. Up to this point, all of the methods have had one thing in common: they begin with a risk-free rate and add one or many factors, based on the risks of the investment. The discounted cash flow (DCF) method is completely different from this.

Although the models used are much different, some of the steps undertaken in estimating the cost of equity capital of a privately held company are the same as those used in the other methods. In particular, the DCF method of estimating cost of capital can be *directly* applied only to publicly traded companies (the current stock price is the essential ingredient here); therefore, for private companies, a set of guideline companies (e.g., those similar to the subject) must be identified. Alternatively, an industry average for companies in the subject's industry may be used as the starting point.

For public companies, the cost of equity estimated by the DCF method represents the *entire* cost of equity. That is, it encompasses in a single number all the factors considered in the build-up and CAPM methods: the risk-free rate, the equity risk premium, the beta, the size effect, and any company-specific factors.

To apply the cost of equity capital developed from public companies to a private company, the characteristics of the public companies must be compared with characteristics of the subject private company. Such comparisons could lead to adjustments for size and/or company-specific risk factors in order to get from the cost of equity estimate for the public companies to an estimate for a particular private company.

THEORY OF THE DCF METHOD

All methods for estimating the cost of capital derive all or part of the expected rates of return from current capital market data. With the exception of possible adjustments for private companies, the DCF method derives all of the implied expected return from current market data used in conjunction with analysts' growth expectations.

In this sense, at least in theory, the DCF method is more direct and simpler than the build-up model or the Capital Asset Pricing Model (CAPM). The important assumption of the DCF method is that the public company's current stock price embodies the market's expectation of the rate of return that will be realized by investing in that stock.

In other words, the assumption is that the current stock price is actually the sum of the present values of the expected future returns to the investors (dividends and stock price change). That is, the implied assumption is that the current stock price is equal to the expected future returns discounted to a present value at a discount rate that represents the equity cost of capital for that company.

The theory of the DCF method to estimate cost of capital is to use the DCF formula for computing present value backward. That is, since the present value (i.e., the current stock price) is known, the calculations are reconfigured to solve for k_e, the cost of equity capital.

The relationship between the DCF method of valuing a business and the DCF method of estimating cost of capital is the matter of which are the known and unknown variables. In using the DCF method to value a company, division, or project, the cost of capital has already been estimated and is given as a known rate in the formula to estimate the present value. In using the DCF method to estimate the cost of capital, the present value (market price of the stock) is known and placed into the formula to then solve for the discount rate (cost of capital).

There are two main types of models used to implement the DCF method as it is applied to estimating cost of capital. The first, and most popular, is the *single-stage model*. The second is the *multistage model*. Although these models can be used to estimate the weighted-average cost of capital, they are typically used to calculate the expected equity rate of return. The discussion that follows is based on equity rates of return only.

SINGLE-STAGE DCF MODEL

The single-stage DCF model is based on a rewrite (an algebraic manipulation) of a constant growth model, such as the Gordon Growth Model, presented earlier as Formula 4.6 and repeated here:

Formula 12.1

$$PV = \frac{NCF_0(1 + g)}{k - g}$$

where:

PV = Present value
NCF_0 = Net cash flow in period 0, the period immediately preceding the valuation date
k = Discount rate (cost of capital)
g = Expected long-term sustainable growth rate in net cash flow to investor

When the present value (i.e., the market price) is known, but the discount rate (i.e., the cost of capital) is unknown, Formula 12.1 can be rearranged to solve for the cost of capital:

Formula 12.2

$$k = \frac{NCF_0(1 + g)}{PV} + g$$

where the variables have the same definitions as in Formula 12.1.

In dealing with public companies, the net cash flow that the investor actually receives is the dividend. We can substitute some numbers to Formula 12.2 and thus illustrate estimating the cost of equity capital for Alpha Utilities, Inc. (AUI), an electric, gas, and water utility conglomerate, by making the following assumptions:

1. *Dividend.* AUI's dividend for the latest 12 months was $3.00 per share.
2. *Growth.* Analysts' consensus estimate is that the long-term growth in AUI's dividend will be 5%.
3. *Present value.* AUI's current stock price is $36.00 per share.

Substituting this information into Formula 12.2, we have the following:

Formula 12.3

$$k = \frac{\$3.00(1 + 0.05)}{\$36.00} + 0.05$$

$$= \frac{\$3.15}{\$36.00} + 0.05$$

$$= 8.8 + 0.05$$

$$= 13.8$$

Thus, according to this computation, AUI's cost of equity capital is estimated to be 13.8% (8.8% dividend yield plus 5.0% expected stock price increase).

The preceding is the formulation used in Ibbotson Associates' *Cost of Capital Quarterly (CCQ)* "Analysts Single-Stage Discounted Cash Flow" cost of equity capital estimate. Ibbotson's source of growth estimates is Standard & Poor's Compustat Analyst's Consensus Estimates (ACE) database. A number of other sources of growth estimates are included in Appendix C, "Data Resources."

This single-stage DCF model is often used in utility rate hearings to estimate a utility's cost of equity.[1]

Like the capitalization "shortcut" version of the discounting model used for valuation, the single-stage DCF model for estimating cost of capital is deceptively simple.

In utility settings, the dividend yield is assumed to be an appropriate estimate of the first input, cash flow yield. This is reasonable, since publicly traded utilities typically pay dividends and these dividends represent a high percentage of available cash flows. In cases where the utility's dividend yield is abnormally high or low, a "normal" dividend yield is used. It is difficult, however, to use dividend yields with all publicly traded companies.

For many companies, dividend payments may have little to do with earnings or cash flows. A large number of companies do not pay dividends or pay only a token amount of dividends. In these cases, theoretically, the growth component, g, will be larger than that of an otherwise similar company that pays higher dividends. In practice, properly adjusting for this lack of dividends is extremely difficult.

One way to avoid the dividend issue is to define cash flows more broadly. That is, instead of considering only the cash flows investors actually receive (dividends), the analyst might define net cash flows as those amounts that could be paid to equity investors without impeding a company's future growth. As noted in Chapter 3, net cash flow is usually defined as:

> Net income (after tax)
>
> + Noncash charges (e.g., depreciation, amortization, deferred revenue, deferred taxes)
> − Capital expenditures*
> − Additions to net working capital*
> ± Changes in long-term debt (add cash from borrowing, subtract repayments)*
> = Net cash flow to equity
>
> *Only amounts necessary to support projected operations

Of course, these cash flows are not those paid to investors, but, presumably, investors will ultimately realize the benefit of these amounts either through higher future dividends, a special dividend, or, more likely, stock price appreciation. Some analysts assume that over the very long run, net (after-tax) income should be quite close to cash flows. Therefore, they assume that net income can be used as a proxy for net cash flow. This assumption should be questioned on a case by case basis. For a growing company, capital expenditure and working capital requirements may make the assumed equivalence of net income and net cash flow so remote as to be irrelevant.

The other, and perhaps more problematic, input is the expected growth rate. An important characteristic of the growth rate is that it is the *perpetual* annual growth rate. Future growth rates do not have to be the same for every year; however, the "average" rate should be equal to this perpetual rate. For example, if a company is expected to grow at 10% per year for the next 4 years and 3% per year thereafter, then the average growth rate into perpetuity could be estimated as about 5%. On the other hand, if the company is expected to grow by 10% per year for the next 20 years and 3% per year thereafter, the average growth rate is probably closer to 9%.

A common approach to deriving a perpetual growth rate is to obtain stock analysts' estimates of earnings growth rates. The advantage of using these growth estimates is that they are prepared by people who follow these companies on an ongoing basis. These professional stock analysts develop a great deal more insight on these companies than a casual investor or valuation analyst not specializing in the industry is likely to achieve.

There are, however, three caveats that should be understood when using this information:

1. These earnings growth estimates typically are for only the next two to five years; they are not perpetual. Therefore, any use of these forecasts in a single-stage DCF model must be tempered with a longer-term forecast.
2. Most published analysts' estimates come from "sell-side" stock analysts. They work for the firms whose business it is to sell stocks. Thus, although their earnings forecasts fall within the range of "reasonable" possibilities, these forecasts may be on the high end of the range.
3. Usually, these estimates are obtained from firms that provide consensus earnings forecasts; that is, they aggregate forecasts from a number of analysts and report certain summary statistics (such as mean, median, etc.) on these forecasts. For a small publicly traded firm, there may be only one or even no analyst following the company. The potential for forecasting errors is greater where the forecasts are obtained from a very small number of analysts. These services typically report the number of analysts who have provided earnings estimates, which should be considered in determining how much reliance to place on forecasts of this type.

Many of the problems inherent in using the single-stage model to estimate cost of capital are addressed by using a multistage model.

MULTISTAGE DCF MODELS

Multistage models come closer to reversing the discounting process than do single-stage models that simply reverse the capitalization process. Multistage models don't go to the extent of incorporating specific expected return amounts for specific years, but they do incorporate different growth rates for different expected growth stages, most often three stages.

Multistage models have one main advantage over single-stage models in that using more than one growth rate reduces reliance on a single such rate. Furthermore, it is unnecessary to compute a blended growth rate.

The main disadvantage of a multistage model is its computational complexity relative to the single-stage model. Unlike the single-stage model, the multistage model must be solved iteratively.

It also differs from the single-stage model in that there is no single form of the multi-stage model. There are two main factors that determine the form of the model. The first is the number of growth stages—usually either two or three. The second factor is the length of each stage—usually between three and five years.

In a three-stage model the discounting formula that must be reversed to solve for k, the cost of capital, looks like this:

Formula 12.4

$$PV = NCF_0 \times \sum_{i=1}^{5} \frac{(1 + g_1)^i}{(1 + k)^1} \quad \text{(first stage)}$$

$$+ NCF_0 \times \frac{(1 + g_1)^5}{(1 + k)^5} \times \sum_{i=1}^{5} \frac{(1 + g_2)^i}{(1 + k)^1} \quad \text{(second stage)}$$

$$+ NCF_0 \times \frac{(1 + g_1)^5 \times (1 + g_2)^5}{(1 + k)^{10}} \times \frac{1 + g_3}{k - g_3} \quad \text{(last stage)}$$

where:

NCF_0 = Net cash flow (or dividend) in the immediately preceding period

g_1, g_2, and g_3 = Expected growth rates in NCF through each of stages 1, 2, and 3, respectively

k = Cost of capital (discount rate)

As noted earlier, this equation must be solved iteratively for k. Fortunately, many of the spreadsheet software packages, such as Excel, are quite capable of performing this calculation.

Ibbotson, for example, in its *CCQ*, uses two 5-year stages and then a growth rate applicable to earnings over all future years following the first 10 years. In the first and second stages it uses estimated cash flows instead of dividends. Ibbotson defines cash flows for this purpose as net income plus non-cash charges less capital expenditures. This definition comes close to our definition of net cash flow to equity, except that it doesn't subtract additions to working capital nor adjust for changes in outstanding debt principal. Ibbotson's third-stage (long-term) growth rate is the expected long-term inflation forecast plus the historical gross domestic product (GDP) growth rate.

SOURCES OF INFORMATION

If one is going to perform the DCF cost of capital analysis rather than use data compiled by one of the services, a variety of inputs are necessary, including company-specific data, industry outlook data, and long-term macroeconomic forecasts.

Company data can be obtained from Securities and Exchange Commission (SEC) filings or services such as Standard & Poor's, Moody's, and Value Line. Analysts' estimates can be compiled from individual analysts' reports or from one of the four earnings consensus reporting services (First Call, ACE from Compustat, I/B/E/S, and Zacks).

There are a great number of different industry forecasts. For some industries, excellent material is available from industry trade associations, although they tend to focus primarily on revenues rather than cash flows. There is also a wide variety of macroeconomic forecast information. Appendix C, "Data Resources," lists details on many sources providing data in all these categories.

SUMMARY

The DCF method of cost of capital estimation attempts to use current public stock price information to estimate implied costs of equity capital. Single-stage models use a Gordon Growth Model type of formula, with the present value (i.e., the stock price) known, solving for k, the cost of capital. Multistage models use two or more growth estimates for different future periods. As with the CAPM, to apply the method to privately held companies involves using public companies in a similar industry group to develop a proxy starting point, with modifications for differences in the characteristics between the public guideline companies and the subject company.

Analysts can obtain DCF-based cost of capital estimates for public companies and industries from several services that compile them, or can build their own estimates from scratch.

The author is working on a research paper showing examples of applying the DCF method of estimating the cost of capital using several different sources of growth estimates. Readers may obtain a complimentary copy of this research paper when it is completed by contacting the author at the address shown in the Preface.

Note

1. For a concise discussion of the use of this model for utility rate setting, see Richard A. Brealey and Stewart C. Myers, *Principles of Corporate Finance*, 5th ed. (New York: McGraw-Hill, 1996), 62–67.

Chapter 13

Using Ibbotson Associates Cost of Capital Data

Michael Annin and Dominic Falaschetti

Notation for This Chapter: The notation used in this chapter is that used in the Ibbotson data sources discussed herein and differs slightly from the notation used elsewhere in this book. There are, however, no conceptual discrepancies between equations in this chapter and similar equations elsewhere in this book.

Ibbotson Associates is a financial software, data, and consulting firm located in Chicago, Illinois. Established in 1977 by Roger Ibbotson, then of the University of Chicago, Ibbotson Associates is a leading provider of financial information to business valuation analysts, corporate finance professionals, and investment analysts. Ibbotson Associates produces three publications that valuation and corporate finance professionals at all levels have found useful in the estimation of cost of capital for companies of various industries and sizes.

The first of these publications, the *Stocks, Bonds, Bills, and Inflation Yearbook,* is based on Roger Ibbotson and Rex Sinquefield's original 1976 study of long-term market returns. The publication has become an industry standard and is updated annually by Ibbotson Associates. *Stocks, Bonds, Bills, and Inflation (SBBI)* is the leading data source for historical equity risk premium and firm size stock premium statistics that frequently serve as the foundation for discount rate, capitalization rate, and cost of capital estimates. The book also contains other useful historical data analysis, market commentary, and a statistical guide.

Ibbotson Associates' *Cost of Capital Quarterly (CCQ)* is the second publication geared directly to analysts engaged in business valuation and corporate finance decisions. *CCQ*, which Ibbotson Associates has produced since 1994, is an industry analysis publication that produces cost of capital and other financial information useful in the valuation and corporate financial analysis processes. It is organized by Standard Industrial Classification (SIC) code.

Ibbotson's most recent addition to its library of publications is the *Beta Book*. The *Beta Book*, published since 1995, provides beta and three-factor model information by company. The goal of the *Beta Book* is to allow practitioners to develop their cost of capital estimates based on company-specific information. This chapter discusses all three Ibbotson Associates' publications in detail.

STOCKS, BONDS, BILLS, AND INFLATION

Stocks, Bonds, Bills, and Inflation (SBBI) is one of the most commonly cited reference sources in valuation reports. Published since 1983, *SBBI* provides equity risk premium and firm size premium data essential for the estimation of discount rates and capitalization rates based on historical return premium data.

Equity Risk Premium

The equity risk premium is the reward that investors require to accept the uncertain outcomes associated with owning equity securities. The equity risk premium is measured as the extra return that equity holders expect to achieve over risk-free assets on average.

The equity risk premium (ERP) is calculated by Ibbotson Associates using the returns on the Standard & Poor's (S&P) 500 over the income return on the appropriate horizon Treasury security. Ibbotson provides equity risk premium calculations for short-, intermediate-, and long-term horizons. Usually, companies are entities that have no defined life span and are assumed to be going concerns for extended time periods. In estimating a company's value, it is important to use a long-term discount rate if the life of the company is assumed to be infinite. Ibbotson's position is that this holds true even if the time horizon of the investor is a short amount of time. For this reason, it is appropriate in most cases to use the long horizon equity risk premium for business valuation.

The long horizon ERP is simply the arithmetic average total return for the S&P 500 less the average annual income return of long-term Treasury bonds, measured from 1926 to the present. (The income return is used because it is considered more representative of expectations than the total return, which includes some gains and losses resulting from unexpected changes in interest rates.) An ERP estimate is necessary for both the Capital Asset Pricing Model (CAPM) and the build-up approach to estimating equity.

There are several points to note about the *SBBI* equity risk premium. First, the Ibbotson ERP covers the time period from 1926 to the present. Second, it is calculated using *arithmetic* averages of stock and bond returns over that time period. Third, the Ibbotson ERP uses the S&P 500 as the benchmark for equity returns and the income return on the 20-year Treasury bond as the benchmark for the risk-free rate. All of these factors have an impact on the ultimate equity risk premium calculation and how it should be applied in the business valuation or capital budgeting setting.

The *SBBI* equity risk premium covers the time period from 1926 to the present. The original data source for the time series comprising the equity risk premium is the Center for Research in Security Prices (CRSP) at the University of Chicago. The CRSP time series start in 1926 because this is when good quality data first became available. This period was also chosen because it includes one full business cycle before the 1929 market crash. In basic terms, these are the reasons that the Ibbotson ERP calculation window starts in 1926.

The period from 1926 to the present is relevant because of the number of different economic scenarios included in this time period. Some practitioners argue for a shorter historical period, such as just the last 30 years. Their argument is based on the notion that it is unlikely for the unique economic conditions present before the more recent period to be repeated in the future. Yet even recent periods can be characterized as unique in one way or another (e.g., the Gulf War, the Dow Jones Industrial Average one-day drop of over 500 points in 1987). Relatively recently there have been periods of recession and boom, low and high inflation, low and high interest rates, and even a period of stagflation in the 1970s. By including market data measured over the entire set of economic scenarios available, Ibbotson believes that the model can better anticipate similar events in the future.

It is difficult even for economists to predict the economic environment of the future. For example, if one were analyzing the stock market preceding the crash in 1987, it would be statistically improbable to predict such short-term volatility in the market without considering the stock market crash and volatility of the market over the 1929–1931 period. The Ibbotson Associates' position is that the entire time horizon is relevant and therefore should be included.

It is also important to note that the *SBBI* equity risk premium is an *arithmetic average* risk premium, as opposed to a *geometric average* risk premium. It is Ibbotson's position that it is always appropriate to use an arithmetic average in discounting future cash flows. This assumes that the cash flow figure being discounted for each period is the mathematical expected value of the probability distribution of possible outcomes for that period. (This assumes probabilistic forecasts, which most analysts do not do on any rigorous basis. However, understanding the theory may help the analyst adjust for any difference there might be between the forecast used and a rigorous probabilistic forecast.[1]) The geometric average is more appropriate for demonstrating past performance, inasmuch as it represents the compound average return.

If the geometric average is employed, the assumption is that the equity risk premium will be the same for all future time periods. This, of course, will never be the case. The arithmetic average represents the estimate of the equity risk premium over future time periods *on average*. In some periods the equity risk premium will be higher, and in other periods it will be lower. The average of such values over these future time periods will be the arithmetic average. Because of the underlying volatility in the ERP, the arithmetic average will always be higher than the geometric average.

A third crucial aspect of the equity risk premium is the data components that comprise it: the total return on the S&P 500 and the income return on the long-term Treasury bond. The S&P 500 was selected as the appropriate market benchmark because it is representative of a large sample of companies across a large number of industries. In short, the S&P 500 is a good measure of the equity market as a whole.

The S&P 500 is composed of the largest publicly traded companies in the United States and is therefore a large company index. Yet many valuation professionals are faced with valuing small companies. Small companies have different risk and return characteristics than large companies. These characteristics are addressed in the next section, which discusses the small stock premium.

Ibbotson Associates uses a 20-year bond to measure the income return in computing the long-horizon risk premium. This is an interesting fact, because the Treasury currently does not issue a 20-year bond. Use of the 30-year bond that the Treasury currently issues would be theoretically more correct because of the long-term nature of business valuation. However, Ibbotson Associates instead creates a series of returns using bonds on the market with approximately 20 years to maturity. The reason for the use of a 20-year maturity is that 30-year Treasury securities have been issued only over the relatively recent past. Ibbotson Associates has persisted in using a 20-year bond to keep the basis of the time series consistent across time.

Finally, the income return of the 20-year Treasury is used in calculating the ERP rather than the total return, as it represents the truly riskless portion of the return. Because yields have been rising generally over the period 1926–1996, there has been negative capital appreciation on the long-term bond series. This negative return is due to the risk of unanticipated yield changes. Any anticipated changes in yields will already have been priced by the market into the bond. Therefore, the total return on the bond series does not represent the riskless rate of return. The income return better represents the riskless rate of return, inasmuch as an investor can hold a bond to maturity and be entitled to the income return with no capital loss.

Firm Size Premium

SBBI has published a small stock premium for several years. In recent years, the small stock analysis in *SBBI* has been refined to show the firm size premiums by mid-cap, low-cap, and micro-cap stocks. In short, all but the very largest companies require an upward adjustment to their cost of capital simply because they are small companies.

What is firm size premium? Historically, small capitalization stocks have shown both greater risk and provided greater returns than large capitalization stocks. In other words, as an asset class, small capitalization stocks are riskier than large capitalization stocks, but have also provided greater returns to investors than large capitalization stocks.

In an effort to better explain the phenomenon of small capitalization stocks, *SBBI* provides a study of stocks on the New York Stock Exchange (NYSE) from 1926 to the present, based on data from the Center for Research in Security Prices (CRSP) at the University of Chicago. The *SBBI* small capitalization study sorts the NYSE into 10 different portfolios, or deciles, with the companies ranked by equity capitalization. The excess returns of the 10 portfolios are tracked over time in a fashion similar to the ERP calculations outlined in the previous section of this chapter.

The next step in the *SBBI* small capitalization study is to calculate betas on these 10 different portfolios across the same 1926–present time horizon. These betas are not the traditional 60-month betas that are normally calculated. Instead, they are betas that cover the entire time horizon.

The final step of the study is to calculate the returns for each portfolio predicted by the beta of the portfolio. The return predicted by beta is compared with the actual return that the portfolio or decile achieved for the time period. What the study shows is that the returns predicted by beta underestimated the actual returns of all but the largest capitalization decile.

Exhibit 13.1 is a graph from the *SBBI 1997 Yearbook* that shows the actual returns achieved by the 10 portfolios and the security market line on which the CAPM would predict the portfolios would fall. If the CAPM were functioning properly for the small companies, all of the portfolios would fall on the line indicated in the graph. Instead, most of the portfolios are above the line, indicating that the CAPM underreports the cost of equity for all but the largest companies. Therefore, a size premium should be added for all CAPM calculations for all but the largest of companies.

Exhibit 13.2 is a table from the *SBBI 1997 Yearbook* that is a numerical representation of the graph depicted in Exhibit 13.1. Exhibit 13.2 also shows the mid-cap, micro-cap, and low-cap results. The mid, low, and micro distinctions are attempts to consolidate the deciles into larger groups where generalizations about the data are possible. For instance, the micro-cap designation is a combination of the ninth and tenth deciles. Exhibit 13.2 shows the returns for the 10 deciles as they actually performed and as the CAPM predicted they would perform. The size premium is the difference between actual returns and returns predicted by the CAPM. This is a very important distinction.

The size premium that is shown in *SBBI* is a CAPM size premium. If you are using the CAPM, this is the premium that should be added to your cost of equity

Exhibit 13.1   Size-Decile Portfolios of the NYSE, Security Market Line

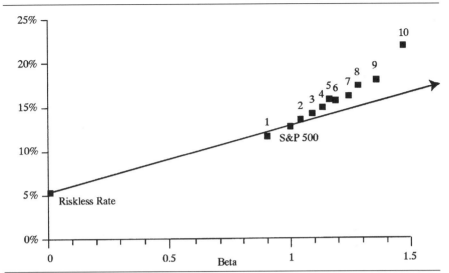

Exhibit 13.2   Size-Decile Portfolios of the NYSE, Long-Term Returns in Excess
of CAPM

Decile	Beta*	Arithmetic Mean Return	Actual Return in Excess of Riskless Rate**	CAPM Return in Excess of Riskless Rate**	Size Premium (Return in Excess of CAPM)
1	0.90	11.56%	6.38%	6.75%	−0.36%
2	1.04	13.45	8.28	7.82	0.47
3	1.09	14.14	8.96	8.19	0.77
4	1.13	14.80	9.62	8.50	1.13
5	1.16	15.62	10.45	8.73	1.72
6	1.19	15.60	10.42	8.91	1.52
7	1.24	16.13	10.96	9.31	1.65
8	1.28	17.27	12.10	9.62	2.47
9	1.35	17.98	12.81	10.16	2.65
10	1.46	21.92	16.75	10.97	5.78
Mid-Cap, 3–5	1.12	14.60	9.42	8.38	1.04
Low-Cap, 6–8	1.22	16.10	10.92	9.18	1.75
Micro-Cap, 9–10	1.38	19.02	13.85	10.37	3.47

 * Betas are estimated from monthly returns in excess of the 30-day U.S. Treasury bill total return,
   January 1926–December 1996.
** Historical riskless rate measured by the 71-year arithmetic mean income return component of
   20-year government bonds (5.17%).

calculation. It could be argued that this is also the size premium that should be incorporated in the build-up approach. Alternatively, it could be argued that the size premium for micro-cap stocks using the build-up approach would be the actual return in excess of the riskless rate less the ERP. Or, by numerical example, 13.85% − 7.5% = 6.35%. (The latter would seem more logical to me.)

Note from Exhibit 13.2 that micro-cap stocks actually have an average return in excess of the riskless rate of 13.85%. Deducting the ERP translates into a size premium of 6.35%. Note also that the micro-cap portfolio has a beta of 1.38. Using a size premium of 3.47% in the build-up approach makes no assumption regarding the overall risk level of the subject company you are valuing (e.g., it implies beta = 1.0). Using the risk premium of 6.35% assumes that the risk of the company you are valuing is greater than that of the overall market. Unfortunately, there is no easy way to gauge the level of risk inherent in most private small companies. Therefore, the very conservative solution to incorporating the size premium in the build-up approach is to use the micro-cap size premium of 3.47%. (*SP note:* This is "conservative" in the sense that it results in a lower discount rate. However, a lower discount rate applied to a set of cash flows results in a higher indicated present value, so it is not "conservative" with respect to the resulting indicated value.)

A common question among practitioners is whether the tenth decile could or should be used instead of the micro-cap premium that combines the ninth and tenth deciles. This is an important question, because the size premium shown in the *SBBI 1997 Yearbook* is 2.65% for the ninth decile and 5.78% for the tenth decile. Stated another way, for the smallest companies on the NYSE, the mismeasurement of the CAPM is the greatest.

Although it appears that the size premium becomes larger as companies become smaller, Ibbotson Associates has taken the conservative approach of combining the ninth and tenth deciles to form the micro-cap group. The micro-cap size premium includes a broader sample of companies, encompassing some larger companies. However, it is possible that the size premium for smaller companies could be much larger than the micro-cap size premium shown in the *SBBI*. (*SP note:* Many analysts would use the tenth decile premium rather than the micro-cap (ninth and tenth deciles combined) premium for a small company.)

Another common question is why the Ibbotson small-cap study focuses on the NYSE. Many business appraisers and valuation practitioners perform valuations on companies much smaller than NYSE companies. The equity values for companies included in the tenth decile reach in excess of $90 million, much larger than that of the typical company that is the subject of many business appraisals.

The Ibbotson study results shown in Chapters 7 and 8 of the *1997 SBBI Yearbook* focus on the NYSE because of concerns for data quality. Although the American Stock Exchange and, especially, the Nasdaq contain a number of smaller companies, the data for these companies are not always complete. There are Nasdaq companies whose shares do not trade for weeks at a time. Using such data would distort the results of the study. Therefore, the sample size was limited to the NYSE companies.

Ibbotson Data and Minority Discount Rate

There is quite a bit of confusion among valuation practitioners regarding the use of data derived from public companies and whether or not a minority discount is implicit in those data. This is a critical issue that must be addressed by the valuation professional, because employing a minority discount or a control premium in a valuation can have a material impact on the ultimate estimate of value derived in the appraisal.

The Ibbotson Associates' long horizon equity risk premium is derived from the returns on the S&P 500 versus the income return on a long-term Treasury bond. The Ibbotson Associates' micro-cap stock premium is derived from the returns on the ninth and tenth deciles of the New York Stock Exchange. Both the S&P 500 and the NYSE include a preponderance of companies that are minority held (i.e., most, and in fact usually all, of the stockholders are minority stockholders).

Because most of the companies in both the S&P 500 and NYSE are minority held, some valuation professionals assume that the ERP and size premium derived from them represent minority returns and therefore have a minority discount implicit in them. In other words, the value that is derived using Ibbotson Associates' data is a minority interest value. Although this assumption is technically correct, Ibbotson Associates does not believe that a control premium is necessarily warranted if the data are being used to reach a control value.

The returns that are generated by the S&P 500 and ninth and tenth deciles of the NYSE represent returns to equity holders in large-cap and small-cap stocks, respectively. Although most of these companies are minority held, there is no evidence that supports the fact that majority shareholders would earn higher rates if all of these companies were suddenly acquired by majority shareholders. Furthermore (for these publicly traded companies) there is no evidence that control shareholders are exploiting minority shareholders to any control owners' benefit. The ERP and small-cap premiums represent expected premiums that holders of securities of a similar nature can expect to achieve on average into the future. Therefore, for these publicly traded companies, there is no distinction between minority owners and controlling owners.

It is important to remember what the discount rate is meant to represent — the underlying risk of being in a particular industry or line of business. There are instances in which a majority shareholder can acquire a company and improve the cash flows generated by that company. However, this is not necessarily the case and does not necessarily have an impact on the general risk level of the cash flows generated by that company.

In performing income approach valuation analysis, adjustments for minority or controlling interest value should be made to the projected cash flows of the subject company instead of making arbitrary adjustments to the discount rate. (*SP note:* There is wide agreement that adjustments to reflect control or minority within the discounted present value formula generally should be made to the expected cash flows rather than to the discount rate. However, not all analysts would agree that the aggregate market value of the shares of a publicly traded company should not be distinguished from control value. In reality, added value for control should be dependent on what a buyer could do with that control. Many analysts would consider adding a control premium to the aggregate value of publicly traded minority shares, making the decision as to whether and, if so, how much, on a case-by-case basis.)

Ibbotson Data and Taxes

The statistics included in any Ibbotson Associates' publication are derived from data on publicly traded companies that are after corporate income taxes but before personal taxes. These returns are derived from dividends and capital appreciation credited to investors after the corporations have paid their income taxes. Therefore, for valuation purposes, the numbers from the Ibbotson Associates' publications are after-tax numbers and should be applied to cash flows that are also after-tax cash flows. (This means after corporate level taxes, not taxes at the individual level.)

There is no easy way to accurately modify the Ibbotson data to a pretax basis. This modification would require estimating pretax returns for all of the publicly traded companies that comprise the Ibbotson data. There is, however, no practical way to do this. Therefore, there is no easy way to calculate a before-tax equity risk premium.

Most valuation settings rely on after-tax cash flows. Yet there are some instances (usually for reasons deriving from regulatory or legal statutes) in which it is necessary to calculate a value based on pretax economic income. In these cases a pretax cost of capital or discount rate should be employed. Although not completely correct, the easiest way to convert an after-tax discount rate to a pretax discount rate is to divide the after-tax rate by (1 minus the tax rate). However, take note that this is a "quick and dirty" way to approximate pretax discount rates. (While this basically works for capitalization rates, where growth is implied to be constant, there is not a convenient way to convert the discount rate in a multiperiod model.)

COST OF CAPITAL QUARTERLY

The *Cost of Capital Quarterly (CCQ)* is an industry publication that provides cost of equity, cost of capital, and other financial information organized by SIC code. The intent of *CCQ* is to provide practitioners with comprehensive cost of capital information by industry. *CCQ* takes the information from approximately 3,500 companies and consolidates it into more than 300 different SIC code designations.

General Content of *CCQ*

The focus of *CCQ* is on the industry level, in an effort to provide the practitioner with an overview of how different cost of capital and other financial information varies for a number of similar companies. The idea behind the *CCQ* is to compensate for the fact that cost of equity models for individual companies can produce erratic data. By looking at the performance of a cost of equity model across an industry, the practitioner can determine a cost of capital range for that industry. From the industry information, a cost of capital estimate for the individual company in question can be proxied and compared with other analysis performed as part of the engagement.

Industries are organized by Standard Industrial Classification (SIC) code, a four-digit classification system developed by the federal government. The SIC codes displayed in *CCQ* range from one digit (the most general) to four digits (the most specific).

The classification procedure is set up in such a way that all companies of a similar type can be grouped together in a systematic fashion. For instance, companies engaged in the business of natural gas transmission are located in SIC 4922. On a less specific level, all companies included in gas production and distribution are included in SIC 492. SIC 49 includes companies engaged in electric, gas, and sanitary services. Finally, SIC 4 includes all forms of utilities and is titled "Transportation, Communications, Electric, Gas, and Sanitary Services." Other SIC codes operate in a similar fashion.

Companies Included in *CCQ*

The main data source for *CCQ* is the Compustat database. Compustat includes data on more than 7,000 publicly traded entities, but not all of them are included in *CCQ*. In an effort to provide the purest industry data possible, *CCQ* includes in a particular industry only those companies that derive at least 75% of their sales from that industry.

The way companies are analyzed is shown best by an example. The following table presents the business segment SIC codes and dollar sales (in millions) for Dover Corporation and Johnson Controls.

Dover Corporation		Johnson Controls	
SIC	$ Sales	SIC	$ Sales
3443	473	2531	3,836
3533	573	3085	1,192
3534	1,485	369	672
3559	603	3822	2,630

For Dover Corporation, industry 3534 represents 47% of sales for the business segments listed. At the two-digit level, industry 35 represents 85% of Dover's sales.

Therefore, in *CCQ*, Dover will appear in industries 35 and 3, but not in 3534 or 353. For Johnson Controls, the picture is not as clear. For the business segments presented, industry 2531 represents 46% of sales and industry 3 represents only 54% of sales. Johnson Controls, therefore, does not meet the 75% of total business segment sales and is excluded from the *CCQ* industry analysis.

Industries have different characteristics, including different levels of profitability, capitalization requirements, capital structure, and risk. *CCQ* attempts to summarize as many of these financial parameters as possible for as many industries as possible. The presentation of cost of equity capital by industry also shows how the different models work across industries. The unique aspect of *CCQ* is that, in addition to providing a summary of industry financial information, it also provides cost of equity information under five different models for each industry.

Cost of Equity Models

There are currently five different cost of equity models employed in *CCQ*. Two are CAPM-based, two are discounted cash flow (DCF)-based, and one is a three-factor model. One of the advantages of *CCQ* is that it provides industry cost of capital estimates for multiple models, given the same set of companies.

A quick glance at *CCQ* tells the reader that there is not necessarily consistent cost of equity information provided across models for a given industry. This is not surprising, given the number of inputs required for the different models and their level of sophistication.

The Capital Asset Pricing Model (CAPM)

Most practitioners are familiar with CAPM. It is referred to in the *CCQ* analysis as the OLS (ordinary least squares) Capital Asset Pricing Model and follows the method of calculating the cost of capital developed by William Sharpe and John Linter, the original founders of the model. (The theory behind the OLS calculation is that the market-required return for accepting risk is a linear function of the systematic risk, as measured by beta.) The formula for CAPM is stated as:

Formula 13.1

$$R_i = R_f + (B_i * R_p)$$

where:

R_i = Cost of equity capital for company i
R_f = The risk-free yield
B_i = The beta of company i
R_p = Expected equity risk premium

If you are using a *CCQ* cost of equity and would like to update the risk-free rate from the one included in the publication, it is possible to substitute the yield from the 20-year Treasury bond for the yield included in the *CCQ* calculation. If you are using *CCQ* and would like to modify the CAPM assumptions that are included in the publication, all of the necessary information, including the industry betas, have been provided.

The expected equity risk premium is the long-horizon equity risk premium from the *SBBI Yearbook*, as discussed previously in this chapter. The risk-free rate and equity risk premium numbers are the same for all of the CAPM models included in *CCQ*.

The two CAPM models utilize the OLS beta and are identical, except that one of them also adds on the appropriate size premium for the companies included in the industry. This allows the reader to see how the cost of equity varies across the industry with the standard CAPM and the CAPM corrected for size.

If a practitioner is using *CCQ* to compile a cost of equity estimate using the CAPM model with the OLS beta, it would be most appropriate to determine the cost of equity for the company in question using the OLS model that does not incorporate the size premium. Once the cost of equity has been determined using this model, the appropriate size premium should then be added to the cost of equity based on the size of the subject company. The OLS beta CAPM adjusted for size is meant to show only the impact of that size on the cost of equity across the entire industry. This impact will vary per company depending on the subject company's size.

Fama-French Three-Factor Model

The Fama-French Three-Factor Model is a multiple linear regression model developed by Eugene Fama and Kenneth French. The coefficients for the model are estimated by running a time series multiple regression for each company. The dependent variable is the company's monthly excess stock returns over Treasury bill returns. The independent variables include:

1. The monthly excess return on the market over Treasury bills
2. SMB—Small minus big, the difference between the monthly return on small-cap stocks and large-cap stocks
3. HML—High minus low, the difference between the monthly return on high book-to-market stocks and low book-to-market stocks

The Fama-French Three-Factor Model is shown in the following equation:

Formula 13.2

$$k_i = R_f + (b_i * ERP) + (s_i * SMBP) + (h_i * HMLP)$$

where:

k_i = Cost of equity capital for company i
R_f = Risk-free rate
b_i = Market coefficient in the Fama-French regression
ERP = Expected equity risk premium
s_i = Small-minus-big coefficient in the Fama-French regression
$SMBP$ = Expected small-minus-big risk premium, estimated as the difference between the historical average annual returns on the small-cap and large-cap portfolios
h_i = High-minus-low coefficient in the Fama-French regression
$HMLP$ = Expected high-minus-low risk premium, estimated as the difference between the historical average annual returns on the high book-to-market and low book-to-market portfolios

The idea behind the Fama-French model is to improve on the CAPM regression by incorporating more than one factor into the regression formula. CAPM is a single-factor cost of equity model in that the cost of equity of the stock is driven by how the stock reacts to movements in the overall market. The addition of the size premium to the CAPM is an attempt to correct the CAPM for its mismeasurement of company size.

Fama and French have attempted to address firm size in a different fashion by including it as a factor in the regression equation. They have also added the book-to-market ratio as an additional factor impacting the magnitude of cost of equity.

Discounted Cash Flow Models

In addition to the two CAPMs and the Fama-French model, CCQ includes two discounted cash flow models. The DCF framework is built around the idea that a company's value is simply the present value of the cash flows accruing to the shareholders of that company. Therefore, to determine a company's value, you need to know the cash flows accruing to shareholders this year, how fast those cash flows will accrue in future periods, and the appropriate discount rate in order to discount each of the expected future cash flows to a present value.

DCF cost of equity models turn this logic around by stating that if you know the value of a company today, and you know what cash flows are being generated by that company, all you need is an estimate of the growth rate of cash flows in order to solve for the cost of equity. In this case, the growth rates are obtained by a consensus of earnings growth rates from stock market analysts following the company.

All DCF cost of equity capital models are rooted in the Gordon Growth Model, which is stated as:

Formula 13.3

$$P_i = D_i / (k_i - g_i)$$

where:

P_i = Price per share for company i
D_i = Dividend per share for company i at the end of year 1
k_i = Discount rate for company i
g_i = Dividend growth rate for company i

If we want to utilize the Gordon Growth Model to calculate the cost of equity capital, the model has to be rewritten as:

Formula 13.4

$$k_i = \{[D_i * (1 + g_i)] / P_i\} + g_i$$

It is evident from this model that if a company does not pay dividends, its cost of equity becomes its growth rate. This is a rather simplistic view and calls into question the value of the model for use in analysis. The single-stage model is shown in *CCQ* more as a point of reference and comparison, not as an endorsement that this level of analysis is all that is necessary in determining the cost of equity.

One effort that can be undertaken to improve the cost of equity figures produced by the DCF analysis is to modify the growth rates that are used in the model. Although it may be realistic to assume that dividends or cash flows will grow at a certain rate for three to five years, it is probably not realistic to assume that growth will continue indefinitely through time at the same rate.

To get around the constant rate assumption of the single-stage model, different growth rates can be estimated for different future time periods. In *CCQ* we have included for each industry the results of a three-stage DCF model that assumes the cash flows will grow at the analyst's company-specific rates for five years, an industry average growth rate for five years, and then an economy-wide average growth rate (real growth rate plus an inflation estimate) for all other time periods. The results of this model can be seen in the column labeled "DCF 3-Stage" in Exhibit 13.3.

An example of an industry included in *CCQ* is shown in Exhibit 13.3.

THE IBBOTSON *BETA BOOK*

The Ibbotson *Beta Book* is a company-specific publication that shows only the ordinary least squares CAPM, sum beta (including lag), and Fama-French regression factors for more than 5,000 individual companies. For practitioners who would like to build their own peer groups for cost of capital analysis, the Ibbotson *Beta Book* provides the information necessary to calculate cost of equity under different cost of equity models or assumptions.

Using similar methodologies to calculate beta and Fama-French data as *CCQ*, the *Beta Book* allows practitioners to see the data behind the calculations for each

Exhibit 13.3   Sample Page from *Cost of Capital Quarterly*

STATISTICS FOR SIC CODE 3663   Radio and Television Broadcasting and Communications Equipment

This Industry Comprises 31 Companies

Industry Description

Establishments primarily engaged in manufacturing radio and television broadcasting and communications equipment. Important products in this industry are closed-circuit and cable television equipment; studio equipment; light communications equipment, transmitters; transceivers and receivers; cellular radio telephones.

Sales ($millions)

Total	3,211
Average	103.6
Three Largest Companies	
SCIENTIFIC-ATLANTA INC	1,146.5
CALIFORNIA MICROWAVE	467.9
GLENAYRE TECHNOLOGIES INC	172.1
Three Smallest Companies	
ANDREA ELECTRONICS CORP	3.3
CIRCUIT RESEARCH LABS INC	2.0
ACTV INC	0.9

Total Capital ($millions)

Total	5,962
Average	192.3
Three Largest Companies	
GLENAYRE TECHNOLOGIES INC	2,291.3
SCIENTIFIC-ATLANTA INC	1,357.8
CALIFORNIA MICROWAVE	361.5
Three Smallest Companies	
CABRE CORP	7.2
OPTELECOM INC	4.5
CIRCUIT RESEARCH LABS INC	1.1

Annualized Statistics For Last 10 Years (%)

	Average Return	Standard Deviation
S&P 500	15.18	16.71
Ind. Composite	41.39	41.04
Lg. Composite	40.22	51.43
Sm. Composite	48.33	135.24

Distribution of Sales ($millions)

	Latest	5 Yr. Avg.
90th Percentile	157.0	120.7
75th Percentile	101.1	80.0
Median	36.1	33.1
25th Percentile	13.4	10.2
10th Percentile	3.3	4.9

Distribution of Total Capital ($millions)

	Latest	5 Yr. Avg.
90th Percentile	304.9	166.6
75th Percentile	154.7	85.7
Median	53.5	35.3
25th Percentile	14.2	12.5
10th Percentile	10.1	8.9

Industry Sales and Income ($billions)

	Sales	Operating Income	Net Income
Current Yr.	3.2	0.3	0.1
Last Yr.	2.5	0.2	0.0
2 Yrs. Ago	2.1	0.1	0.0
3 Yrs. Ago	2.0	0.1	0.0
4 Yrs. Ago	1.8	0.1	0.0

Industry Market Capitalization ($billions)

	Equity	Debt
Current Yr.	5.8	0.2
Last Yr.	4.8	0.2
2 Yrs. Ago	3.0	0.2
3 Yrs. Ago	2.1	0.2
4 Yrs. Ago	1.5	0.2

Number of Companies & Total Capital ($billions)

	Large Cap	Mid Cap	Low Cap	Micro Cap	Total Cap
AAA, AA, A					
	0	0	0	0	0
	0.0	0.0	0.0	0.0	0.0
BBB					
	0	0	0	0	0
	0.0	0.0	0.0	0.0	0.0
BB, B, CCC, CC, D					
	0	0	0	1	1
	0.0	0.0	0.4	0.0	0.4
Not Rated					
	0	2	3	25	30
	0.0	3.6	0.7	1.3	5.6
Totals					
	0	2	4	25	31
	0.0	3.6	1.1	1.3	6.0
					☐ S&P Rating

Growth Over Last 5 Years (%)

	Net Sales	Operating Income	Net Income
75th Percentile	18.56	25.08	34.57
Median	5.81	0.82	3.23
25th Percentile	-1.39	-13.87	-29.78
Ind. Composite	14.23	25.48	47.47
Lg. Composite	23.47	40.61	46.74
Sm. Composite	3.88	-21.44	-21.88

Compound Annual Equity Return (%)

	5 Yrs.	10 Yrs.
75th Percentile	27.83	9.39
Median	6.31	3.22
25th Percentile	-0.03	-5.38
Ind. Composite	50.05	35.70
Lg. Composite	51.08	31.38
Sm. Composite	78.20	19.59

Betas (in Decimal)

	Unlevered Asset Beta	Levered Equity Beta
	1.36	1.48
	0.68	0.72
	0.22	0.35
	1.25	1.32
	1.46	1.49
	1.15	1.19

Margins (%)

	Operating Margin Latest	Operating Margin 5 Yr. Avg.	Net Margin Latest	Net Margin 5 Yr. Avg.	Return On Assets Latest	Return On Assets 5 Yr. Avg.	Return On Equity Latest	Return On Equity 5 Yr. Avg.
75th Percentile	12.40	9.73	5.57	4.05	9.32	5.79	5.98	3.77
Median	7.46	8.13	2.14	1.91	3.01	2.32	1.99	2.51
25th Percentile	3.72	4.69	-0.49	-2.70	-0.83	-3.04	-0.68	-1.95
Ind. Composite	10.09	8.12	3.79	1.76	5.21	2.29	2.08	1.28
Lg. Composite	11.69	9.48	4.97	4.03	6.93	5.34	2.18	2.25
Sm. Composite	-111.00	-47.57	-120.00	-63.76	-56.45	-40.86	-7.82	-6.42

Capital Structure Ratios (%)

	Debt/Total Capital Latest	Debt/Total Capital 5 Yr. Avg.	Debt/MV Equity Latest	Debt/MV Equity 5 Yr. Avg.
75th Percentile	16.17	14.95	19.41	17.60
Median	4.39	5.85	4.59	6.22
25th Percentile	0.17	1.88	0.17	1.92
Ind. Composite	3.61	5.55	3.68	5.88
Lg. Composite	1.80	2.85	1.82	2.93
Sm. Composite	2.56	2.20	2.63	2.25

Equity Valuation Ratios (in Decimal)

	Price/Earnings Latest	Price/Earnings 5 Yr. Avg.	Market/Book Latest	Market/Book 5 Yr. Avg.	Price/Sales Latest	Price/Sales 5 Yr. Avg.
75th Percentile	NMF	NMF	3.69	3.39	2.13	1.52
Median	61.73	39.84	1.91	2.17	0.92	1.01
25th Percentile	15.75	26.56	0.96	1.29	0.53	0.58
Ind. Composite	48.08	78.13	3.79	2.72	1.82	1.38
Lg. Composite	44.84	44.44	4.55	3.39	2.22	1.79
Sm. Composite	NMF	NMF	9.04	8.30	15.42	9.94

DCF Growth Rates (%)

	Analysts
75th Percentile	24.27
Median	24.27
25th Percentile	24.27
Ind. Composite	24.27
Lg. Composite	24.77
Sm. Composite	24.27

Yields (% of Price)

	Dividends Latest	Dividends 5 Yr. Avg.	Cash Flow Latest	Cash Flow 5 Yr. Avg.
75th Percentile	0.00	0.00	4.13	2.95
Median	0.00	0.00	0.53	1.15
25th Percentile	0.00	0.00	-3.75	-2.42
Ind. Composite	0.09	0.19	0.54	0.26
Lg. Composite	0.12	0.20	0.82	1.08
Sm. Composite	0.00	0.00	-7.29	-5.44

Cost Of Equity Capital (%)

	CAPM S-L Form	CAPM S-L Sm Cap	3-Factor F-F	DCF Analysts	DCF 3 Stage
75th Percentile	17.79	19.71	26.15	24.27	17.32
Median	12.16	15.41	18.33	24.27	13.95
25th Percentile	9.42	13.00	12.75	24.27	10.17
Ind. Composite	16.61	18.31	17.98	24.38	8.94
Lg. Composite	17.85	19.01	15.07	24.91	10.91
Sm. Composite	15.62	19.20	69.48	24.27	NMF

Cost of Debt (%)

	Analysts
	9.40
	9.06
	7.98
	7.19
	3.89
	NMF

Weighted Average Cost Of Capital (%)

	CAPM S-L Form	CAPM S-L Sm Cap	3-Factor F-F	DCF Analysts	DCF 3 Stage
75th Percentile	16.80	19.15	22.65	24.24	15.99
Median	11.47	14.55	15.87	23.14	13.59
25th Percentile	8.75	11.62	11.28	19.05	10.15
Ind. Composite	16.18	17.83	17.51	23.68	8.79
Lg. Composite	17.57	18.71	14.84	24.51	10.76
Sm. Composite	15.22	18.71	67.70	23.65	NMF

Copyright © 1996
Ibbotson Associates

Cost of Capital Quarterly
1996 Yearbook

Source: *Cost of Capital Quarterly*, 1996 Yearbook (Chicago: Ibbotson Associates, 1996), 3-47. Used with permission. All rights reserved.

company. A sample page from the Ibbotson Associates' *Beta Book* is shown in Exhibit 13.4. The *Beta Book* contains more companies than *CCQ* because the *Beta Book* has no industry requirements. Therefore, conglomerates and diversified companies that are excluded from *CCQ* are included in the *Beta Book*.

The *Beta Book* is organized into three distinct sections for each company. The first section provides the ordinary least squares (OLS) beta for each company, the t-statistics, R-squared, peer group beta, and adjusted OLS beta. The second section provides the sum beta, t-statistics, R-squared, peer group beta, and adjusted sum beta. The final section provides all three Fama-French Three-Factor Model factors and their respective t-statistics as well as the R-squared for the overall Fama-French regression. The *Beta Book* provides both the betas and the relevant regression figures in an attempt to show the user the statistical significance and goodness of fit for each regression.

The *Beta Book* provides the user with several different beta measures. The OLS beta is a traditional 60-month beta regression with no adjustment. It also provides an adjusted OLS beta. The adjustment procedure forces the company beta to be closer to the average of the peer group companies for that company. The amount of the adjustment depends on the statistical confidence of the regression equation. In other words, for companies whose beta calculations have little statistical confidence, their betas will be significantly adjusted toward the peer average. For companies whose beta calculations have high statistical confidence, their betas may also be adjusted toward the peer average, but not nearly as much.

Another beta that the *Beta Book* provides is the sum beta. A sum beta is based on the concept that not all companies react to market movements at the same time. Some companies, especially small companies, may actually lag behind the movement of the market. One factor contributing to this lag is that many small companies are not traded regularly enough for their prices to reflect immediate reactions to changes in the overall market.

Traditional beta measurement methodologies have no way of picking up a lagged reaction to market movements. The sum beta methodology attempts to pick up this lagged price reaction. The sum beta can also be adjusted toward the peer average in a fashion similar to that described for the OLS beta. (These adjusted betas can then be used the same way as traditional betas in the CAPM.)

The *Beta Book* also provides the factor weightings for the Fama-French Three-Factor Model. Using the *Beta Book,* the practitioner can see how much weight is given to each of the three factors in the Fama-French model and the statistical significance of each weight.

SUMMARY

Ibbotson Associates provides valuation and corporate finance practitioners with three valuable reference resources for calculating discount rates, capitalization rates, and cost of capital. *SBBI* provides equity risk premium and firm size premium esti-

Exhibit 13.4   Excerpt from First 1997 *Beta Book*

Ibbotson Associates' Beta Book
Copyright © 1997

First 1997 Edition
Data Through December 1996

Ticker	Company	CAPM: Ordinary Least Squares					CAPM: Sum Beta (Including Log)					Fama-French Three-Factor Model						
		OLS Beta	t-Stat	R-Sqr	Pr Grp Beta	Adj Beta	Sum Beta	t-Stat	R-Sqr	Pr Grp Beta	Adj Beta	FF Beta	FF t-Stat	SMB Prem	SMB t-Stat	HML Prem	HML t-Stat	FF R-Sqr
MRBK	MERCANTILE BANKSHARES CORP*	1.10	4.26	0.24	1.00	1.07	1.31	3.35	0.25	1.33	1.32	1.17	4.25	-0.36	-0.37	1.25	0.93	0.26
MST	MERCANTILE STORES CO INC	1.23	3.62	0.18	0.94	1.12	1.36	2.64	0.19	0.76	1.13	1.20	3.48	2.69	2.17	-1.24	-0.74	0.28
MERCS	MERCER INTL INC	2.02	2.57	0.10	0.79	1.06	2.43	2.04	0.11	0.95	1.30	2.74	3.59	9.60	3.51	8.57	2.31	0.28
MBVT	MERCHANTS BANCSHARES INC/VT	1.15	2.09	0.07	1.00	1.05	2.04	2.47	0.10	1.33	1.61	1.25	2.10	1.45	0.68	1.05	0.36	0.08
MGP	MERCHANTS GROUP INC	0.38	1.00	0.02	1.08	0.69	0.47	0.83	0.02	1.04	0.72	0.63	1.61	2.80	2.00	3.10	1.63	0.08
MBNY	MERCHANTS N Y BANCORP INC	0.08	0.31	0.00	1.00	0.32	0.15	0.39	0.00	1.33	0.44	0.30	1.18	1.66	1.82	3.00	2.42	0.11
MRK	MERCK & CO	1.29	4.64	0.27	1.12	1.24	1.52	3.60	0.28	1.20	1.42	1.03	3.68	-2.43	-2.41	-3.36	-2.46	0.37
MAX	MERCURY AIR GROUP INC	0.30	0.51	0.00	0.88	0.68	0.85	0.97	0.02	0.89	0.88	0.25	0.41	2.42	1.10	-1.44	-0.48	0.04
MFN	MERCURY FINANCE CO	1.40	2.93	0.13	1.41	1.40	0.81	1.13	0.15	1.40	1.13	1.69	3.37	1.82	1.01	4.14	1.69	0.17
MCY	MERCURY GENERAL CORP	0.68	1.45	0.03	1.08	0.90	1.42	2.03	0.07	1.04	1.22	0.86	1.71	0.85	0.47	2.59	1.06	0.05
MERQ	MERCURY INTERACTIVE CORP*	0.96	0.90	0.02	1.06	1.05	0.71	0.44	0.02	1.43	1.32	0.59	0.49	-2.06	-0.32	-7.33	-0.81	0.04
MDP	MEREDITH CORP	1.22	3.36	0.16	0.82	1.05	1.19	2.17	0.16	0.74	1.01	1.25	3.21	1.60	1.15	-0.06	-0.03	0.19
MDCD	MERIDIAN DATA INC*	1.06	0.77	0.01	1.25	1.23	2.88	1.37	0.04	1.47	1.60	1.10	0.72	10.35	1.32	-1.79	-0.16	0.05
KITS	MERIDIAN DIAGNOSTICS INC	0.58	0.81	0.01	1.12	0.98	0.62	0.57	0.01	1.20	1.04	1.05	1.40	-0.53	-0.20	7.45	2.05	0.10
MDG	MERIDIAN GOLD INC	0.55	0.84	0.01	0.53	0.53	0.75	0.75	0.01	0.76	0.75	0.74	1.05	2.20	0.87	2.37	0.69	0.03
MIGI	MERIDIAN INS GROUP INC	0.05	0.15	0.00	1.08	0.41	0.69	1.53	0.06	1.04	0.81	0.26	0.79	1.27	1.09	2.92	1.85	0.06
MTEC	MERIDIAN MEDICAL TECH INC	0.85	1.18	0.02	1.06	1.00	2.03	1.89	0.06	1.20	1.42	1.31	1.78	6.85	2.60	5.15	1.44	0.13
MRCO	MERIDIAN NATIONAL CORP	0.79	0.44	0.00	1.00	0.99	0.42	0.15	0.00	1.24	1.20	2.41	1.30	12.73	1.92	21.78	2.41	0.11
MPTBS	MERIDIAN POINT REALTY TR 83	-0.60	-0.47	0.00	0.43	0.33	0.30	0.16	0.01	0.91	0.85	-0.84	-0.61	2.25	0.46	-4.46	-0.67	0.02
MPH	MERIDIAN POINT VIII	-1.50	-0.83	0.01	0.43	0.33	0.67	0.25	0.03	0.91	0.90	-2.04	-1.07	3.84	0.56	-9.74	-1.05	0.05
MERS	MERIS LABORATORIES INC	0.57	0.50	0.00	1.06	1.00	0.44	0.25	0.00	1.27	1.16	0.04	0.03	0.86	0.20	-8.57	-1.46	0.05
MSEL	MERISEL INC	1.01	1.05	0.02	1.02	1.02	1.26	0.86	0.02	1.31	1.30	1.53	1.67	13.13	3.98	4.31	0.96	0.24
MMSI	MERIT MEDICAL SYSTEMS INC	1.00	1.17	0.02	1.06	1.05	2.18	1.70	0.05	1.20	1.40	0.87	1.00	6.13	1.95	-3.85	-0.90	0.13
MERI	MERITRUST FEDERAL SVGS BANK*	0.08	0.15	0.00	1.00	0.64	0.94	1.23	0.06	1.33	1.17	0.15	0.25	1.98	0.64	0.79	0.18	0.01
MRLL	MERRILL CORPORATION	2.13	3.84	0.20	0.82	1.29	2.06	2.45	0.20	0.69	1.21	2.48	4.55	6.67	3.41	3.62	1.36	0.34
MER	MERRILL LYNCH & CO	1.84	6.19	0.40	1.88	1.85	2.20	4.92	0.41	2.34	2.25	1.88	5.87	0.77	0.67	0.42	0.27	0.40
MRAM	MERRIMAC INDUSTRIES INC	1.19	2.11	0.07	1.29	1.25	2.24	2.68	0.12	1.83	1.99	1.09	1.82	1.98	0.92	-2.15	-0.74	0.11
MRY	MERRY LAND & INVT CO INC	0.25	0.67	0.01	0.43	0.33	0.15	0.27	0.01	0.91	0.47	0.44	1.12	2.10	1.49	2.42	1.26	0.05
MESA	MESA AIR GROUP INC	0.78	0.91	0.01	1.41	1.29	1.08	0.83	0.02	1.68	1.56	0.96	1.10	8.06	2.57	0.44	0.10	0.13
MXP	MESA INC	1.09	0.89	0.01	0.97	0.98	1.16	0.63	0.01	1.10	1.11	0.93	0.70	-1.91	-0.40	-2.01	-0.31	0.02
MLAB	MESA LABORATORIES INC	0.80	1.30	0.03	1.06	0.98	2.13	2.36	0.09	1.20	1.52	0.61	1.05	6.21	3.00	-4.81	-1.71	0.27
MTR	MESA ROYALTY TRUST	-0.20	-0.88	0.01	0.43	-0.06	-0.42	-1.22	0.03	0.91	-0.13	-0.19	-0.79	-0.79	-0.90	0.38	0.32	0.04
MAIR	MESABA HOLDINGS INC	-0.61	-0.72	0.01	1.41	1.02	1.45	1.18	0.09	1.68	1.63	-0.62	-0.68	3.94	1.22	-1.19	-0.27	0.04
MSB	MESABI TRUST	0.39	0.62	0.01	0.43	0.42	1.04	1.08	0.02	0.91	0.95	0.93	1.41	2.73	1.15	7.65	2.38	0.10
MCC	MESTEK INC	0.82	2.54	0.10	1.23	0.98	1.23	2.53	0.12	1.47	1.31	0.88	2.52	0.46	0.36	0.81	0.48	0.10
METS	MET-COIL SYSTEMS CORP	1.01	0.74	0.01	1.25	1.23	-1.18	-0.58	0.04	1.47	1.22	1.62	1.14	10.66	2.08	6.54	0.94	0.08
MPR	MET-PRO CORP	0.43	0.94	0.02	1.25	0.88	1.03	1.49	0.04	1.47	1.26	0.45	0.93	2.87	1.67	-0.61	-0.26	0.08
MTLM	METAL MANAGMENT INC	2.00	2.33	0.09	1.25	1.39	3.09	2.41	0.11	1.47	1.81	2.07	2.24	2.27	0.69	0.48	0.11	0.09
MTLC	METALCLAD CORP	-0.90	-0.90	0.01	0.46	0.26	0.08	0.34	0.04	0.82	0.77	-0.26	-0.27	12.48	3.57	6.46	1.36	0.20
META	METATEC CORP	0.43	0.54	0.01	1.29	1.10	0.80	0.66	0.01	1.83	1.60	1.10	1.35	6.51	2.22	8.61	1.70	0.12
METHA	METHODE ELECTRONICS -CLA	0.31	0.61	0.01	1.29	0.90	-0.33	-0.44	0.03	1.83	0.91	0.68	1.31	5.10	2.76	4.22	1.68	0.13
MCOM	METRICOM INC*	1.27	1.11	0.02	1.29	1.28	2.07	1.16	0.03	1.83	1.86	1.23	1.14	17.26	3.36	0.12	0.02	0.25
MTRO	METRO TEL CORP	-0.02	-0.02	0.00	1.29	1.03	0.08	0.00	0.00	1.83	1.46	0.05	0.05	0.95	0.29	0.74	0.17	0.00
MCLL	METROCALL INC*	1.34	1.64	0.06	0.91	1.00	1.80	1.46	0.07	0.97	1.16	1.26	1.50	6.91	1.59	6.46	1.36	0.23
MMG	METROMEDIA INTERNATIONAL GRP	3.05	4.38	0.25	1.21	1.70	3.35	3.18	0.25	1.56	2.06	3.23	4.40	4.46	1.70	-4.97	-0.77	0.29

MERCANTILE BANKSHARES CORP   METROMEDIA INTERNATIONAL GRP mates. *CCQ* provides the industry financial information and cost of capital estimates by SIC code. The *Beta Book* provides the company-specific information necessary to calculate cost of equity for more than 5,000 different companies, using different cost of equity assumptions.

In an effort to improve access to valuation and investment information, Ibbotson Associates is developing new and different ways to distribute information. The worldwide web is becoming an increasingly important tool for providing data. Much of the data that has been discussed in this chapter, as well as papers presented at conferences and new developments in cost of capital, can be found at www.ibbotson.com.

Note

1. The theory and our example of probabilistic forecasts is included in Chapter 3.

Chapter 14

The Arbitrage Pricing Model

Explanation of the APT Model (APM)
The APM Formula
Summary

The concept of the *arbitrage pricing theory* (APT) was introduced by academicians in 1976.[1] However, it was not until 1988 that data in a commercially usable form became generally available to permit the application of the theory to the estimation of required rates of return in day-to-day practice. In spite of the longevity of the theory's existence, it still is not widely used by practitioners today.

EXPLANATION OF THE APT MODEL (APM)

As noted in Chapter 9, the CAPM is a univariate model; that is, CAPM recognizes only one risk factor—systematic risk relative to a market index. In a sense, APT is a multivariate extension of the CAPM. APT recognizes a variety of risk factors that may bear pervasively on an investment's required rate of return, one of which may be a CAPM-type "market" or "market timing" risk. It may be argued that the CAPM and APT are not mutually exclusive, nor is one of greater or lesser scope than the other. It can also be argued that the CAPM beta implicitly reflects the information included separately in each of the APT "factors." However, in spite of its more limited use, most academicians consider the Arbitrage Pricing Model (APM) richer in its information content and explanatory and predictive power.

Whereas the nature of the CAPM is a single regression, the nature of the APM is a multiple regression. In the APM, the cost of capital for an investment varies according to that investment's sensitivity to each of several different risk factors.

The model itself does not specify what the risk factors are. Most formulations of the APM consider only risk factors that are of a pervasive macroeconomic nature, such as:

- *Yield spread.* The differential between risky and less risky bonds as a measure of investors' consensus confidence in economic prosperity
- *Interest rate risk.* Measured by the difference between long-term and short-term yields

- *Business outlook risk.* Measured by changes in forecasts for economic variables such as gross national product (GNP)
- *Inflation risk.* Measured by changes in inflation forecasts

The beta used in the CAPM may or may not be one of the risk factors included in any particular practitioner's version of the APM. In some versions, more industry-specific factors may be included, such as changes in oil prices. Exhibit 14.1 explains one version of APT risk factors.

THE APM FORMULA

In terms of a formula, the econometric estimation of the Arbitrage Pricing Model with multiple risk factors yields the following:

Formula 14.1

$$E(R_i) = R_f + (B_{i1}K_1) + (B_{i2}K_2) + \ldots + (B_{in}K_n)$$

where:

$E(R_i)$ = Expected rate of return on the subject security
R_f = Rate of return on a risk-free security
$K_1 \ldots K_n$ = Risk premium associated with factor K for the average asset in the market
$B_{i1} \ldots B_{in}$ = Sensitivity of security i to each risk factor relative to the market average sensitivity to that factor

Ibbotson and Brinson make the following observations regarding APT:

In theory, a specific asset has some number of units of each risk; those units are each multiplied by the appropriate risk premium. Thus, APT shows that the equilibrium expected return is the risk-free rate plus the sum of a series of risk premiums. APT is more realistic than CAPM because investors can consider other characteristics besides the beta of assets as they select their investment portfolios.[2]

Research has shown that the cost of equity capital as estimated by the APM tends to be higher for some industries (e.g., oil) and lower for others (e.g., certain utility groups) than the cost of equity capital using the CAPM. Early research also suggests the multivariate APT model explains expected rates of return better than the univariate CAPM.[3]

So, if the APM is more powerful than the CAPM, why isn't the APM used more? For one thing, the variables aren't specified. Also, there is no universal consensus as to which ones are likely to have the greatest efficacy. Furthermore, it is complicated in the sense that coefficients for several factors, rather than just one factor, must be worked out for each company for each specific time it is going to be applied.

Exhibit 14.1   Explanation of APT Risk Factors

Confidence Risk

Confidence Risk is the unanticipated changes in investors' willingness to undertake relatively risky investments. It is measured as the difference between the rate of return on relatively risky corporate bonds and the rate of return on government bonds, both with 20-year maturities, adjusted so that the mean of the difference is zero over a long historical sample period. In any month when the return on corporate bonds exceeds the return on government bonds by more than the long-run average, this measure of Confidence Risk is positive. The intuition is that a positive return difference reflects increased investor confidence because *the required yield on risky corporate bonds has fallen relative to safe government bonds.* Stocks that are positively exposed to the risk then will rise in price. (Most equities *do* have a positive exposure to Confidence Risk, and small stocks generally have greater exposure than large stocks.)

Time Horizon Risk

Time Horizon Risk is the unanticipated changes in investors' desired time to payouts. It is measured as the difference between the return on 20-year government bonds and 30-day Treasury bills, again adjusted to be mean zero over a long historical sample period. A positive realization of Time Horizon Risk means that the price of long-term bonds has risen relative to the 30-day Treasury bill price. This is a signal that investors require a lower compensation for holding investments with relatively longer times to payouts. The price of stocks that are positively exposed to Time Horizon Risk will rise to appropriately decrease their yields. (Growth stocks benefit more than income stocks when this occurs.)

Inflation Risk

Inflation Risk is a combination of the unexpected components of short- and long-run inflation rates. Expected future inflation rates are computed at the beginning of each period from available information: historical inflation rates, interest rates, and other economic variables that influence inflation. For any month, Inflation Risk is the unexpected surprise that is computed at the end of the month, i.e., it is the difference between the actual inflation for that month and what had been expected at the beginning of the month. Since most stocks have negative exposures to inflation risk, a positive inflation surprise causes a negative contribution to return, whereas a negative inflation surprise (a deflation shock) contributes positively toward return.

Industries whose products tend to be "luxuries" are most sensitive to Inflation Risk. Consumer demand for "luxuries" plummets when real income is eroded through inflation, thus depressing profits for industries such as retailers, services, eating places, hotels and motels, and toys. In contrast, industries least sensitive to Inflation Risk tend to sell "necessities," the demands for which are relatively insensitive to declines in real income. Examples include foods, cosmetics, tire and rubber goods, and shoes. Also companies that have large asset holdings such as real estate or oil reserves may benefit from increased inflation.

Business Cycle Risk

Business Cycle Risk represents unanticipated changes in the level of real business activity. The expected values of a business activity index are computed both at the beginning and end of the month, using only information available at those times. Then, Business Cycle Risk is calculated as the difference between the end-of-month value and the beginning-of-month value. A positive realization of Business Cycle Risk indicates that the expected growth rate of the economy, measured in constant dollars, has increased. Under such circumstances firms that are more positively exposed to business cycle risk — for example, firms such as retail stores that do well when business activity increases as the economy recovers from a recession — will outperform those such as utility companies that do not respond much to increased levels in business activity.

Market Timing Risk

Market Timing Risk is computed as that part of the S&P 500 total return that is not explained by the first four macroeconomic risks and an intercept term. Many people find it useful to think of the APT as a generalization of the CAPM, and by including this Market Timing factor, the CAPM becomes a special case: If the risk exposures to all of the first four macroeconomic factors were exactly zero, then Market Timing

Risk would be proportional to the S&P 500 total return. Under these extremely unlikely conditions, a stock's exposure to Market Timing Risk would be equal to its CAPM beta. Almost all stocks have a positive exposure to Market Timing Risk, and hence positive Market Timing surprises increase returns, and vice versa.

A natural question, then, is: "Do Confidence Risk, Time Horizon Risk, Inflation Risk, and Business Cycle Risk help to explain stock returns better than I could do with just the S&P 500?" This question has been answered using rigorous statistical tests, and the answer is very clearly that they do.

Source: Presented in a talk based on a paper, "A Practitioner's Guide to Arbitrage Pricing Theory," by Edwin Burmeister, Richard Roll, and Stephen A. Ross, written for the Research Foundation of the Institute of Chartered Financial Analysts, 1994. The exhibit is drawn from Notes for "Controlling Risks Using Arbitrage Pricing Techniques," by Edwin Burmeister. Reprinted with permission.

Alcar, for example, provides APT and CAPM cost of equity capital estimates for about 9,000 public companies. A sample of Alcar's data for one company is shown in Exhibit 14.2.

Exhibit 14.2   APT and CAPM Cost of Equity Capital Estimates Example

APT Estimated Cost of Equity for Air Prods & Chems Inc.

	Beta	+	Risk Premium	= Contribution	
Risk-Free Rate	N/A		N/A	10.00%	
+ CAPM Equity Premium	1.09		3.00%	3.26%	
+ Large Capitalization	(0.58)		(0.23)%	0.13%	APT uses additional
+ Small Capitalization	0.36		3.30%	1.19%	portfolios to
+ High Cash Flow/Price	0.00		2.53%	0.01%	overcome limitations
+ Low Cash Flow/Price	0.43		(3.76)%	(1.64)%	of CAPM
APT Cost of Equity					
				12.95%	
Business Risk (Unlevered Ke)				12.41%	Three ways to look
+ Financial Risk				0.54%	at equity risk
APT Cost of Equity					
				12.95%	
Risk-Free Rate				10.00%	APT techniques link
+ Short-Term Inflation				(0.40)%	the cost of equity to
+ Long-Term Inflation				0.24%	underlying economic
+ Interest Yield Term				0.20%	factors. This
+ Default Risk				2.47%	business is quite
+ Monthly Production				0.43%	sensitive to "default
APT Cost of Equity					risk," or investor
					confidence in the
				12.95%	economy (the spread
					between high- and
					low-grade bonds)

Selected Yield Term:	20 years
Selected Market Risk Premium:	Alcar Forecast
Debt/Equity Ratio:	33.69%
R-Squared:	43%
Specific Risk:	5%

Exhibit 14.2 *(continued)*

Estimated Cost of Equity for Air Prods & Chems Inc.

CAPM/APT Reconciliation

——————— Economic Factors ———————

Portfolio Factors	Short-term Infl.	Long-term Infl.	Interest Yield Term	Default Risk	Monthly Prodn.	TOTAL	Memo: Average Risk Premia	
Risk-free Rate						10.00%		"Small capitalization," or small stock, premium is due to this company's higher sensitivity to default risk
CAPM Eq. Prem.	-0.13%	0.47%	0.49%	1.84%	0.58%	3.26%	3.00%	
CAPM Ke						⟨13.26%⟩		
Large Cap	0.02%	0.02%	0.02%	0.06%	0.02%	0.13%	-0.23%	This Low Cash Flow-to-Price effect indicates stability and lower risk which more than offsets the small cap. effect, resulting in a lower estimated cost of equity under APT than CAPM
Small Cap	0.11%	0.10%	0.08%	⟨0.73%⟩	0.16%	1.19%	3.30%	
High CF/Price	0.00%	0.00%	0.00%	0.00%	0.00%	0.01%	2.53%	
Low CF/Price	-0.40%	-0.36%	-0.39%	-0.17%	-0.33%	⟨-1.64%⟩	-3.76%	
Difference	-0.27%	-0.24%	-0.28%	0.63%	-0.15%	-0.31%		
APT Ke	-0.40%	0.24%	0.20%	2.47%	0.43%	⟨12.95%⟩		
Memo: Avg. Risk Premia	-0.25%	0.31%	0.19%	3.99%	0.60%			

Selected Yield Term:	20 years
Selected Market Risk Premium:	Alcar Forecast
Debt/Equity Ratio:	33.69%
APT R-squared improvement:	7%

Source: Exhibit Highlights from *APT*. Alcar's Financial Policy Information Service. Reprinted with permission.

Two sources of information for inputs to the APM are BIRR Portfolio Analysis, Inc. and the Alcar Group. Contact addresses and phone numbers are given in Appendix C, "Data Resources."

SUMMARY

The Arbitrage Pricing Model is a multivariate model for estimating the cost of equity capital. The risk factor variables are not specified, but most formulations use macroeconomic factors that may impact different companies' rates of return to different degrees. The beta in the CAPM may or may not be one of the factors.

Partly because of lack of consensus on the specific factors and the complexity of the model, it has not enjoyed wide usage up to this time. Moreover, the macroeconomic factors used in current applications of APT may have a considerably less significant systematic impact on the cost of capital for smaller companies or on individual divisional or project decisions than for large national companies.

Notes

1. Stephen A. Ross, "The Arbitrage Theory of Capital Asset Pricing," *Journal of Economic Theory*, (December 1976): 241–260; and Stephen A. Ross, "Return, Risk, and Arbitrage," in *Risk and Return in Finance*, Irwin I. Friend and I. Bisksler, eds. (Cambridge, MA: Ballinger, 1977), 189–218. See also Stephen A. Ross, Randolph W. Westerfield, and Jeffrey F. Jaffe, *Corporate Finance*, 3d ed. (Burr Ridge, IL: McGraw-Hill, 1993), Chapter 11, 315–337.

2. Roger G. Ibbotson and Gary P. Brinson, *Investment Markets* (New York: McGraw-Hill, 1987), 32. For a more extensive discussion of APT, see Frank K. Reilly, *Investment Analysis and Portfolio Management*, 4th ed. (Fort Worth, TX: The Dryden Press, 1994), 288–291.

3. Tom Copeland, Tim Koller, and Jack Murrin, *Valuation: Measuring and Managing the Value of Companies*, 2d ed. (New York: John Wiley & Sons, 1994), 267.

PART III

Other Topics Related to Cost of Capital

Chapter 15

Minority Versus Control Implications of Cost of Capital Data

There is much confusion as to whether the results of applying cost of capital data, as discussed in this book, in the context of a company or stock valuation produces a minority value or a control value. The difference between the per share value of a share that represents control and the value of a share that represents a minority interest can be quite significant. (See, for example, the traditional levels of value chart, Exhibit 15.1.) As with many such questions in economics and finance, the answer is, *it depends*.

More than anything else, when the cost of capital is used in the context of valuation, the question as to whether the result of discounting or capitalizing represents a minority or a control value depends primarily on *the nature of the cash flows being discounted or capitalized, rather than on the discount or capitalization rate.*

In some cases, the answer to this question may hinge on the definition of value being sought, for example, fair market value (the value to a *hypothetical* buyer and/or seller) or investment value (the value to a *particular* buyer and/or seller).[1]

MINORITY VERSUS CONTROL HAS LITTLE OR NO IMPACT ON COST OF CAPITAL

Regardless of which of the major approaches is being used to estimate cost of capital (e.g., build-up model, CAPM, DCF model, or APM), the information is

Exhibit 15.1   Example of Relationships Between Control Ownership Premiums, Minority Ownership Interest Discounts, and Discounts for Lack of Marketability

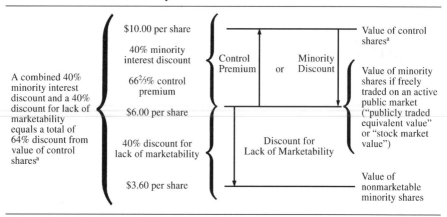

[a] Control shares in a privately held company may also be subject to some discount for lack of marketability, but usually not nearly as much as minority shares.

Source: Jay E. Fishman, Shannon P. Pratt, J. Clifford Griffith, and Mark Wells, *Guide to Business Valuations*, 7th ed. (Fort Worth, TX: Practitioners Publishing Company, 1997), 8–15. Reprinted with permission of Practitioner's Publishing Company. Copies of this Guide can be ordered by calling PPC at (800) 323-8724.

derived from publicly traded stocks. Because these public market transactions represent minority ownership interests, some analysts think that the cost of capital should be adjusted downward in valuing a controlling ownership interest.

This generally is not true!

Recall that the discounting method of valuation and the capitalization method of valuation have two basic elements in common:

1. A numerator consisting of an amount or amounts of expected economic income
2. A denominator consisting of a rate of return at which the economic income is discounted or capitalized

Almost all the difference in the control value versus the minority value in the income approach to valuation is found in the numerator—the expected economic income available to the investor—rather than in the denominator—the discount or capitalization rate.

As Roger Ibbotson has succinctly stated the case:

> When you are purchasing a company you are acquiring the ability to potentially control future cash flows. To acquire this option to exercise control, you must pay a premium. Holding all else constant, it should not impact the discount rate.[2]

Generally speaking, investors will not accept a lower expected rate of return for purchase of a controlling interest than for purchase of a minority interest. Control buyers pay premiums because they expect to do something to increase the cash flows, not because they are willing to accept a lower expected rate of return. What they may do to increase cash flows can range anywhere from eliminating Grandma from the payroll to drastically increasing prices for products or services of both acquirer and target as a result of absorbing a direct competitor.

Of course, we've seen many a public stock take a huge tumble in its market price as a result of an acquisition. This usually is because the acquisition failed to achieve the expected increase in cash flows for the target and/or the acquirer, but those are stories for another day. If the market perceives that the returns a company is likely to achieve will fall short of the market's required rate of return, then the market simply adjusts the stock price downward until the expected returns *do* meet the market's required rate of return.

COMPANY EFFICIENCY VERSUS SHAREHOLDER EXPLOITATION

Benefits available to a minority shareholder are a function of two distinct factors:

1. Efficiency at the overall company level
2. Differential benefits between control stockholders and minority stockholders (e.g., cash flow that could be available for dividends used for extra compensation to controlling owners)

Controlling stockholders enjoy a number of prerogatives of control, which can have an impact on both of the aforementioned factors as they affect minority stockholders. The following are some of the more common prerogatives of control:

1. Appoint management
2. Determine management compensation and perquisites
3. Set policy and change the course of business
4. Acquire or liquidate assets
5. Select people with whom to do business and award contracts
6. Make acquisitions
7. Liquidate, dissolve, sell out, or recapitalize the company
8. Sell or acquire Treasury shares
9. Register the company's stock for a public offering
10. Declare and pay dividends
11. Change the articles of incorporation or bylaws
12. Block any of the preceding actions[3]

It is apparent that exercise of some of these prerogatives may have an impact on the total cash flows available to the firm, and others will affect the relative benefits ultimately realized by control shareholders versus minority shareholders. It should also be apparent that in projecting expected cash flows, the amounts available to a control owner may not be the same as those available to a minority owner. For example, in many companies control owners set their own compensation (often reflecting their own perceived genius) rather than having an independent compensation committee. In any case, whether a result of company efficiency or differential shareholder benefits, it is the expected cash flows to the investor that drive the value to the investor, not differences in cost of capital as between minority investors and control investors.

The exploitation of minority shareholders is far less prevalent in public companies than in private companies, at least in larger public companies. If company cash flows are already maximized and the returns are already distributed pro rata to all shareholders, then there may be no difference between a control value and a minority value.

IMPACT OF THE STANDARD OF VALUE

Some analysts suggest that the appropriate cost of capital for an acquisition should be that of the acquirer rather than the target. This position departs from the standard of *fair market value* (the price at which the property would change hands between *hypothetical* buyers and sellers, with no special motivations) and introduces an element of *investment value* (the value to a *particular* buyer or seller). If the standard of value is fair market value, then the principle that "The cost of capital is a function of the investment, not the investor," clearly applies.

The idea of fair market value is that there is a consensus value that, in economic terms, "clears the market." If the cost of capital is a function of the investment, not the investor, then it is conceivable that the risk perceived by one investor may depart from the market consensus regarding the investment's risk. If the estimated cost of capital for a particular investment for a particular investor is driven by a view which departs from the market consensus, then we are moving away from the standard of fair market value (a consensus value) and toward investment value (value to some particular investor, driven by that investor's unique perceptions or circumstances).

UNDER WHAT CIRCUMSTANCES SHOULD A CONTROL PREMIUM BE APPLIED?

We have made the case that the cost of capital is the same or nearly the same for controlling interests as for minority interests. But we know that acquisitions are made at prices reflecting a control price premium over public market minority share trading prices.[4] So if we are valuing a controlling interest by the discounting or capitalizing method, and if we are using the cost of capital that we have estimated, under what circumstances should we add a control premium?

Projected Income May Not Reflect What a Control Owner Would Achieve

We said earlier that the control premium would be reflected as a result of the increased cash flows that a control owner would expect to achieve. If such control cash flows have been either discounted or capitalized, then no further control premium should be applied. However, if the projected cash flows used do *not* reflect a control owner's expectation, then a control premium may be warranted.

Investment Value Reflecting Synergies

If a buyer may achieve strategic or synergistic benefits by an acquisition, then that buyer may be willing to pay a control premium. For example, if the target is a direct competitor, then the buyer may benefit by raising *his own* prices as well as those of the target. Remember, however, that a price premium reflecting benefits to such a *particular* buyer bring in the element of investment value as opposed to a pure fair market value.

In the context of this thinking, with many synergistic acquisitions in the 1990s, some versions of the "levels of value" chart (Exhibit 15.1) add another level at the top, "synergistic value," reflecting a potential premium over control value on a stand-alone basis.

Factors Affecting a Control Premium a Financial Buyer Might Pay

Financial buyers sometimes pay control premiums, even if they do not have any opportunities for synergistic benefits, albeit typically much lower premiums than those paid by synergistic buyers. For example, one control prerogative that control owners can implement that minority owners cannot is to register a public offering. Other control prerogatives would be to sell interests to employees or to others, to repurchase outstanding minority interests, or to recapitalize. Some will pay a premium to "call the shots." Some may perceive psychological advantages to control of some companies.

SUMMARY

As a generality, the cost of capital is the same for minority interest investments as for controlling interest investments. Investors typically do not reduce their required rate of return because they are buying a controlling interest rather than a minority interest.

Therefore, although empirical data used to estimate the cost of capital are drawn almost entirely from the public stock market (which represents transactions in minority shares), the cost of capital thus estimated is applicable to either control or minority investments. Premiums above current market trading prices often are paid to acquire controlling interests. However, these premiums are paid because of anticipated increases in the cash flows available to the controlling investors, not because of a lower cost of capital.

Increased cash flows to control buyers may come as a result of improved operating efficiency, synergies with a buying company, or redistribution of already available cash flows to new control owners.

The standard of value conceivably could affect the cost of capital. *Fair market value* assumes a market consensus cost of capital, whereas an *investment value* standard may reflect a cost of capital driven by a particular investor's perceptions or circumstances, which may depart from the market consensus.

Notes

1. For a detailed discussion of definitions of various standards of value in commonly encountered legal contexts, see "Standards of Value" in Shannon P. Pratt, Robert F. Reilly, and Robert P. Schweihs, *Valuing a Business: The Analysis and Appraisal of Closely Held Companies*, 3d ed. (Burr Ridge, IL: McGraw-Hill, 1996), 23–28.
2. *Ibbotson Associates Cost of Capital Workshop*, Chapter 1 (Chicago: Ibbotson Associates, 1998), 12.
3. Pratt, Reilly, and Schweihs, *Valuing a Business*, 301.
4. See, for example, *HLHZ Control Premium Studies* (Los Angeles: Houlihan, Lokey, Howard, & Zukin, published quarterly).

Chapter 16

Handling the Discount for Lack of Marketability

As noted earlier, whether the cost of capital estimation is based partly on historical market data or entirely on current market data, the data represent publicly traded stock transactions in the highly liquid U.S. public stock markets. Investors in companies without an established trading market for their stock place a high premium on liquidity or, conversely, demand a high discount for lack of liquidity, as compared with companies with an established trading market for their stock.

Having estimated required rates of return from market data for publicly traded stocks, there are two ways you can adjust for the lack of liquidity for closely held stock:

1. After estimating a value as if publicly traded, subtract a percentage discount for lack of marketability.
2. Build the lack of marketability factor into the discount rate by adding some number of percentage points into the discount or capitalization rate, developed from any of the models discussed in earlier chapters of this book.

DISCRETE PERCENTAGE DISCOUNT FOR LACK OF MARKETABILITY

The most common way to handle the lack of marketability issue is by a percentage deduction from the value indicated after discounting or capitalizing expected cash flows at a rate derived from public market data.

Minority Ownership Interests

Many empirical studies have provided extensive transaction data to help quantify the amount of such a discount in the case of minority interest transactions. The studies consistently show a central tendency for discounts for lack of marketability for minority interests to be 30% to 50% from the value as if they were publicly traded. However, it is noteworthy that there are many transactions above and below this range.

Controlling Ownership Interests

The case for discounts for lack of marketability for controlling interest transactions is not as clear. A controlling interest holder cannot merely call the friendly stockbroker, execute a transaction in seconds, and have cash in hand within three business days. It may take months to get a controlling interest ready to sell, incurring significant legal, accounting, and management time costs in the process. Furthermore, as compared with public companies, most private companies have much less ready access to the capital markets to raise additional equity and/or debt capital.[1]

In spite of these limitations, some analysts would say that discounts for lack of marketability are not applicable to controlling interests. These same analysts may, however, recognize the realities of these factors under the rubric of "liquidity." Frequently, courts have recognized discounts for lack of marketability for controlling stock interests held in estates. Discounts for lack of liquidity (marketability) for controlling ownership interests, when appropriate (such as those recognized in the U.S. Tax Court), are often in the range of 10% to 25%,[2] not as great as for minority ownership interests.

BUILDING THE DISCOUNT FOR LACK OF MARKETABILITY INTO THE DISCOUNT RATE

Venture Capitalists' Required Rates of Return

Venture capitalists typically say that they look for expected rates of return between 30% and 50% on their portfolios, which means higher rates on very risky start-ups. One of the reasons that these rates are so high is the illiquidity of the companies and securities in which they invest, even though they virtually always have some sort of exit strategy in place if everything works out as projected. Unfortunately, there are no data available to indicate how much of their required rate of return is for the liquidity factor. (If any readers can shed some light on this question, please contact the author at the phone number or address shown in the Preface.)

Quantifying the Marketability Factor

In building the lack of marketability factor into the discount rate, the question of how many percentage points to add to the discount rate is difficult and quite subjective. Chris Mercer has compiled a list of factors to consider, generally adding somewhere between zero and four percentage points for each factor considered important in the particular case. This list is shown in Exhibit 16.1. In most of his examples, he considers about four to six factors, and his cumulative adjustments tend to run between one and six percentage points.[3] The applicable cash flow for Mercer's "Quantitative Marketability Discount Model" discount rate are those expected to be available to the minority investor.

Exhibit 16.1   Estimating Cost of Capital, Including Illiquidity Factor

		Range of Returns	
Components of the Required Holding Period Return		Lower	Higher
Base equity discount rate (adjusted Capital Asset Pricing Model)			
Current yield-to-maturity composite long-term Treasuries		0.0%	0.0%
+ Adjusted Ibbotson large stock premium	0.0%		
× Applicable beta statistic	× 1.0		
= Beta-adjusted large stock premium		0.0%	0.0%
+ Adjusted Ibbotson small stock premium		0.0%	0.0%
= Base equity discount rate		0.0%	0.0%
Investment-Specific Risk Premiums — Factors to Consider			
Uncertainties related to length of expected holding period			
General illiquidity of the investment			
Lack of expected interim cash flow			
Uncertainties related to expected interim cash flow			
Potential for adverse cash flow from tax pass-through entity			
Uncertainties related to potential for favorable exit from investment			
General unattractiveness of the investment			
Lack of diversification of assets			
Unattractive asset mix			
Unlikely candidate for merger/sale/acquisition/initial public offering			
Uncertainties related to buy-sell agreement			
Small shareholder base			
Adjustment for large size of the entity			
Large size of the investment limits market			
Other			
Range of specific risk premiums for the investment		0.0%	0.0%
Initial range of required returns		0.0%	0.0%
Concluded range of required holding period returns		0.0%	0.0%

Source: Z. Christopher Mercer, *Quantifying Marketability Discounts* (Memphis: Peabody Publishing, 1997), 312. Reprinted with permission.

SUMMARY

Investors, especially in the United States, cherish liquidity and abhor illiquidity. Because our empirical data to estimate cost of equity capital all come from the public stock market, the comparative lack of liquidity must be addressed in using cost of capital data to estimate value for privately held interests or companies.

There are two ways to handle the liquidity difference between public company interests and private company interests:

1. *Use a discrete percentage discount for lack of marketability.* Value the interest as if it were publicly traded, and then subtract a discount for lack of marketability from the estimated publicly traded equivalent value.

2. *Adjust the discount rate.* Add percentage points to the discount rate used to discount the expected cash flows to present value.

The notes at the end of this chapter provide reference sources for assistance in implementing either one of these methods.

Notes

1. For a concise but comprehensive summary of the quantification of discounts for lack of marketability, see Chapter 15, "Discounts for Lack of Marketability," in Shannon P. Pratt, Robert F. Reilly, and Robert P. Schweihs, *Valuing a Business: The Analysis and Appraisal of Closely Held Companies*, 3d ed. (Burr Ridge, IL: McGraw-Hill, 1996), 331–365.
2. See reference in note 1, plus Brad Fowler, "How Do You Handle It—Lack of Marketability: Discounts on Minority Interests," *Shannon Pratt's Business Valuation Update* (July 1997), 1–2.
3. Z. Christopher Mercer, *Quantifying Marketability Discounts* (Memphis: Peabody Publishing, 1997). This book also comprehensively covers empirical studies of discounts for lack of marketability, conducted over the last 30 years.

Chapter 17

How Cost of Capital Relates to the Excess Earnings Method of Valuation

The excess earnings method of valuation was originally created for the purpose of valuing intangible assets, specifically intangible value in the nature of goodwill. It was devised in order to determine how much the U.S. government would compensate brewers and distillers for the economic loss of their goodwill as a result of Prohibition.

This valuation method has since been embodied in Revenue Ruling 68-609, included here in Exhibit 17.1. Although it was originally designed to value only intangible assets, it is widely used (and misused) today in the valuation of small businesses and professional practices.

This chapter has a single point: An estimate of the cost of capital, developed by methods discussed in this book, can be used as a test of the reasonableness of the assumptions and results achieved by using the excess earnings method. This test can be applied either by a person preparing an excess earnings method valuation, or by someone reviewing an excess earnings method valuation prepared by someone else.

This chapter gives only enough of the skeletal basics of the excess earnings method to allow the reader to understand how to apply the reasonableness test proposed herein. Most basic texts on business valuation contain a full chapter, or major portion of a chapter, on the excess earnings method.[1]

Exhibit 17.1   Revenue Ruling 68-609

The "formula" approach may be used in determining the fair market value of intangible assets of a business only if there is no better basis available for making the determination; A.R.M. 34, A.R.M. 68, O.D. 937, and Revenue Ruling 65-192 superseded.

SECTION 1001. — DETERMINATION OF AMOUNT OF AND RECOGNITION OF GAIN OR LOSS

26 CFR 1.1001-1: Computation of gain or loss. Rev. Rul. 68-609[1]
(Also Section 167; 1.1679(a)-3.)

The purpose of this Revenue Ruling is to update and restate, under the current statute and regulations, the currently outstanding portions of A.R.M. 34, C.B. 2, 31 (1920), A.R.M. 68, C.B. 3, 43 (1920), and O.D. 937, C.B. 4, 43 (1921).

The question presented is whether the "formula" approach, the capitalization of earnings in excess of a fair rate of return on net tangible assets, may be used to determine the fair market value of the intangible assets of a business.

The "formula" approach may be stated as follows:

A percentage return on the average annual value of the tangible assets used in a business is determined, using a period of years (preferably not less than five) immediately prior to the valuation date. The amount of the percentage return on tangible assets, thus determined, is deducted from the average earnings of the business for such period and the remainder, if any, is considered to be the amount of the average annual earnings from the intangible assets of the business for the period. This amount (considered as the average annual earnings from intangibles), capitalized at a percentage of, say, 15 to 20 percent, is the value of the intangible assets of the business determined under the "formula" approach.

The percentage of return on the average annual value of the tangible assets used should be the percentage prevailing in the industry involved at the date of valuation, or (when the industry percentage is not available) a percentage of 8 to 10 percent may be used.

The 8 percent rate of return and the 15 percent rate of capitalization are applied to tangibles and intangibles, respectively, of businesses with a small risk factor and stable and regular earnings; the 10 percent rate of return and 20 percent rate of capitalization are applied to businesses in which the hazards of business are relatively high.

The above rates are used as examples and are not appropriate in all cases. In applying the "formula" approach, the average earnings period and the capitalization rates are dependent upon the facts pertinent thereto in each case.

The past earnings to which the formula is applied should fairly reflect the probable future earnings. Ordinarily, the period should not be less than five years, and abnormal years, whether above or below the average, should be eliminated. If the business is a sole proprietorship or partnership, there should be deducted from the earnings of the business a reasonable amount of services performed by the owner or partners engaged in the business. See *Lloyd B. Sanderson Estate v. Commissioner*, 42 F. 2d 160 (1930). Further, only the tangible assets entering into net worth, including accounts and bills receivable in excess of accounts and bills payable, are used for determining earnings on the tangible assets. Factors that influence the capitalization rate include (1) the nature of the business, (2) the risk involved, and (3) the stability or irregularity of earnings.

The "formula" approach should not be used if there is better evidence available from which the value of intangibles can be determined. If the assets of a going business are sold upon the basis of a rate of capitalization that can be substantiated as being realistic, though it is not within the range of figures indicated here as the ones ordinarily to be adopted, the same rate of capitalization should be used in determining the value of intangibles.

Accordingly, the "formula" approach may be used for determining the fair market value of intangibles of a business only if there is no better basis therefor available.

See also Revenue Ruling 59-60, C.B. 1959-1, 237, as modified by Revenue Ruling 65-193, C.B. 1965-2, 370, which sets forth the proper approach to use in the valuation of closely held corporate stocks for estate and gift tax purposes. The general approach, methods, and factors, outlined in Revenue Ruling 59-60, as modified, are equally applicable to valuations of corporate stocks for income and other tax purposes as well as for estate and gift tax purposes. They apply also to problems involving the determination of the fair market value of business interests of any type, including partnerships and proprietorships, and of intangible assets for all tax purposes.

A.R.M. 34, A.R.M. 68, and O.D. 937 are superseded, since the positions set forth therein are restated to the extent applicable under current law in this Revenue Ruling 65-192, C.B. 1965-2, 259, which contained restatements of A.R.M. 34 and A.R.M. 68, is also superseded.

----
[1]Prepared pursuant to Rev. Proc. 67-6, C.B. 1967-1, 576.

Source: Rev. Rul. 68-609, 1968-2, C.B. 327.

BASIC "EXCESS EARNINGS" VALUATION METHOD

The excess earnings method is a form of a capitalization method requiring separate estimation of *two* capitalization rates. The reason for the two rates is that the income stream being capitalized is broken down into two parts:

1. *Income attributable to tangible assets.* Less risky, lower required rate of return
2. *Income attributable to intangible assets.* More risky, generally higher required rate of return

In this regard, the rule is simply that the weighted average of the two rates based on asset components (weighted at market values, of course) should approximately equal capitalization rates based on capital structure components estimated by methods discussed in this book.

Conceptual Basis for the Method

The *Guide to Business Valuations* explains the concept of the excess earnings method as follows:

> The model for the excess earnings method computes the company's equity value based on the "appraised" value of tangible assets, plus an additional amount for intangible assets. A company's tangible assets should provide a current return to the owner. Since there are risks associated with owning the company's assets, the rate of return on those assets should be commensurate with the risks involved. That rate of return should be either the prevailing rate of return required to attract capital to that industry or an appropriate rate above the risk-free rate. Any returns produced by the company above the rate on tangible assets are considered to arise from intangible assets. Accordingly, the weighted average capitalization rate for tangible assets and intangible assets should be equivalent to the capitalization rate for the entire company.[2]

Steps in Applying the Excess Earnings Method

The *Guide to Business Valuations* lists the steps required in implementing the excess earnings method as follows:

Step 1. Obtain the company's financial statements. Apply the necessary generally accepted accounting principles (GAAP) and normalization adjustments (including adjustments for nonoperating assets). Recompute federal and state income taxes, if necessary, based on normalized pre-tax earnings.

Step 2. Determine the value of the company's net tangible assets.

Step 3.   Determine a reasonable rate of return (as of the valuation date) on the appraised value of the company's net tangible assets.

Step 4.   Multiply the reasonable rate of return (Step 3) times the company's net tangible asset value (Step 2). That amount is the "reasonable return" on those assets.

Step 5.   Subtract the calculated reasonable return (Step 4) from normalized net earnings (Step 1). That difference is the company's "excess earnings."

Step 6.   Determine an appropriate capitalization rate (as of the valuation date) for the company's excess earnings, which are assumed to be attributable to goodwill or other intangible assets.

Step 7.   Capitalize the excess earnings (divide excess earnings by the capitalization rate).

Step 8.   Add the amount computed in Step 7 and the value of the net tangible assets (Step 2).

Step 9.   Perform "sanity checks" to determine the reasonableness of the value determined in Steps 1 through 8.[3]

A very good "sanity check," as referred to in Step 9, is the cost of capital reasonableness check outlined in this chapter.

An Example of the Excess Earnings Method

For an example, we will use a company with 100% equity in its capital structure. This simplifies the example, although it works just as well in valuing overall invested capital. As a practical matter, a majority of the companies to which this method is applied have no long-term debt anyhow. We are reviewing an excess earnings method valuation prepared by Sam Shoveler for a company owner's wife in a divorce proceeding.

The company is Kenny's Landscaping Mob (KLM), a sole proprietorship with several years of history in a residential area primarily populated by employees of lumber, plywood, and papermill companies. Mill shutdowns are frequent, impacting KLM's business, and there has even been talk of permanent closures. Kenny, now 45, supervises a high-turnover work force whose members are paid a small fraction of the hourly rate that Kenny charges his clients for the gardening and landscaping work performed. There is substantial client turnover, but Kenny advertises heavily and finds new customers, at least when the mills are fully operating.

To illustrate a simple valuation of KLM by the excess earnings method, we will make the following assumptions:

1. An appraiser accredited by the American Society of Appraisers in Machinery and Equipment Appraisal and with experience in landscaping and gardening equipment has appraised KLM's tangible assets on a value-in-use basis at $200,000.

2. Shoveler has determined that a reasonable rate of return on the company's net tangible assets is 8%.
3. Shoveler has also determined that an appropriate capitalization rate for the company's excess earnings is 20%.
4. Normalized net cash flow for KLM, after reasonable compensation to Kenny, is $50,000 per year.
5. Because Kenny is always scrambling for both customers and workers, and because the community's industrial base is flat at best, growth in net cash flow is expected to be only at the rate of inflation, estimated at 3%.

Shoveler's summary of the excess earnings method of valuation of KLM is as follows:

Tangible asset value		$200,000
Net cash flow	$50,000	
Required return on tangible assets:		
0.08 × $200,000	16,000	
Return attributable to intangible assets	$34,000	
Intangible asset value (capitalized excess earnings)		
$34,000 ÷ 0.20		170,000
Total value of KLM		$370,000

THE COST OF CAPITAL REASONABLENESS CHECK

The cost of capital reasonableness check is a fairly simple two-step process:

1. Estimate a reasonable capitalization rate for the subject company by one or more of the cost of capital estimation methods discussed in this book.
2. Compute the weighted average capitalization rate (the weighted average of the returns on tangible assets and excess earnings, the latter representing the return on intangible assets) implied in the excess earnings valuation, and compare it with the capitalization rate estimate in Step 1.

If the results of Step 1 and Step 2 are close to each other, this implies passing marks on one test of the reasonableness of the rates used in the excess earnings method. (The analyst should recognize, of course, that the weighted average of the excess earnings method rates could have been close to the overall capitalization rate by accident, and that different tangible asset values or cash flows could still produce an unreasonable result.)

Estimating a Capitalization Rate

For a very small company like KLM, the build-up method, as presented in Chapter 8, is usually the best method for estimating an equity capitalization rate. To implement the build-up method, we'll make the following assumptions:

1. *Risk-free rate.* At the valuation date, 7.0%
2. *Equity risk premium.* Arithmetic average from *SBBI Yearbook*, 7.5%
3. *Size premium.* Ibbotson's 10th decile size premium from *SBBI Yearbook*, 6.35%
4. *Specific company risk premium.* The company is tiny as compared with Ibbotson's 10th-decile NYSE stocks. The company has high specific risk because of lack of stability of customer base, and economic vulnerability of its customer base because of conditions in the industry on which it is dependent. In addition, there's a key person issue: how easily could Kenny be replaced? Although this decision is quite subjective, it seems conservative to add a specific risk factor of 5.0%.

Adding up the pertinent factors gives us a discount rate as follows:

Risk-free rate	7.00%
Equity risk premium	7.50
Size premium	6.35
Company-specific premium	5.00
Estimated KLM cost of equity (discount rate)	25.85%

We then subtract the estimated growth rate from the discount rate to get the estimated capitalization rate:

Estimated Capitalization Rate for KLM Cash Flows

Discount rate	25.85%
− Estimated long-term growth rate	3.00
= Estimated capitalization rate	22.85%

Computing the Weighted Average Excess Earnings Capitalization Rate

Going back to the excess earnings method valuation, we see that the company's estimated value of $370,000 was composed of $200,000 tangible asset value and $170,000 intangible asset value. Computing the relative weights of these asset values, we have the following:

Tangible assets	$200,000 ÷ $370,000 = 54.1%
Intangible assets	$170,000 ÷ $370,000 = 45.9
	100.0%

Weighting the required rates of return on the tangible and intangible asset value components gives us the following:

Tangible asset value	$0.541 \times 0.08 = 0.043$
Intangible asset value	$0.459 \times 0.20 = 0.092$
Weighted asset-based capitalization rate	$= 0.135$

A 13.5% asset-based capitalization rate certainly is significantly different from a 22.85% capitalization rate based on capital structure components. If we divided the $50,000 cash flow by the 13.5% asset-based capitalization rate, we would, of course, get the excess earnings method value of $370,000 ($50,000 ÷ 0.135 ≅ $370,000).

If we divided the $50,000 by the 22.85% build-up method capitalization rate, we would get an indicated value of $218,818 ($50,000 ÷ 0.2285 ≅ $218,818).

Which do you believe?

Discussion of the Example

Considering the risks involved, it is unlikely that anyone would pay $170,000 for the blue sky in KLM. And it can be argued that the 22.85% capitalization rate is an already conservative capitalization rate itself.

Obviously, the capitalization rates for tangible assets and excess earnings used by Mr. Shoveler in his excess earnings exercise are considerably too low. Note that the asset appraisal assumes value *in use*. This is the value to an operating business, not a liquidation value. There appears to be plenty of risk associated with these tangible assets. Accordingly, one point over the risk-free rate is not nearly an adequate risk premium. Capitalizing excess earnings at 20% implies that a buyer will pay for five years of expected excess earnings (1 ÷ 0.20 = 5). Typically, buyers will pay that implied multiple for only a very stable customer base. The KLM customer base certainly is not stable.

Obviously, this is an extreme example. Its purpose is merely to illustrate the mechanics of using cost of capital as a reasonableness check on an excess earnings method valuation. However, there have been worse abuses. There are even people who think that the 30-day U.S. Treasury bill rate is a satisfactory return rate of the tangible assets employed in a business. Watch out for such abuses!

VAGARIES OF THE EXCESS EARNINGS METHOD

Revenue Ruling 68-609 is not very specific on many points, such as how income is to be defined. Definitions of income other than net cash flow may require some adjustment to the capitalization rate, as we illustrated its development.

The many vagaries of the excess earnings method have been explored at great length and are beyond the scope of this book.[4] The purpose here is simply to show the mechanics of demonstrating whether the weighted capitalization rate implied in an excess earnings valuation is or is not within a reasonable range.

SUMMARY

The excess earnings method uses two capitalization rates:

1. A required return on tangible assets.
2. A rate at which to capitalize "excess earnings," returns over and above amounts necessary to support the tangible assets in a business.

The position presented in this chapter is that the weighted average of these two rates (weighted at market value, of course) should be approximately equal to a company's capitalization rate as we have discussed developing it in this book. This chapter has illustrated the mechanics of how to make such a comparison.

To explore the many vagaries of implementation of the excess earnings valuation method, readers are encouraged to avail themselves of the references listed in the notes at the end of this chapter.

Notes

1. See, for example, Jay E. Fishman, Shannon P. Pratt, J. Clifford Griffith, and Mark Wells, *Guide to Business Valuations*, 7th ed. (Fort Worth, TX: Practitioners Publishing Company, 1997, updated annually in May), 7-20–7-33; Shannon P. Pratt, Robert F. Reilly, and Robert P. Schweihs, *Valuing Small Businesses and Professional Practices*, 3d ed. (New York: McGraw-Hill, 1998), Chapter 23, "Excess Earnings Method"; Shannon P. Pratt, Robert F. Reilly, and Robert P. Schweihs, *Valuing a Business: the Analysis and Appraisal of Closely Held Companies*, 3d ed. (Burr Ridge, IL: McGraw-Hill, 1996), Chapter 13, "The Excess Earnings Method."
2. Fishman, Pratt, Griffith, and Wells, *Guide to Business Valuations*, 7-20.
3. Ibid.
4. See the preceding references plus "Practitioners Disagree Strongly on Excess Earnings Methodology," *Shannon Pratt's Business Valuation Update* (April 1997): 1–3.

Chapter 18

Common Errors in Estimation and Use of Cost of Capital

The purpose of this chapter is to call attention to some of the errors that we frequently encounter in estimation and applications of the cost of capital. We point out these errors partly so that readers won't fall into the same traps themselves when they are estimating or using cost of capital. Another reason is to help readers readily spot such errors when reviewing the work of others, and have an understanding as to how the errors should be corrected.

CONFUSING DISCOUNT RATES WITH CAPITALIZATION RATES

The *discount rate* is the cost of capital, and it applies to *all* prospective economic income. This includes all distributions and realized or readily realizable capital appreciation. The *capitalization rate* is a divisor applied to some particular economic income (e.g., earnings, cash flow, and so on, for the latest 12 months, coming 12 months, or some other period). Only when the expected level of economic income is constant in perpetuity are these two rates equal, other than by sheer coincidence.

Nevertheless, some analysts fall into the trap of using the discount rate (i.e., cost of capital) as a capitalization rate. We also see the opposite from time to time: the use of a capitalization rate to discount prospective cash flow or other expected economic income to a present value.

The relationship between discount rates and capitalization rates is the subject of Chapter 4.

USING THE FIRM'S COST OF CAPITAL TO EVALUATE A MORE OR LESS RISKY ACQUISITION OR PROJECT

We have emphasized throughout this book that the cost of capital is market driven, and that it is a function of the investment, not the investor.

If an acquirer uses its own cost of capital to set an acquisition price by discounting the expected cash flows of a more risky acquiree, then the result will be some increase in the risk of the acquiring company after the acquisition. This will result in an increase in the company's overall risk and cost of capital, to which the market would be expected to respond by reducing the stock price. Decreases in acquirers' stock prices as a result of acquisitions is a very common phenomenon, although it is not possible to sort out the extent to which this is a result of perceived overestimation of future cash flows or a market adjustment to the company's cost of capital.

The same principle applies to internal capital budgeting and project selection as to acquisitions. If the project under consideration is more or less risky than the activities of the company as a whole, then the expected cash flows from the project should be evaluated by a correspondingly higher or lower discount rate. In deciding among competing potential projects, an analyst should be certain to appropriately reflect the risk of each project in the discount rate applied to the respective project.

MISTAKING HISTORICAL RATES OF RETURN FOR EXPECTED RATES OF RETURN

Remember, cost of capital is a forward-looking concept. Cost of capital is the *expected* rate of return that the market requires to induce investment in a subject security.

One of the most common errors is to take the recent average historical rates of return that have been achieved for an industry, often from a source of industry composite statistics such as Robert Morris Associates' *Annual Statement Studies*, and to assume that this average is the expected return required to attract investment in that industry. The returns actually achieved for a particular industry in recent past years may be well above or below the level of expected return required to attract capital to the industry, and certainly do not represent a reliable indicator of the cost of capital. Furthermore, returns shown in sources such as annual Statement Studies are based on book values, whereas the relevant measure is return on market values. (This is not intended to totally eliminate *all* consideration of historical returns, such as a long-term average equity risk premium.)

MISMATCHING THE DISCOUNT RATE WITH THE ECONOMIC INCOME MEASURE

The most common type of error in application of the income approach to valuation is to use a discount or capitalization rate that is not appropriate for the definition of economic income being discounted or capitalized. This general category of error has almost infinite variations. Those discussed in the following paragraphs are only a few.

Using a Safe Rate to Discount or Capitalize a Risky Return

Although not the most common version of the mismatching error, the use of a safe rate to discount or capitalize a risky return certainly is one of the most egregious. On occasion, I have seen analysts erroneously discount a highly risky series of projected economic income by the U.S. Treasury bill rate!

Applying a Discount Rate in Real Terms to an Economic Income Projection in Nominal (Current) Terms

Some analysts erroneously subtract the anticipated inflation rate from the discount rate and then apply the adjusted discount rate to an economic income projection that includes inflation (and vice versa). It is noteworthy that all the Ibbotson data are presented in nominal terms—that is, they include inflation. The most common way of performing the income approach to valuation in the United States and in other mature economies is to express the cash flows in nominal terms (including the effect of inflation) and use a nominal discount rate. In countries with hyperinflation, it is more common to express expected cash flows in real terms, and to use a discount rate not including expected inflation.

Applying Costs of Capital Derived from After-Tax Returns to Pretax Returns

Whether costs of capital are estimated by the build-up model, the Capital Asset Pricing Model (CAPM), or the discounted cash flow (DCF) method, in all cases they are returns realized *after* the payment of corporate-level income taxes. If the entity being valued is subject to entity-level income taxes, then it is inappropriate to apply the cost of capital estimated by those methods to pretax return flows.

Subtracting a Short-Term Supergrowth Rate from the Discount Rate to Get a Capitalization Rate

Converting a discount rate to a capitalization rate involves subtracting an esti-mate of the *long-term sustainable growth rate*. Many companies expect high short-term growth that will tend to dampen over time. If the high short-term growth rate is subtracted from the discount rate, the proper capitalization rate will be understated, resulting in overvaluation. In such circumstances, a two-stage or three-stage DCF valuation model will usually produce a more valid valuation than a straight capitali-zation model.

PERFORMING AN EXCESS EARNINGS METHOD VALUATION THAT RESULTS IN AN UNREALISTIC COST OF CAPITAL

One very useful application of the cost of capital analysis is to do a sanity check on the reality of a valuation performed by the excess earnings method, as discussed in the previous chapter.

In the excess earnings method, two capitalization rates are estimated:

1. A capitalization rate for tangible assets
2. A capitalization rate for excess earnings (return over and above the amount re-quired to support the company's tangible assets)

The excess earnings method derives its capitalization rates by very different methods from those discussed earlier in this book. It is based on required returns to categories of assets, rather than on required returns to categories of capital. Never-theless, at the end of the day, the value as estimated by the excess earnings method should reflect a capitalization rate very similar to that which would be derived if we developed a discount rate by any of the cost of capital estimation methods presented in this book and subtracted a reasonable estimate of long-term sustainable growth.

The following is an example of such a sanity check:

Sanity Check: Is the overall equity capitalization rate approximately equal to what you would expect using a build-up capitalization rate?

1. Analysis of overall equity cap rate using excess earnings method:
   Net cash flow to equity $270
   Divided by: indicated equity value $1,205
   Equals implied cap rate on equity: 22.4%
      ($270 ÷ $1,205 = 22.4%)

2. Build-up cap rate:

20-year government bond rate	7.0%
Small stock equity risk premium (combined general equity	
premium and small stock premium)	15.8%
Specific risk premium for subject	5.0%
Total required rate of return (discount rate)	27.8%
Less: expected sustainable growth rate	4.0%
Equals cap rate applicable to net cash flow:	23.8%

According to the sanity check, the results of the excess earnings method seem reasonable. If we capitalize the $270 net cash flow to equity at 23.8%, we would have an indicated value of $1,134, as compared with $1,205 achieved by the excess earnings method. This is a reasonable range of difference. If the results were significantly different, we would reexamine all our calculations and assumptions.

In the above example, we only dealt with a capitalization rate for equity. This is because most of the data sources used to perpetrate this error show only returns to equity rather than returns to total capital. However, the excess earnings method is used more often to value controlling interests than minority interests. Therefore, the return to total capital, as measured by the weighted average cost of capital (WACC), is relevant. Thus, the capitalization rate for overall invested capital also should be considered in the reasonableness test.

This use of cost of capital as a reasonableness check for an excess earnings method valuation was the subject of Chapter 17.

PROJECTING GROWTH BEYOND THAT WHICH THE CAPITAL BEING VALUED WILL SUPPORT

As businesses expand, they typically need additional working capital and capital expenditures to support the increased level of operations. One of the many advantages of using net cash flow as the prospective economic income measure is that it forces the analyst to explicitly consider these needs. Nevertheless, they often are underestimated.

When cost of capital is used for valuation, it values only the investment as of the valuation date. The calculation of net cash flow allows for reinvestment for capital expenditures and additions to working capital necessary to support projected operations. However, if the projections being discounted will *not* be totally supported by the capital expenditure and working capital allowances in the net cash flow projections, and additional investment will be required to achieve those projected results, then the *existing* investment will be overvalued.

INTERNALLY INCONSISTENT CAPITAL STRUCTURE PROJECTION

Methods using weighted average cost of capital and betas adjusted for leverage require projections about the subject company's capital structure. These projected capital structures are on the basis of market value. Analysts often assume a capital structure in the process of estimating a market value of equity, and the resulting estimated market value of equity makes the capital structure, at the estimated market value, different from that which was assumed.

In such cases, the projected capital structure has to be adjusted and the process iterated until the estimated market value of equity results in a capital structure consistent with that which is projected in estimating the cost of capital.

What is even worse, of course, is to not even estimate a market value capital structure, but to simply use book value. If the company is earning good returns, then the market value of equity is likely to exceed book value. This is true not only for the subject company, but also for peer companies that may be used to estimate an industry-average capital structure. If the market value of equity is understated, then the assumed proportion of low-cost debt in the capital structure will be too high. This will result in an understatement of the weighted average cost of capital (WACC) and an overstatement of value.

ASSUMPTIONS THAT PRODUCE A STANDARD OF VALUE OTHER THAN THAT CALLED FOR IN THE VALUATION ENGAGEMENT

A common error is to project a capital structure other than the company's actual capital structure (thereby deriving a weighted average cost of capital different from the company's actual WACC) when the standard of value is fair market value on a minority basis. If an acquirer were to use its own WACC, then the implied result would be *investment value* to that acquirer instead of fair market value. Moreover, if the equity ownership interest is a minority interest, the holder could not force a change in capital structure.

SUMMARY

Cost of capital is one of the most critical components in valuation, capital budgeting, and other financial decision making. There are many ways to err in both estimating the cost of capital and applying it in practice. The errors regularly seen in actual practice are prolific. The following indicate some of the major areas that require careful consideration:

- Properly distinguishing between discount rates and capitalization rates

- Making sure that data supporting discount and capitalization rates are representative of *expected* returns (current market-required returns), not some returns that were realized in a past period that is not representative of future expectations
- Making sure that the discount or capitalization rate used *matches* the definition of expected returns being discounted or capitalized
- Making sure that the implied weighted capitalization rate used in an excess earnings valuation procedure is reasonably close to capitalization rates developed by the cost of capital estimation methods discussed in this book
- Being careful that projected returns being discounted or capitalized can be achieved without having to dilute the existing capital with additional outside capital
- Being sure that capital structure assumptions fully reflect the *market values* of the capital structure components
- Being sure that valuation results are estimated in a way that is consistent with the definition of value called for in the valuation assignment

Avoid all of these traps and you get a gold star! More important, your company and your clients will be well served, and your cost of capital work should stand up to rigorous scrutiny.

Chapter 19

Cost of Capital in the Courts

Cost of capital is getting ever increasing attention in the courts within many contexts. These include valuations for many judicial purposes, allowed rates of return as a component in rate setting, and other applications.

This chapter touches briefly on many of the contexts in which many millions of dollars' worth of court decisions hinge significantly on the court's determination of the relevant cost of capital. For each context, we have cited one or more cases that are typical of contemporary court deliberations on the subject.

COST OF CAPITAL IN SHAREHOLDER DISPUTES

Delaware has traditionally been the case law trendsetter regarding shareholder disputes. A landmark Delaware Supreme Court case in 1983 reversed a lower court case because it did not take into consideration future earnings projections. The court made the point that a determination of fair value (the statutory standard of value in Delaware, as well as in most other states, for dissenting stockholder actions) "must include proof of value by any techniques or methods which are generally considered acceptable in the financial community."[1]

Since that time Delaware courts have increasingly embraced the discounted cash flow (DCF) method of valuation. In a case heard not long before this book went to press, the Delaware Chancery Court characterized the DCF method as "increasingly the model of choice for valuations in this court."[2]

COST OF CAPITAL IN THE TAX COURT

Both the IRS and the U.S. Tax Court have traditionally leaned more toward the market approach than the income approach. This is partly because of language in Revenue Ruling 59-60, written before the development of modern capital market theory, which evolved particularly in the 1960s. It is also partly because of concern about possible manipulation of both cash flow forecasts and discount rates in the DCF method. Nonetheless, as the DCF method has achieved greater utilization in the professional financial community, it has also achieved greater acceptance in the Tax Court.

In a 1985 case the IRS challenged income tax returns reflecting deductions for a company's contributions to the employee stock ownership trust at $61.35 per share, based on the fair market value arrived at by an independent appraisal firm. The IRS asserted that the value was between $5.36 and $8.00 per share. The independent appraisal gave heavy emphasis to earning power and dividend-paying capacity, whereas the IRS stressed net asset value (book value was $7.05 per share).

The court found itself in agreement with the emphasis placed on the earning power and dividend-paying capacity. The court was somewhat concerned "that the appraisal took into account a 20-year earnings projection" but thought it was "not unreasonable in light of past earnings increases." The court concluded that "the only reasonable appraisal presented to it was the one at $61.35 per share."[3]

Yet the Tax Court has *rejected* the DCF method in cases where it believed that the model used by the expert was far too sensitive to minor changes in assumptions, such as the discount rate and/or the growth rate.[4]

The Tax Court has also been known to reach its conclusion by giving partial weight to a DCF method and partial weight to a market approach method. For example, one case gave 70% weight to the market method and 30% weight to the DCF method.[5]

COST OF CAPITAL IN FAMILY LAW

Cost of capital is getting increasing attention in family law courts as those courts are becoming more receptive to the DCF method of valuation of closely held businesses for marital property divisions.

In a 1996 Ohio case, for example, the trial judge stated from the bench that the DCF method had never been used before within her family law jurisdiction. She was willing to consider it, based on testimony that members of the professional financial community would be likely to use the method in valuing a company of the particular type. Ultimately, the court not only accepted the method, but used the value indicated by the DCF method as its final conclusion of value. The case was appealed and upheld.[6] Other courts have similarly followed suit.[7]

COST OF CAPITAL IN BANKRUPTCY REORGANIZATIONS

The concept of the cost of capital as described in this book is recognized for the purpose of setting interest rates in the case of a bankruptcy reorganization. For example, the U.S. Court of Appeals rejected a trustee's notion that the interest rate a creditor should receive should be the Treasury bill rate.

The court stated that the creditor was entitled to "indubitable equivalence of its property interest, which means a stream of payments including interest that adds up to the present value of its claim. . . . The creditor must get the market rate of interest . . . for loans of equivalent duration and risk."

The court then added, "To say that the lender is limited to its 'cost of capital' is therefore to say that the lender is entitled to the market rate of interest, for that is what the cost of capital is: the price it must pay to its own lenders, plus the costs of making and administering loans, plus reserves for bad debts (that is, the anticipated rate of nonpayment).[8]

Another Court of Appeals case in another circuit stated the same concept. In considering a reorganization plan involving interest payments, it said that "the question is whether the interest rate provides the plaintiffs with the 'present value' of their claims pursuant to 11 U.S.C. § 1325(a)(5)(B)(ii)." The court explained, " 'Present value' is a market rate concept, determined by an interest rate which fairly compensates the creditor for not receiving the full amount of its secured claim upon confirmation of the debtor's plan."

The same court added, "An entity forced to delay payment that it is entitled to receive is, in effect, extending a loan. . . . The purpose is to put the secured creditor in an economic position equivalent to the one it would have occupied had it received the allowed secured amount immediately. . . . The appropriate rate of interest is that which the secured creditor would charge at the effective date of the plan, for a loan similar in character, amount and duration to the credit which the creditor would be required to extend under the plan."[9]

The preceding case quoted the Third Circuit's case of first impression on this issue, a case frequently quoted. In effect, the case rejected use of the prime lending rate and required a market rate for similar credits.

Some courts, including the bankruptcy court in the cases we are here reviewing, have suggested a "cost of funds" theory which would determine present value by looking to the creditor and the market in which the creditor borrows capital. . . .

There is more involved, however, than the mere cost of funds. . . .

It is only by acknowledging the coerced loan aspects of a cramdown and by compensating the secured creditor at the rate it would voluntarily accept for a loan of similar character,* amount and duration that the creditor can be placed in the same position he would have been in but for the cramdown.

We hold that the bankruptcy and district courts erred in utilizing the prime rate to determine whether the proposed plan, as required by § 1325(a)(5)(B)(ii), provided for payments to the creditor having a present value equal to the value of its allowed secured claim. The appropriate interest rate for this purpose is the rate of interest currently being charged by the creditor in the regular course of its business for loans similar in character, amount and duration to the loan being coerced in the cramdown.[10]

---

* By a loan of "similar character" we mean a loan that the creditor regularly extends to other debtors who are not in bankruptcy but who are otherwise similarly situated to the debtor who is the recipient of the loan coerced by the Chapter 13 proceeding and who are seeking the same kind of credit (e.g., auto loan, home equity loan, etc.).

The Fifth Circuit reached a similar conclusion in a case decided September 8, 1997.[11]

COST OF CAPITAL INCLUDED IN DAMAGES

In a District of Columbia case, the plaintiff appealed the district court's decision to award the cost of its lost capital, calculated on the basis of the total amount of damages.

The Court of Appeals ruled, "It remains unclear whether prejudgment interest (interest from the time of the tort to the date of court judgment) is available in a negligence action. Nonetheless, . . . in addition to finding Williams negligent, the district court found that Straight had breached its contract with Smoot. Further, because Williams agreed to indemnify Straight in full, the court did not err by including the cost of capital in the damage award assessed against Williams — whether or not District of Columbia law allows a cost of capital award in a negligence action."

The Court of Appeals did, however, require an adjustment in the district court's calculation of the time period for which portions of the cost of capital was awarded. The district court had awarded cost of capital on the full amount of the damages (caused by collapse of a steel structure) and up through the last day of the trial. The Court of Appeals noted, however, that portions of the damages, such as increased insurance premiums and legal fees, were incurred over an extended period of time, and ordered a recalculation based on time of actual incurrence of damages.[12]

COST OF CAPITAL IN UTILITY RATE SETTING

Many providers of essential services are subject to federal or state regulation in respect to the rates they can charge for their services. In setting rates, it is virtually universally recognized that one of the costs the service provider is entitled to recover is its cost of capital. This is generally interpreted to mean its weighted average cost of capital (WACC), as discussed in Chapter 7.

This principle was articulated by the U.S. Supreme Court more than 50 years ago:

> The Supreme Court has stated that a just and reasonable rate should be "sufficient to assure confidence in the financial integrity of the enterprise, so as to maintain its credit

and to attract capital"; the rate should also be "commensurate with returns on investments in other enterprises having corresponding risks."[13]

The following quote from a case appealing a Federal Communications Commission rate order is typical:

> The FCC relied on "classic" DCF methodology, which assumes that the price of a share of stock is equal to the present value of the cash flows the stock will generate. J. Bonbright et al., *Principles of Public Utility Rates* 318 (2d ed. 1988).* These cash flows are in the form of dividends.** Because a dollar available now is worth more than a dollar available only later, the future cash flows must be reduced by a rate that reflects investors' opportunity costs, i.e., their required rate of return or discount rate, Id. Assuming that this discount rate and the growth rate of dividends both remain constant, one calculates the price of the stock using the following formula: $P = D/(r - g)$, where P is the current price of the stock, D is the total dividend in the first year, r is the rate of return, and g is the expected annual growth of dividends. Id.; see also A. Kolbe et al., *The Cost of Capital: Estimating the Rate of Return for Public Utilities* 53-54 (1984). Since regulatory commissions are interested in the rate of return, they rearrange the equation to solve for r: $r = D/P + g$.

> * The DCF method "has become the most popular technique of estimating the cost of equity, and it is generally accepted by most commissions. Virtually all cost of capital witnesses use this method, and most of them consider it their primary technique." Id. at 317-18.
> ** Cash flows also result from the ultimate sale of the stock. R. Brealey and S. Myers, *Principles of Corporate Finance* 49 (4th ed. 1991). However, the theory is that the next investor will be willing to buy the stock at a price based on his estimate of future dividends and the price at which he will be able to sell; so too the third investor and the fourth, ad infinitum. The most basic form of the DCF model therefore assumes that the stock is held forever. Bonbright et al., supra at 318. For a detailed explanation, together with the mathematics, see 1.[14]

Similarly, a case challenging a Federal Energy Regulatory Commission rate order supports the use of the Gordon Growth Model version of DCF analysis for estimating the cost of equity. Courts reviewing rate decisions generally will not require an agency to use one method rather than another to estimate the cost of equity capital, but will accept methods in common use in the financial community. The following excerpt is typical of approval of regulatory methodology:

> In fact, the Commission appears quite wedded to DCF analysis and to efficient market theory as its theoretical mainstay. In Montaup Electric Co., 38 FERC ¶ 61,252 (1987), for example, the Commission adopted the DCF methodology over risk premium analysis for a period of rapidly declining interest rates and reasoned that "a market-oriented analysis such as a DCF analysis accounts for all risk factors perceived by investors." Id. at 61,866. At about the same time as this court's first remand, it published its third annual "generic Determination of Rate of Return on Common Equity for Public Utilities," in which it defended the use of the DCF methodology against attacks based on criticism of the Efficient Market Hypothesis. Order No. 461, III FERC Regulations Pre-

ambles ¶ 30,722 (1987). It declared enthusiastically, "The concept of an efficient market is astonishingly simple and remarkably well supported by the facts."[15]

TAXICAB LEASE RATES

The City of Chicago Commissioner of Consumer Services retained a consulting firm to recommend the rate of return on invested capital that Yellow Cab Company should be allowed to include in its maximum allowable lease rate for taxicabs. The commissioner adopted the consultant's recommended rate of 14 percent, and Yellow Cab appealed to the U.S. District Court.

According to the court, "Based on extensive research and the concept of a weighted average cost of capital, which resulted in a 12 percent rate of return assigned to the debt and a 20 percent rate of return given to the equity, (the consultant) determined that the maximum lease rates should afford a 14 percent rate of return."

Yellow Cab's actual cost of debt at the time was 7.25 percent, so the cost of capital was based on the risks and costs of the lease transaction, not on Yellow's debt cost. In granting summary judgment for the defendants, the Court stated, "Yellow Cab did not show that the risk of the taxicab industry in Chicago entitled it to a rate of return exceeding 20 percent."[16]

SUMMARY

In matters such as valuation and allowed rates of return or interest rates, courts attempt to reflect the realities of financial decision making as practiced in the contemporary financial environment. This includes the attempt to embrace modern capital market theory in reaching determinations of the appropriate cost of capital in many contexts.

These contexts include, but are not limited to:

- Shareholders disputes
- Gift and estate tax valuations
- Marital property valuations
- Bankruptcy reorganizations
- Damage awards
- Rate setting

Courts are moving away from arbitrary cost of capital decisions and relying heavily on expert witnesses who use current market data in conjunction with the cost of capital estimation methods discussed in this book.

Notes

1. *Weinberger v. U.O.P., Inc.*, 457 A.2d 701 (Del. Sup. Ct. 1983).
2. *Charles L. Gaines v. Vitalink Communications Corporation*, No. 12334, Del. Ch., 1997 WL 538676 (August 28, 1997).
3. *Las Vegas Dodge, Inc. v. U.S.*, 85-2 U.S.T.C. Paragraph 9546 (1985).
4. *Nathan and Geraldine Morton v. Commissioner*, T.C. Memo 1997-166, 1997 WL 148312 (April 1, 1997).
5. *Estate of Ross H. Freeman v. Commissioner*, T.C. Memo 1996-372, 1996 WL 453872 (August 13, 1996).
6. *Sergi v. Sergi*, No. 17476 Ohio App. 9th Dist., 1996 WL 425914 (July 31, 1996). Discussion of statement from bench from *Shannon Pratt's Business Valuation Update* (September 1996): 9.
7. See, for example, *Guiffre v. Baker*, No. 95-G-1984 Ohio App. 11th Dist., 1996 WL 535254 (August 30 1996).
8. *Koopmans v. Farm Credit Services of North America*, 102 F.3d 874, U.S. App. 7th Cir. (December 10, 1996).
9. *Rankin v. DeSarno*, 89 F.3d 1123, U.S. App. 3rd Cir. (July 30, 1996).
10. *General Motors Acceptance Corporation v. Alphonso Jones*, 999 F.2d 63, U.S. App. 3rd Cir. (July 20, 1993).
11. *Green Tree Financial Servicing Corporation v. Ruben R. Smithwick, Jr.*, 121 F.3d 211, U.S. App. 5th Cir. (September 8, 1997).
12. *Williams Enterprises, Inc. v. The Sherman R. Smoot Company*, 938 F.2d 230, 290 U.S. App. D.C. 411 (October 8, 1991).
13. *FPC v. Hope Natural Gas Co.*, 320 U.S. 591, 64 S. Ct. 281, 88 L. Ed. 333 (1944) ("Hope"). Quoted in *Illinois Bell Telephone Company, et al. v. Federal Communications Commission*, 988 F.2d 1254, 300 U.S.App.D.C. 296 (April 2, 1993).
14. *Id.*
15. *Tennessee Gas Pipeline Company v. Federal Energy Regulatory Commission*, 926 F. 2d 1206, 288 U.S.App.D.C. 333 (March 5, 1991).
16. *Yellow Cab Company v. City of Chicago*, 938 F.Supp. 500, U.S. Dist. N.D. Ill. (September 10, 1996).

Chapter 20

Cost of Capital in Ad Valorem Taxation

Carl R.E. Hoemke

INTRODUCTION TO AD VALOREM TAXATION

Ad valorem taxation is a process whereby government entities assess a tax or levy on the value of property. Of the three basic types of taxes—the tax on wealth, the tax on income, and the tax on transactions, or excise taxes—the tax on wealth or property is the oldest and provides the revenue foundation for local governments. This tax is assessed as per value, thus the Latin term *ad valorem*. Property value is determined by the taxing jurisdiction, and a rate or levy is applied to the value for assessment. Proceeds are collected and used to fund services to the population of the entity. These services may include police and fire protection, school funding, road funding, governmental administration, and others.

Many states have constitutional and statutory provisions that establish terms to define the value to be used by the assessor for tax purposes. The terms *full cash value*, *actual cash value*, *fair cash value*, *fair value in exchange*, *value in exchange*, and *true and fair value* are among those most commonly used. The courts have consistently interpreted these terms as indicating the same kind of value, which is value in exchange or value in the marketplace, normally termed *market value*. Therefore, we may consider that the basis of assessment is market value and that the assessor's task is to estimate the market value of property. For this reason, there is a great need to estimate accurately the value of property so that it can be fairly applied within its context.

The process of valuation has been described as an art form rather than a science. The appraiser's final conclusion must be made by judgment to determine value. The assessment of value is therefore limited by its tendency to be somewhat subjective; thus governmental authorities have attempted to make the process of assessment more objective through policy-making. Some of the policies that have been created to simplify and standardize the application of variables to value have served only to increase the complexity in the way cost of capital should be measured. The scope of this chapter is to identify the adjustments to the cost of capital as applied in the income approach. The increased complexity derives from the fact that standardization forces the analyst to deviate from preferred measurements of income.

There are three approaches to value: income, cost, and market. Properties that are not frequently sold in the markets but have income streams are the best candidates for the income approach to value. The income approach to value is a useful, although sensitive, appraisal tool. It is useful because, for most types of property, it is the most valid approach to value; it is sensitive and therefore must be used with care, because any small original error will be compounded.

One of the parameters of concern in the income approach is the cost of capital. A basic assumption of the income approach is that people purchase property for the income it will yield. A different way of stating the assumption is that the value of the property depends on the income it produces. In valuing income-producing property, the valuation of an income stream is a function of the level of income that is being measured. The level of income corresponds to ownership rights to the cash flows.

The preferred measure of return is the return as measured by net cash flow. There is certainly much discussion and many theories on this measure, as previous chapters so eloquently identify. Using this return requires that the income to discount is the net cash flow income (see Chapter 3 for definition). Both creditors and shareholders expect to be compensated for the opportunity cost of investing their funds in one particular business instead of others with equivalent risk. In terms of ad valorem taxation, the level of income to discount is dependent on the limits placed on it by statutory requirements. Because of legislative constraints on the definition of income, adjustments must be made to the net cash flow return to give it comparability with the measure of income to discount.

SOME EXAMPLES OF LAW THAT PROMULGATES THE DEFINITION OF INCOME TO DISCOUNT

In many instances, limits or standards have promulgated the measurement of income. For instance, if a governing body limits the definition of income to be discounted to the earnings before depreciation, interest, and taxes (EBDIT), then the analyst must recognize these barriers and make opposing adjustments in the cost of capital to compensate for the recognition of taxes and capital expenditures. Another example: If statutory requirements or practices require the subtraction of book depreciation from EBDIT, then changes in the rate are necessary to match that specific level of income as compared with net cash flow measurements. It is easy to see how statutory requirements can dramatically alter the cost of capital and leave the analyst with many adjustments to the standard net cash flow cost of capital. It is essential that the analyst fully understand the cost of capital and its basis, then make any adjustments that make it comparable with the income that is being measured.

GENERAL CATEGORIES OF LEGISLATIVE CONSTRAINTS WHERE ADJUSTMENTS TO THE COST OF CAPITAL ARE NECESSARY

A good rule to use in making these adjustments is that any change made to the return on net cash flow should ultimately result in a value that would have been arrived at by measuring the present value of the net cash flow under unconstrained circumstances. Here are a few situations in which adjustments to the cost of capital are necessary:

- Cost of capital is used as a capitalization rate.
- Earnings are used as a proxy for free cash flow.
- Before-tax cash flow is used as the proxy for income.
- Adjustments are made for flotation costs.
- Adjustments are made for book value capital structure.
- Adjustments are made in the cost of capital for unaccounted capital expenditures in the cash flow.

COST OF CAPITAL IN A CONSTANT, PERPETUAL CASH FLOW SCENARIO

In its simplest form the cost of capital is a function of a numerator income and a denominator value. It expresses the relationship of income to value.

The preferred level of income to discount is the net cash flow. Net cash flow is the income available for the equity investor after he or she has satisfied all obligations for other forms of capital. The discount rate applicable to this level of income is the rate that is the subject of discussion in this book. If the expected net cash flows are constant and perpetual, then the discount rate (k) is simply the constant annual net cash flow (NCF) divided by the present value (PV) of all future net cash flows.

Formula 20.1

For a constant and perpetual income (*NCF*):

$$k = \frac{NCF}{PV}$$

Under these assumptions any changes to the numerator will result in a direct and proportional change in *k*.

DIFFERENT TYPES OF ADJUSTMENTS

This section addresses how the changes in *k* influence the rate and how we may adjust accordingly. The discussion covers several areas:

1. Income adjustments
2. Changes in relation to a percentage of value
3. Handling a combination of income and value adjustments

Each of these areas is elaborated in regard to both multiplicative and linear adjustments. A *multiplicative adjustment* is the application of a factor or percentage to the numerator and/or denominator. Similarly, a *linear adjustment* is one whereby a variable is added or subtracted to the numerator and/or denominator. Within the discussions of multiplicative and linear adjustments are analyses of the effects of changing variables.

Multiplicative Income Adjustments

The primary adjustment associated with a multiplicative income adjustment is the effect of income taxes on the discount rate. Before-tax income is multiplied by an effective tax rate to determine the after-tax income. The simplifying assumption here is that tax-deductible items and other non-cash items do not materially affect the multiplicative relationship with before-tax income. For instance, "after-tax income is equal to 60% of before-tax income" is a muliplicative proposition. This is synonymous with "before-tax income is reduced by a 40% tax rate." The tax rate in this case is not necessarily the actual income tax rate on the taxable income. This rate is a rate that takes into account the comparison of after-tax income with before-tax income, which is not necessarily taxable income.

Accounting for Income Tax Within the Cost of Capital.   If the numerator in Formula 20.1 is changed to before-tax net cash flows, then the numerator is increased by the annual amount of income tax. If the before-tax income is NCF_{pt} and after-tax income is *NCF*, then the tax rate (*t*) on before-tax income is $1 - NCF/NCF_{pt}$. Therefore:

Formula 20.2

$$k = \frac{NCF}{PV} \text{ or } \frac{NCF_{pt} \times (1 - t)}{PV}$$

$$k = \frac{NCF_{pt}}{PV} \text{ or } \frac{NCF \div (1 - t)}{PV}$$

Let us assume that annual net cash flow (NCF) is $84, the effective income tax rate on before-tax income is 40%, and the net present value (NPV) is equal to $1,000. If k were converted to a before-tax rate (k_{pt}), then the numerator would change from $84 to $140, or $84 ÷ (1 − 40%). The cost of capital increases by the annual tax divided by the present value, or 56 ÷ 1000, or 5.6%.

Formula 20.3

$$k = \frac{\$84}{\$1,000} = 8.40\%$$

$$k_{pt} = \frac{\$84 \div (1 - 40\%)}{\$1,000} = 14.00\%$$

Accounting for Income Tax Within the Individual Components of the WACC. Alternatively, income tax adjustments can be measured directly in the weighted average cost of capital (WACC) under the assumption of constant and perpetual net cash flows.

The After-Tax Measurement of WACC. The weighted cost of each security is expressed as follows:

Formula 20.4

$$WACC = \left(k_e \times W_e\right) + \left(k_p \times W_p\right) + \left(k_d \times W_d\right)$$

Each component is expressed in after-tax terms.

After-Tax Cost of Equity (k_e). Unless otherwise stated, the cost of equity (k_e) is generally assumed to be the discount rate applicable to net cash flow available to common equity. Therefore, because this rate is in after-tax terms, no adjustment is necessary.

After-Tax Cost of Preferred Stock of (k_p). Preferred stock is a hybrid between debt and equity. Under certain provisions preferred stock dividends are tax-deductible, and under other circumstances they are not. The analyst must determine the nature of the taxability. If it has tax-deductible components, then its cost should be treated like debt; otherwise, it requires no adjustment.

After-Tax Cost of Debt (k_d).   Comparatively, the cost of debt (k_d) should be expressed in after-tax terms. The rate of interest on debt is measured in terms of the yield to maturity. Because interest on debt is tax-deductible, the net cost of debt to the company is reduced by the tax rate. Therefore, an adjustment to the yield rate must be made to convert the yield rate to an after-tax debt cost. This adjustment is the before-tax rate of debt multiplied by 1 minus the marginal tax rate $(1 - t)$. The marginal tax rate is the rate that equates to the incremental tax associated with the inclusion of the additional profit to the purchasing company. Typically, this rate is assumed to be the top corporate tax rate that is levied by the federal government. If the property's income is subject to state income tax, then that rate must also be included in the tax rate. Because state taxes are typically deductible from federal taxes, the state taxes must be tax effected before adding them to the total marginal rate.

Formula 20.5

$$k_d = k_{d(pt)} \times (1 - t)$$

Therefore:

    if: $k_{d(pt)}$ = 8%

           t = 40% (combined federal 35% and state 5%)

    then: k_d = 4.8%

Therefore:

    if: k_e = 12%

         k_d = 4.80%

         W_e = 0.50

         W_d = 0.50

    then: $WACC$ = 8.40%

Although it is true that this is the after-tax cost of debt, one must be sure that the correct level of income is measured in utilizing this rate. A common error in discounting net cash flow to invested capital is that the interest expense is added back at its face amount and not measured net of the tax deduction resulting from interest as a tax-deductible expense. If before-tax interest is added back to the net cash flow to invested capital, then the before-tax cost of debt must be used to discount the income.

For instance, if earnings before interest and taxes (*EBIT*) equals the pretax income, and interest is tax-deductible, then *EBIT* less interest equals the taxable income (*EBT*). An income tax rate (t) multiplied by *EBT* is the income tax (*T*). Subtracting *T* from *EBT* equals net income. If the desired income to discount is the net operating income (*EBI*), then an amount of interest must be added to the net income. Algebraically, the equation is as follows:

$$(EBIT - I)\,(1 - t) = NI$$

Alternately:

Formula 20.6

$$EBIT\,(1 - t) - I\,(1 - t) = NI$$

If the desired income is earnings before interest but after-tax or *EBI*, then the equation can be rewritten as:

Formula 20.7

$$EBI = NI + I\,(1 - t)$$

Therefore, the tax-affected interest is correctly added back to net income to result in the desired income.

Special Case After-Tax Cost of Capital (WACC).   In many appraisals of companies subject to regulatory accounting, the level of income measured is the net operating income. In regulatory filing the net operating income is measured by subtracting the income tax from the operating income. This is mathematically equivalent to adding back the full interest expense (before-tax impacted) to the net income. Thus, in cases where this occurs the before-tax cost of debt is the correct measure; otherwise the taxes must be adjusted to remove the effect of interest's being tax-deductible.

In the special case after-tax cost of capital, the cost of each security is appropriately expressed as follows:

Formula 20.8

$$WACC = \left(k_e \times W_e\right) + \left(k_{d(pt)} \times W_d\right)$$

Therefore:

if: k_e = 12%
    $k_{d(pt)}$ = 8%
    W_e = 0.50
    W_d = 0.50

then: $WACC = 10\%$

The Before-Tax Measurement of k: *Constant Level Income*

Before-Tax Cost of Capital (WACC$_{pt}$). The cost of each security is appropriately expressed as follows:

Formula 20.9

$$WACC_{pt} = \left(k_{e(pt)} \times W_e\right) + \left(k_{d(pt)} \times W_d\right)$$

Before-Tax Cost of Debt (k$_{d(pt)}$). Because the cost of debt (k$_d$) is calculated in before-tax terms as stated earlier, no adjustment is necessary.

Before-Tax Cost of Equity (k$_{e(pt)}$). The cost of equity (k$_e$) must be adjusted because it is measured in after-tax terms. With the assumption that the cash flows are constant and perpetual, the adjustment is simply the cost of equity k$_e$ divided by 1 minus the tax rate (note that by using these assumptions the capitalization rate is equal to the cost of capital):

Tautology:

Formula 20.10

$$c_{e(pt)} = \frac{c_e}{(1 - t)}$$

Under the given assumptions that cash flows are constant and perpetual, the capitalization rate is equal to the discount rate. The before-tax cost of equity can be expressed as follows:

Formula 20.11

$$k_{e(pt)} = \frac{k_e}{(1 - t)}$$

Therefore:

    if: k_e = 12%
          t = 40%
    then: $k_{e(pt)}$ = 20%

Therefore:

    if: $k_{e(pt)}$ = 20%
          $k_{d(pt)}$ = 8%
          W_e = 0.50
          W_d = 0.50

    then: $WACC_{pt}$ = 14%

The Impact of Taxes on the Equity Cost of Capital: The Growth Variant. As identified earlier, the calculations presented here are for determining a before-tax cost of capital under constant cash flow assumptions. For calculation of the before-tax cost of capital where a constant growth rate is present, the rate can be determined by expanding on the preceding tautology. The before-tax equity capitalization rate $(c_{e(pt)})$ is equal to the after-tax equity capitalization rate (c_e) divided by 1 minus the effective tax rate on the income to be capitalized:

Tautology:

Formula 20.12

$$c_{e(pt)} = \frac{c_e}{(1 - t)}$$

Therefore, since:

$$c_{e(pt)} = k_{e(pt)} - g_{e(pt)}$$
$$c = k_e - g_e$$

where:

g_e = growth rate in after-tax equity income
$g_{e(pt)}$ = growth rate in before-tax equity income

The tautology can be rewritten to account for growth:

Formula 20.13

$$k_{e(pt)} - g_{e(pt)} = \frac{k_e - g_e}{(1 - t)}$$

Then rearranging and solving for $k_{e(pt)}$:

Formula 20.14

$$k_{e(pt)} = \frac{k_e - g_e}{(1 - t)} + g_{e(pt)}$$

This calculation requires an analyst to calculate the growth rate on after-tax income and before-tax income. Differences in the two growth parameters can arise from several circumstances. One circumstance in particular is the effect of accelerated tax depreciation. Normally, the effective tax rate on before-tax income is smaller in the initial years and grows with each year until it reaches a constant level. This difference can serve to reduce growth on after-tax cash flows, because it allows for a higher after-tax income in the near-term years and a lower income in the later years, offsetting some of the normal inflationary changes in the before-tax income. Otherwise, growth patterns in the two levels of income are typically not widely divergent. When comparing the changes in growth to a simple nongrowth model, the following observations can be made:

1. Growth tends to reduce the impact of taxes on the before-tax cost of capital.
2. Conversely, decline increases the cost of capital.

For example, assume the growth rates of pretax and after-tax cash flows are equal:

If $k =$ 15%, $t = 40\%$, and
$g =$ 10%, then $k_{ebt} = 18.33\%$
$g =$ 0%, then $k_{ebt} = 25.00\%$
$g =$ -10%, then $k_{ebt} = 31.67\%$

Linear Income Adjustments: Constant Perpetual Income

The primary adjustment associated with a linear income adjustment originates with the differences between nonoperating cash outflows and noncash items — specifically, capital expenditures, depreciation, and accrual versus cash accounting. This adjustment is necessary in capitalizing a level of income that includes any items that should or should not be included in net cash flow. Some assessor practices have traditionally excluded adjustments for depreciation, other non-cash items, and capital expenditures. In many cases the income identified as the income to capitalize or discount is the earnings before interest (EBI), otherwise known as net operating income (NOI). Consider Formula 20.1 again:

$$k = \frac{NCF}{PV}$$

Again, the same assumptions must hold true (constant and perpetual income). Thus, if a constant e (any adjustment to NCF required by the assessor) is added to the numerator to represent a linear adjustment, then it too must be added to k to maintain the integrity of the calculation. Where k_q is the adjusted discount rate:

Formula 20.15

$$k_q = k + \frac{e}{PV} = \frac{NCF + e}{PV}$$

Notice how the addition of a constant e affects the left side of the equation, as compared with Formula 20.1. The constant's relation to present value (PV) linearly changes the rate. In most cases, constant e represents the difference between book depreciation and capital expenditures. In other words, if annual depreciation is equal to 4% of the value and capital expenditures are equal to 5% of the value, then the discount rate increases by 1%. This is consistent with real experiences of deficient book depreciation as compared with capital expenditures. Inflation, deflation, or incorrect estimates of the service life of an asset can cause these differences.

In other cases assessors require adding back depreciation to NOI or EBI. To further complicate the equation, capital expenditures are not subtracted from the cash flow, resulting in the necessity of a large e adjustment. The e in this scenario is comparable to what is called a recapture rate. Some analysts add back the annual straight-line depreciation rate. For example, if a project has a 20-year life with no salvage value, it depreciates 5% per year. Ideally, the rate in this instance should be equal to the ratio of capital expenditures to value.

Linear Income Adjustments with a Growth Variant

Inflation or deflation can account for differences in capital expenditures and depreciation. The preceding formula accounts for a constant and perpetual difference. This constant difference is also paired with a constant net cash flow. A variant to this equation is the influence of growth. Refer again to Formula 20.1:

$$k = \frac{NCF}{PV}$$

As identified, k represents a rate that is true for a constant and perpetual income stream. Alternately, if the rate of income is growing at a constant rate into perpetuity, then this equation can be altered to account for the constant growth component:

Formula 20.16

$$c_q = k - g = \frac{NCF}{PV}$$

and, $\qquad k_q = c_q + g$

thus, $\qquad k_q = k$

where:

c_q = capitalization rate
$k\ $ = unadjusted discount rate
k_q = adjusted discount rate
$g\ $ = constant growth in NCF

Adding a linear parameter to the numerator is allowed only if that parameter is growing at the same rate as the income. The formula is restated to account for this constant where k_q is the adjusted discount rate:

Formula 20.17

$$c_q = k - g + \frac{e}{PV} = \frac{NCF + e}{PV}$$

and $$k_q = c_q + g$$

thus, $$k_q = k + \frac{e}{PV}$$

where:

e = linear parameter

g = growth in both NCF and e

Otherwise, if the growth rate of NCF and e differ, then the equation becomes much more complex. Essentially, the problem is to solve for the discount rate necessary to discount the two separate income streams (NCF and e) sufficiently, to equal the present value of NCF discounted with the return on net cash flow rate. To represent this formula, let the adjusted discount rate be equal to k_q. The equation can be demonstrated as follows:

Formula 20.18

$$\frac{NCF}{k_q - g} + \frac{e}{k_q - g_e} = \frac{NCF}{k - g}$$

where:

k_q = adjusted discount rate for the inclusion of e

g_e = growth in e

g = growth rate in NCF

Solving for k_q mathematically is difficult because the equation is in a polynomial form. The easiest way to solve for k_q is to use a solver function in a spreadsheet.

The Random Income Variant

Because both net cash flow and adjusted income are subject to the same parameters, both are subject to a variety of variables, which sometimes makes it difficult to fit the streams into rigid constant formulas. As noted in earlier sections, the formula constrains the analyst with measurements available only in a sterile environment. It requires constant levels of growth and perpetuity incomes. For situations that fall outside this environment, there is no "quick and dirty" estimate that one can perform. The only way to determine the effect of the adjustment on the discount rate when the subject falls outside the constraints is to use internal rate of return calculations.

The *internal rate of return* is the discount rate necessary to convert future income into the investment. The tools available to calculate the cost of capital on an after-tax basis have been widely established; therefore, it is easier to simply discount the preferred level of income (net cash flow). Once the present value of the net cash flow is calculated, the result can be used for determination of the discount rate. This discount rate would then be the appropriate rate to use in the alternate income streams. By using methods of determining the internal rate of return, one can specifically measure the effect of a desired variable on the cost of capital.

Therefore, let us observe the given income streams on the investment proposed earlier:

Year	Net Cash Flow	Before-Tax Income
0	($1,000)	($1,000)
1	77	133
2	81	137
3	85	141
4	89	145
5	1,081	1,137

Observations:

1. Year 0 is the investment or the present value of cash flows.
2. Year 5 is a reversion value plus Year 5's income.
3. The difference between each cash flow and the next is $56. This difference is the annual tax associated with each respective cash flow.
4. The net present value in the net cash flow was determined by using an 8.4% discount rate.
5. The internal rate of return for the before-tax income, using $1,000 as the investment, is 14.0%.
6. The incremental effect to the cost of capital for adding back the income tax is 5.6%.

This process will return a rate equivalent to the before-tax discount rate. This is the desired method of calculating the true effect of taxes on the discount rate. Several things are occurring here that lead to a result on a before-tax basis. Generally, the reason for calculating the internal rate of return (IRR) is that inconsistent growth rates between net cash flow and before-tax income are difficult to model in an easy-to-understand formula. Unfortunately, the downside to this process is that it is more complex and a little more difficult to explain.

Multiplicative Value Adjustments

Ad Valorem Tax Addback.   The most common multiplicative value adjustment in ad valorem assessment is the addback of ad valorem taxes. Many assessors want to remove the historical bias resulting from prior valuations. Therefore, they may prefer to account for property tax within the discount rate. They do so by adding back the percent relationship of tax to market value, to the discount rate. This adjustment is most similar to the linear adjustment in income. The difference is that the adjustment is a direct function of value. In other words, if the value goes up, the adjustment goes up directly with the value, and vice versa. This can be demonstrated by the following formula:

Formula 20.19

$$k_q = k + (o \times PV) \div PV = \frac{1 \div (o \times PV)}{PV}$$

thus, $k_q = k + o$

where:

o = percent of tax to value

And with the addition of a growth component (g), the formula expands to:

Formula 20.20

$$k_q - g = k - g + o$$

thus, $k_q \quad = k + o$

The same formula can be used for any adjustment that is equal to a percentage of value. This holds true even in random changes in value. The only caveat is that the percent relationship to value must remain constant. This adjustment is quite powerful and easy to demonstrate, which is likely the reason for its popularity.

Flotation Costs.   Another type of multiplicative value adjustment is flotation costs. Flotation costs occur when new issues of stock or debt are sold to the public. The firm usually incurs several kinds of flotation or transaction costs, which reduces the actual proceeds received by the firm. Some of these are direct out-of-pocket outlays, such as fees paid to underwriters, legal expenses, and prospectus preparation costs. Because of this reduction in proceeds, the firm's required returns on these proceeds equate to a higher return to compensate for the additional costs. Flotation costs can be accounted for either by amortizing the cost, thus reducing the cash flow to discount, or by incorporating the cost into the cost of capital. Because flotation costs are not typically applied to operating cash flow, one must incorporate them into the cost of capital.

The cost of flotation is a function of size and risk. The larger the issuance, the lower the cost as a percentage of the issuance price. Flotation costs are the greatest for equity and the least for debt issuance. Preferred stock flotation costs tend to be somewhere in between. The following table shows examples of the relation of flotation cost to size of an issuance of stock that occurred during 1996 and 1997.

Company	Total Issuance	Total Flotation
Excite	39,100,000	9.46%
Team Rental	52,000,000	6.76%
Amazon	54,000,000	8.57%
IXC	89,600,000	8.67%
General Cigar	108,000,000	8.28%
Ciena	115,000,000	7.96%
Capstar	166,500,000	7.68%
General Cable	354,900,000	5.94%
Sabre	545,400,000	5.77%
Hartford Life	649,750,000	6.50%

OTHER ADJUSTMENTS TO THE COST OF CAPITAL

In the property tax arena traditional techniques are king. Any new approaches are met with skepticism, because the results of many new techniques tend to lower the market value of the project and, thus, the taxes. This is true despite the validity of such approaches. The following paragraphs identify four "newer" techniques introduced in the ad valorem arena within the last decade.

Ex Post and Ex Ante Risk Premiums

The expected equity risk premium is unobservable in the market and must be estimated. For both the Capital Asset Pricing Model (CAPM) and the build-up method (BUM) *ex post* and *ex ante* risk premiums are used to obtain estimates for the cost of equity.

An *ex post* risk premium is based on the assumption that historical returns are the best predictor of future returns. It is calculated by subtracting the long-term arithmetic average of the income return on long-term government bonds for the CAPM, or long-term corporate bonds for the measurement of the BUM. Each is measured from the long-term arithmetic average stock market return measured over the same period. The duration of the bond must be the same as that used to estimate the equity risk premium (RP_m).

The *ex ante* risk premium is a forward-looking premium. The Gordon Growth Model is applied to determine the resulting risk premium. The premium is determined by first estimating the cost of equity for the proxy market. The proxy market is a market large enough to remove the effects of non-diversification. Typically, the S&P 500 or the NYSE is used as this proxy. The data necessary for this analysis is more abundant in the S&P 500 because analysts follow these stocks more than any other large grouping of an index, and the size of the index is sufficient for this measurement.

The first parameter of estimate is the expected growth on the dividends of the market. Dividend growth is not typically measured, because it is a function of management decision on capitalization of the firm. The more retention of capital, the greater the growth in dividends; whereas the lower the retention rate, the lower the growth in dividends. If the retention rate remains the same in relation to the net income, then the growth in earnings per share is the best proxy for the growth in dividends.

The first step in deriving the *ex ante* risk premium is to use a single-stage discounted cash flow analysis (otherwise known as the Gordon Growth Model) to calculate the cost of equity for the market proxy (i.e., the S&P 500). The cost of equity is calculated by using the most recent I/B/E/S consensus long-term growth rates for each firm in the S&P 500 and adding it to the dividend growth yield. I/B/E/S is a service that polls analysts about their growth estimates for individual stocks.

The dividend yield for the S&P 500 should be an estimate for Year 1's dividend (D_1). D_1 can be estimated by multiplying the S&P 500's current weighted average dividend yield (D_0) by 1 plus its weighted average long-term earnings growth rate. By adding the weighted average long-term growth rate to the dividend yield at the end of Year 1, the cost of equity is estimated. If, for example, the long-term growth rate is equal to 10% and the current dividend yield is 4%, then the cost of equity is $(4\% \times 1.1) + 10\%$, or 14.40%. This can also be described in the following formula:

Formula 20.21

$$k_{e500} = DY \times (1 + g) + g$$

where:

DY = dividend yield
g = long-term growth rate
k_{e500} = cost of equity for the S&P 500

The second step is to calculate the risk premium of the S&P 500 (RP_{500}). For the CAPM, the *ex ante* risk premium is calculated by subtracting the risk-free rate (R_f), from the cost of equity for the S&P 500. For the build-up method, the *ex ante* risk premium is calculated by subtracting the weighted average bond yield for the S&P 500 from the cost of equity for the S&P 500.

$$RP_{500} = k_{e500} - R_f$$

Size Premium

Many analysts recommend including a size premium in the cost of capital. They support the argument for including this premium with the fact that small companies have historically earned returns that were greater than those explained by the β-times-risk-premium alone. In other words, although betas for small companies tend to be greater than for large companies, they still do not account for *all* of the risks faced by investors in small companies. This premium is directly added to the results obtained using the CAPM. The size premium was discussed earlier in this book and has application in the property tax arena.

Industry Long-Term Capitalization

Traditionally, property tax assessors have used a book value capital structure as the appropriate measure of the employment of capital. This was the result of regulatory influence in the economic analysis. Regulators define the allowed earnings as a return on the original investment. A utility company would receive a return on its investment and a return of its investment. Depreciation serves as a return *of* the investment and net book value (otherwise termed *rate base*) is identified as the basis for the return *on* the investment. Therefore, the utility company would be limited to a return on the net book value, not on the fair market value of the assets. With regulation for telecommunication and electric utility companies coming to an end (as seen in recent state and federal deregulation advances), investors are looking at the returns on the market value of assets out of regulation (i.e., fair market value). Therefore, the cost of capital would be subject to a market-weighted capital structure.

SUMMARY

The use of the cost of capital in ad valorem taxation must be done with care. Because of various legislative caveats and exceptions, analysts must analyze the impacts of different methods and determine whether or not they affect the cost of capital. With the tools given in this chapter, this approach can ease the burden and the complexity of the adjustments to the cost of capital.

Chapter 21

Capital Budgeting and Feasibility Studies

Good cost of capital estimation is essential to sound capital budgeting and feasibility analysis decisions.

INVEST FOR RETURNS ABOVE COST OF CAPITAL

When addressing capital budgeting and feasibility analysis decisions, popular phrases in contemporary corporate finance literature are *shareholder value added* (SVA) and *economic value added* (EVA). The essence of the way to add value is to invest funds in projects that will earn at a rate of return higher than the cost of capital.

As Brealey and Myers word it, in their capital budgeting chapter of their classic text on *Principles of Corporate Finance*, "accept any project that more than compensates for the *project's beta.*"[1]

In the case of selection among multiple potential projects competing for limited funds, analysts recommend investing in those with the highest *net present value* (NPV). Net present value is estimated by discounting the expected cash outflows and expected cash inflows from the project by the project's cost of capital.

Note two important points in the last sentence:

1. *Cash flow* is the preferred measure of economic income.
2. *Project's cost of capital* is the preferred focus, as opposed to the company's cost of capital.

"The company cost of capital rule can get a firm in trouble if the new projects are more or less risky than its existing business. Each project should be evaluated on its *own* opportunity cost of capital."[2]

DCF IS BEST CORPORATE DECISION MODEL

At a "Seminar on Frontiers in Corporate Valuation," Tom Copeland, co-author of *Valuation: Measuring and Managing the Value of Companies*, compared the use of ratios, formulas, and discounted cash flow analysis for purposes of corporate decision-making. In evaluating the three approaches, he noted "The most important criterion for comparing approaches is that they result in good decisions, because the model value is close to the equilibrium market value."[3]

This entire list of criteria is the following:

- How well do model values match market values?
- Is the model logical?
- Is the approach easy to understand and use?
- Does the approach easily lend itself to a wide variety of decision-making applications?

Copeland's list of pros and cons for each of the three approaches to corporate decision-making are shown in Exhibit 21.1. Having listed the pros and cons for each, he concludes unequivocally that the DCF approach is superior.

FOCUS ON NET CASH FLOW

Copeland notes that the DCF approach captures all elements of value. He also states:

Managers who are interested in maximizing share value should use discounted cash flow analysis to make decisions, not earnings per share . . . The market is not fooled by cosmetic earnings increases; only earnings increases that are associated with improved long-term cash flows will increase share prices. The evidence that the market focuses on cash flows can be grouped into four areas, studies showing that:

- Accounting earnings is not very well correlated with share prices
- Earnings "window dressing" does not improve share prices
- The market evaluates management decisions based on their expected long-term cash flow impact, not the short-term earnings impact
- There are many decisions where cash flows and earnings per share give opposing results.[4]

Exhibit 21.1   Pros and Cons of Approaches to Corporate Decision-Making

Ratios are the oldest form of valuation methodology because they are easy to use. They provide a direct, simple link between easy-to-observe variables like earnings and market prices.

Pros and Cons of Ratios

Pros	Cons
• Easy to use • Based on comparables	• Difficult to find exact comparables • Heavily dependent on accounting standards • No logic that leads back to a fundamental understanding (e.g., should earnings in a P/E ratio be normalized?) • P/E ratio does not focus on balance sheet, and market/book ratio does not focus on income statement • Generally low correlation with actual market values • Not particularly useful for day-to-day operating decisions

Formulas are also fairly simple to use, but are crude tools because their simplicity requires that they make strong (often unrealistic) assumptions.

Pros and Cons of Formulas

Pros	Cons
• Easy to use • Logic does tie back to fundamentals (e.g., cash flows to the owner)	• Make strong implicit assumptions (e.g., constant growth forever) • Depend strongly on a point estimate of cash flows or earnings • Require modest amounts of training regarding the underlying math • Not useful for day-to-day operating decisions

Discounted cash flows is best for decision-making, but is more complex than the alternatives.

Pros and Cons of DCF

Pros	Cons
• Clear logical link to the underlying fundamentals • Matches actual market values quite well • Lends itself to a wide variety of decision-making applications • Not dependent on changes in accounting principles, depends only on actual cash flow	• Complex, requires training

Source: Tom Copeland, "Seminar on Frontiers in Corporate Valuation," New York University Leonard H. Stern School of Business, November 6-7, 1997. Reprinted with permission.

ADJUSTED PRESENT VALUE ANALYSIS

Generally speaking, most contemporary corporate finance literature and seminars advocate discounting expected cash inflows and outflows at a weighted average cost of capital (WACC). The characteristics of a project, either risk or special financing opportunities unique to the project, may cause the WACC for the project to differ from the company's overall WACC.

However, a variation on DCF analysis, dubbed *adjusted present value* (APV), advocates taking DCF analysis for project selection in a different direction. Instead of an overall project WACC, the APV approach estimates by a *base-case value*, by unbundling the components of value and analyzing each separately. APV starts with a base-case value, discounting all cash flows from the project as if they were financed by equity. It then adds or subtracts increments or decrements of value from all financing side effects. The list includes:

- Interest tax shields
- Cost of financial distress
- Subsidies
- Hedges
- Issue costs
- Other costs[5]

Timothy A. Leuhrman, author of "Using APV: A Better Tool for Valuing Operations," claims "the particular version of DCF that has been accepted as the standard over the past 20 years — using the weighted average cost of capital (WACC) as the discount rate — is now obsolete ... *Adjusted present value* (APV) is especially versatile and reliable, and will replace WACC as the DCF methodology of choice among generalists."[6]

USE TARGET COST OF CAPITAL OVER LIFE OF PROJECT

In any case, while the consensus advocates focusing on the cost of capital of the project rather than the overall company cost of capital to the extent that there is a difference, the focus should encompass the life of the project rather than any temporary effects. For example, if the project requires an abnormal level of debt financing which would temporarily change the company's capital structure, the WACC should reflect the company's *target* capital structure rather than the abnormal structure when the investment initially is made.

SUMMARY

This has been a short chapter, because the essential principles of using cost of capital for capital budgeting and project selection are essentially the same as for other applications already discussed.

The general consensus is:

- Discounted cash flow is the best model for corporate finance decisions.
- Focus on net cash flow as the economic income variable of choice.
- Each project should be analyzed in light of its own cost of capital characteristics rather than automatically using the company's overall cost of capital.
- The cost of capital used should be the target cost of capital over the life of the project.
- New variations of cost of capital applications are constantly being developed.

Notes

1. Richard A. Brealey and Stewart C. Myers, *Principles of Corporate Finance*, 5th ed. (New York: McGraw-Hill, 1996), 205.
2. Ibid., 204.
3. Tom Copeland, "Seminar on Frontiers in Corporate Valuation," New York University Leonard N. Stern School of Business, November 6–7, 1997.
4. Ibid.
5. Timothy A. Luehrman, "Using APV: A Better Tool for Valuing Operations," *Harvard Business Review*, May–June 1997, 145.
6. Ibid., 145–53.

Appendixes

Bibliography

This bibliography is separated into two sections—books and articles. Appendix B references relevant workshops and conferences, and Appendix C lists data resources for information on cost of capital.

BOOKS

Bierman, Harold, Jr., and Seymour Smidt. *The Capital Budgeting Decision: Economic Analysis of Investment Projects*, 8th ed. New York: Macmillan, 1992.

Brealey, Richard A., and Stewart C. Myers. *Principles of Corporate Finance*, 5th ed. New York: McGraw-Hill, 1996.

Brown, Lawrence D., ed. *I/B/E/S Research Bibliography*, 5th ed. New York: I/B/E/S International, Inc., 1996.

Copeland, Tom, Tim Koller, and Jack Murrin. *Valuation: Measuring and Managing the Value of Companies*, 2nd ed. New York: John Wiley & Sons, 1994.

Cornell, Bradford. *Corporate Valuation: Tools for Effective Appraisal and Decision Making*. New York: McGraw-Hill, 1993.

Damodaran, Aswath. *Damodaran on Valuation: Security Analysis for Investment and Corporate Finance*. New York: John Wiley & Sons, 1994.

_____. *Investment Valuation*. New York: John Wiley & Sons, 1996.

Ehrhardt, Michael C. *The Search for Value: Measuring the Company's Cost of Capital*. Boston: Harvard Business School Press, 1994.

Fishman, Jay E., Shannon P. Pratt, J. Clifford Griffith, and Mark Wells. *Guide to Business Valuations*, 7th ed. Fort Worth, TX: Practitioners Publishing Co., 1997 (updated annually).

Hull, J. *Options, Futures and Other Derivative Securities*. Englewood Cliffs, NJ: Prentice-Hall, 1993.

Ibbotson, Roger G., and Gary P. Brinson. *Global Investing: The Professional's Guide to the World Capital Markets*. New York: McGraw-Hill, 1993.

Mercer, Z. Christopher, *Quantifying Marketability Discounts—Developing and Supporting Marketability Discounts in the Appraisal of Closely Held Business Interests*, Memphis, TN: Peabody Publishing, LP, 1997.

Pratt, Shannon P., Robert F. Reilly, and Robert P. Schweihs. *Valuing a Business: The Analysis and Appraisal of Closely Held Companies*, 3d ed. Burr Ridge, IL: McGraw-Hill, 1996.

———. *Valuing Small Businesses and Professional Practices*, 3d ed. New York: McGraw-Hill, 1998.

Rachlin, Robert, and H. W. Allend Sweeny. *Handbook of Budgeting*, 3d ed. New York: John Wiley & Sons, 1993. See especially Chapter 11, "Determining the Cost of Capital," by Mike Kaufman.

Rapport, Alfred, *Creating Shareholder Value*, revised ed., New York: The Free Press, 1998.

Reilly, Frank K. *Investment Analysis and Portfolio Management*, 4th ed. Fort Worth, TX: Dryden Press, 1994.

Ross, Stephen A., Randolph W. Westerfield, and Jeffrey F. Jaffe. *Corporate Finance*, 4th ed. Burr Ridge, IL: McGraw-Hill, 1996.

Sharpe, William F., and G. J. Alexander. *Investments*, 4th ed. Englewood Cliffs, NJ: Prentice-Hall, 1989.

Williams, John Burr. *The Theory of Investment Value*. Cambridge, MA: Harvard University Press, 1938.

ARTICLES

Abrams, Jay B. "A Breakthrough in Calculating Reliable Discount Rates." *ASA Valuation* (August 1994): 8–24.

———. "The Right Tools Can Simplify Company Valuation." *Accounting Today* (November 6, 1995): 14, 35.

Annin, Michael. "Fama-French and Small Company Cost of Equity Calculations." *Business Valuation Review* (March 1997): 3–13.

———. "Using Ibbotson Associates' Data to Develop Minority Discount Rates." *CPA Expert* (winter 1997): 1–4.

Ashton, D. J. "The Cost of Equity Capital and a Generalization of the Dividend Growth Model." *Accounting & Business Research* (winter 1995): 3–17.

Baptiste, Laurent, Gregory Borges, and Gary Carr. "Utility Bond Ratings and the Cost of Capital." *Public Utilities Fortnightly* (October 27, 1988).

Bendixen, Christian L. "Improved Estimation of Equity Risk Premiums." *Business Valuation Review* (March 1994): 22–32.

Berk, Jonathan B. "Does Size Really Matter?" *Financial Analysts Journal* (September–October 1997): 12–18.

Black, Fischer. "Estimating Expected Return." *Financial Analysts Journal* (September–October 1993): 36–38.

Booth, Laurence, and Cleveland S. Patterson. "Estimating the Cost of Equity Capital of a Non-Traded Unique Canadian Entity: Reply." *Canadian Journal of Administrative Sciences* (June 1993): 122–133.

Botosan, Christine A. "Disclosure Level and the Cost of Equity Capital." *Accounting Review* (July 1997): 323–349.

Boudoukh, Jacob, Matthew Richardson, and Robert F. Whitelaw. "Nonlinearities in the Relation Between the Equity Risk Premium and the Term Structure." *Management Science* (March 1997): 371–385.

Burmeister, Edwin, Richard Roll, and Stephen A. Ross. "A Practitioner's Guide to Arbitrage Pricing Theory." In *A Practitioner's Guide to Factor Models*. Charlottesville, VA: Research Foundation of the Institute of Chartered Financial Analysts, 1994.

Carlton, Willard T., and Josef Lakonishok. "Risk and Return on Equity: The Use and Misuse of Historical Estimates." *Financial Analysts Journal* (January–February 1985): 38–47.

Chen, Nai-fi, Richard Roll, and Stephen A. Ross. "Economic Forces and the Stock Market: Testing the APT and Alternative Asset Pricing Theories." *UCLA Graduate School of Management Working Paper No. 20-83* (December 1983).

Clineball, John M., Douglas R. Kahl, and Jerry L. Stevens. "Time-Series Properties of the Equity Risk Premium." *Journal of Financial Research* (spring 1994): 105–116.

Clubb, Colin D. B., and Paul Doran. "On the Weighted Average Cost of Capital with Personal Taxes." *Accounting & Business Research* (winter 1992): 44–48.

Cornell, Bradford. "Estimating the Cost of Equity Capital." *Proceedings of the 27th Annual Wichita Program: Appraisal for Ad Valorem Taxation*, August 3–7, 1997. Wichita, KS: Wichita State University, 1997.

Cummins, J. David, and Joan Lamm-Tennant. "Capital Structure and the Cost of Equity Capital in the Property-Liability Insurance Industry." *Insurance: Mathematics & Economics* (December 1994): 187–201.

Dempsey, Mike. "The Cost of Equity Capital at the Corporate and Investor Levels: Allowing a Rational Expectations Model with Personal Taxations." *Journal of Business Finance & Accounting* (December 1996): 1319–1331.

Dickerson, Gregg. "Estimating the Cost of Equity or They Ripped Out My CAPM and Stomped That Sucker Flat." *Proceedings of the 27th Annual Wichita Program: Appraisal for Ad Valorem Taxation*, August 3–7, 1997, Wichita, Kansas.

Dilbeck, Harold R. "A Constant-Dollar Discount Rate for Closely Held Businesses Based on Risk Premiums from Five-Year Holding Periods." *Business Valuation Review* (March 1994): 11–18.

Durand, David. "Afterthoughts on a Controversy with MM, Plus New Thoughts on Growth and the Cost of Capital." *Financial Management* (summer 1989): 12–18.

Fama, Eugene, and Kenneth French. "Common Risk Factors in the Returns on Stocks and Bonds." *University of Chicago Working Paper No. 360* (November 1992).

Goldenberg, David H., and Ashok J. Robin. "The Arbitrage Pricing Theory and Cost-of-Capital Estimation: The Case of Electric Utilities." *Journal of Financial Research* (fall 1991): 181–196.

————. "The Cross Section of Expected Stock Returns." *Journal of Finance* 47 (1992): 427–465.

Good, Walter R. "Yes, Virginia, There Is a Risk Premium, But . . ." *Financial Analysts Journal* (January–February 1994): 11–12.

Grabowski, Roger, and David King. "New Evidence on Size Effects and Rates of Return," *Business Valuation Review* (September 1996): 103–115.

Greer, Willis R. "The Growth Rate Term in the Capitalization Model." *Business Valuation Review* (June 1996): 72–79.

Hanley, Frank J., and A. Gerald Harris. "Does Diversification Increase the Cost of Equity Capital?" *Public Utilities Fortnightly* (July 15, 1991): 26–30.

Hawkins, George B. "Critically Assessing a Business Valuation: Is the Capitalization Rate Used Reasonable?" *Internet: http://www.cris.com/ ~ banister/ caprates.htm* (1996): 1–6.

Honnold, Keith L. "The Link Between Discount Rates and Capitalization Rates: Revisited." *Appraisal Journal* (April 1990): 190–195.

Ibbotson, Roger G. "Equity Risk Premium: Where We Stand Today." *Proceedings of the Equity Risk Premium Conference*, University of Chicago, June 6, 1996. Chicago: Ibbotson Associates, 1996.

Jackson, Marcus. "The Gordon Growth Model and the Income Approach to Value." *Appraisal Journal* (January 1994): 124–128.

Joyce, Allyn A. "Why the Expected Rate of Return Is a Geometric Mean." *Business Valuation Review* (March 1996): 17–19.

Julius, J. Michael. "Market Returns in Rolling Multi-Year Holding Periods: An Alternative Interpretation of the Ibbotson Data." *Business Valuation Review* (June 1996): 57–71.

Kairys, Joseph P., Jr. "Predicting Sign Changes in the Equity Risk Premium Using Commercial Paper Rates." *Journal of Portfolio Management* (fall 1993): 41–51.

Kaplan, Paul D. "Why the Expected Rate of Return Is an Arithmetic Mean." *Business Valuation Review* (September 1995): 126–129.

Kenny, Thomas J. "Closely Held Corporation Valuation: Determining a Proper Discount Rate." *Business Valuation Review* (March 1992): 22–30.

Kihm, Steven G. "The Superiority of Spot Yields in Estimating Cost of Capital." *Public Utilities Fortnightly* (February 1, 1996): 42–45.

Kincheloe, Stephen C. "The Weighted Average Cost of Capital — The Correct Discount Rate." *Appraisal Journal* (January 1990): 88–95.

King, David W. "The Equity Risk Premium for Cost of Capital Studies: Alternatives to Ibbotson." *Business Valuation Review* (September 1994): 123–29.

_____. "Recent Evidence on Discount Rates." *Proceedings of the AICPA 1995 National Business Valuation Conference*, New Orleans, LA, December 1995, pp. 12-i–12-13. Available on *Business Valuation Update Online*.

Krueger, Mark K., and Charles M. Linke. "A Spanning Approach for Estimating Divisional Cost of Capital." *Financial Management* (spring 1994): 64–70.

Lally, Martin. "The Accuracy of CAPM Proxies for Estimating a Firm's Cost of Equity." *Accounting & Finance* (May 1995): 63–72.

Lavely, Joe, and Frank Bacon. "Risk and Rate of Return for Electric Utilities." *Public Utilities Fortnightly* (September 1, 1993): 18–20.

Levy, Moshe, and Haim Levy. "The Danger of Assuming Homogeneous Expectations." *Financial Analysts Journal* (May–June 1996): 65–70.

Lippitt, Jeffrey W., and Nicholas J. Mastriacchio. "Developing Capitalization Rates for Valuing a Business." *The CPA Journal* (November 1995): 24–28.

Mard, Michael J., and James S. Rigby. "New Research to Estimate Cost of Capital." *CPA Expert* (fall 1995): 9–12.

Maris, Brian A., and Fayez A. Elayan. "Capital Structure and the Cost of Capital for Untaxed Firms: The Case of REITs." *Journal of the American Real Estate & Urban Economics Association* (spring 1990): 22–39.

Mastriacchio, Nicholas J., and Jeffrey W. Lippitt. "A Comparison of the Earnings Capitalization and the Excess Earnings Models in the Valuation of Closely Held Businesses." *Journal of Small Business Management* (January 1996): 1–12.

Meyer, James E., Patrick Fitzgerald, and Mostafa Moini. "Loss of Business Profits, Risk, and the Appropriate Discount Rate." *Journal of Legal Economics* (winter 1994): 27–42.

Moyer, R. Charles, and Ajay Patel. "The Equity Market Risk Premium: A Critical Look at Alternative Ex Ante Estimates." *Proceedings of the Ibbotson Equity Risk Premium Conference*, University of Chicago, June 6, 1996. Chicago: Ibbotson Associates, 1996. Abstracted in *Shannon Pratt's Business Valuation Update* (August 1996): 1–2.

"New Studies Quantifying Size Premiums Offer Strong Cost of Capital Support." *Shannon Pratt's Business Valuation Update* (August 1997): 1, 3.

Paolo, Stanley B. S. "The Weighted Average Cost of Capital: A Caveat." *Engineering Economist* (winter 1992): 178–183.

Patterson, Cleveland S. "The Cost of Equity Capital of a Non-Traded Unique Entity: A Canadian Study." *Canadian Journal of Administrative Sciences* (June 1993): 115–121.

Pratt, Shannon P. "Evidence Suggests Equity Risk Premium Lower Than Conventional Wisdom Thinks." *Shannon Pratt's Business Valuation Update* (July 1996): 1–5.

_____. "Alternative Equity Risk Premium Measures Unstable; Lack Robust Predictive Power." *Shannon Pratt's Business Valuation Update* (August 1996): 1–2.

_____. "Building Better Betas Is Ibbotson's Answer to Beta Controversy." *Shannon Pratt's Business Valuation Update* (August 1997): 1–2.

Rigby, Jim, and Michael J. Mattson. "Capitalization and Discount Rates: Mathematically Related, but Conceptually Different." *CPA Expert* (fall 1996): 1–3.

Scott, M. F. G. "The Cost of Equity Capital and the Risk Premium on Equities." *Applied Financial Economics* (March 1992): 21–32.

Sharpe, William F. "Factor Models, CAPMs, and the ABT." *Journal of Portfolio Management* (fall 1984): 21–25.

_____. "Capital Asset Prices With and Without Negative Holdings." Nobel Lecture, December 1990. Stockholm: The Nobel Foundation, Royal Swedish Academy of Sciences, 1990.

Sliwoski, Leonard. "Capitalization Rates Developed Using the Ibbotson Associates Data: Should They Be Applied to Pretax or After Tax Earnings?" *Business Valuation Review* (March 1994): 8–10.

Suvas, Arto. "Cost of Equity Capital Redefined." *Quarterly Journal of Business & Economics* (spring 1992): 53–71.

Swad, Randy. "Discount and Capitalization Rates in Business Valuations." *CPA Journal* (October 1994): 40–46.

Thompson, Howard E., and Wing K. Wong. "On the Unavoidability of 'Unscientific' Judgment in Estimating the Cost of Capital." *Managerial & Decision Economics* (February 1991): 27–42.

Yamaguchi, Katsunari. "Estimating the Equity Risk Premium from Downside Probability." *Journal of Portfolio Management* (summer 1994): 17–27.

Workshops, Courses, and Conferences

Ibbotson Associates Workshops
  Basic Cost of Capital Workshop
  Advanced Cost of Capital Workshop
Annual Cost of Capital Conference
Courses by Professional Associations
  American Society of Appraisers
  American Institute of Certified Public Accountants
  Schedules and Other Conferences

IBBOTSON ASSOCIATES WORKSHOPS

Ibbotson Associates conducts two tutorial-type workshops on cost of capital, a basic cost of capital workshop and an advanced cost of capital workshop. Both are one-day sessions, and they are offered back-to-back several times a year at locations in major cities around the country. Information can be obtained by calling (800) 215-2494.

Basic Cost of Capital Workshop

Topics in the basic workshop include the following:

- What is the cost of capital?
- Capital asset pricing model
- Discounted cash flow model
- Arbitrage pricing theory
- Case studies
- Estimating cost of debt
- Weighted average cost of capital
- International cost of capital

Advanced Cost of Capital Workshop

Topics in the advanced workshop include the following:

- Effect of leverage on the cost of capital
- Cost of capital in regulation
- Qualitative cost of capital issues in an international or domestic setting
- Advanced issues relating to the Capital Asset Pricing Model (CAPM)
- Estimating beta
- Limitations of traditional betas
- Multifactor model approaches
- Building better betas

The workshop also sets forth a case example that involves estimating the cost of capital using advanced models.

ANNUAL COST OF CAPITAL CONFERENCE

Ibbotson Associates also sponsors a one-day cost of capital conference, held annually in Chicago in June. The conference is built on papers reflecting original research by practitioners and academicians around the country. For information call (800) 215-2494.

COURSES BY PROFESSIONAL ASSOCIATIONS

Both the American Society of Appraisers (ASA) and the American Institute of Certified Public Accountants (AICPA) offer certain courses with substantial content on cost of capital.

American Society of Appraisers

The income approach to valuation, including estimation and use of cost of capital, is a major part of the ASA's BV202: "Introduction to BV, Part Two." This is a three-day course, plus a half-day exam, offered about a dozen times a year at various cities around the country. For information call (800) ASA-VALU.

American Institute of Certified Public Accountants

The AICPA's basic course, NBV4: "The Income Approach and Asset-Based Approach to Valuation," is primarily on the income approach, including estimation and use of cost of capital. It also covers the excess earnings method. The AICPA's advanced course, ABV-ROR "Advanced Business Valuation-Rate of Return," is devoted to estimating cost of capital and applying it in business valuations. Both are one-day courses, offered frequently at many locations around the country. For information call (800)862-4272.

Schedules and Other Conferences

There often are sessions relating to cost of capital at conferences sponsored by various professional business appraisal organizations and other organizations that utilize the cost of capital.

All new offerings are described as they are announced in the monthly "Association News" or "Cost of Capital" department of *Shannon Pratt's Business Valuation Update*. Conference schedules are included in the monthly "Calendar Update" section.

Data Resources

IBBOTSON ASSOCIATES COST OF CAPITAL DATA

Stocks, Bonds, Bills, and Inflation. Published annually by Ibbotson Associates in April. Includes equity risk premium and size effect data. 1997 edition $99. We highly recommend that analysts using Ibbotson data for cost of capital have the current year's book and thoroughly understand the derivation of the numbers used. See the following note for ordering information.

Cost of Capital Quarterly. Yearbook published annually by Ibbotson Associates. Provides several measures of cost of equity capital by industry group, as well as valuation ratios such as price/earnings, price/book, and price/sales. Also provides industry betas, growth rates, and many other statistics. $395, or yearbook plus three quarterly updates $995. A sample page from the *Cost of Capital Quarterly 1997 Yearbook* is shown in Chapter 13. The *Cost of Capital Quarterly* is now also available on the Internet, priced on a per inquiry basis.

Ibbotson Beta Book. Published semiannually by Ibbotson Associates (February and August). Provides several versions of the Capital Asset Pricing Model (CAPM) betas, as well as Fama-French three-factor cost of equity estimates for each of more than 5,000 public companies. $1,250 for single issue, or $2,000 per year; $60 for reproduction of data, subject to written approval for each request. A sample extract from the *Beta Book* is included in Chapter 13.

The subject of Chapter 13 is the construction, interpretation, and use of these three data sources.

Note: These three resources are available from Ibbotson Associates, 225 North Michigan Avenue, Suite 700, Chicago, IL 60601; (800)215-2494.

BETAS

CompuServe, 5000 Arlington Centre Boulevard, P.O. Box 20212, Columbus, OH 43220; (800)848-8990.

Ibbotson Associates, 225 North Michigan Avenue, Suite 700, Chicago, IL 60601; (800)215-2494—*Beta Book*: Individual Company Betas; *Cost of Capital Quarterly:* Industry betas.

Merrill Lynch, Merrill Lynch Capital Markets, Global Securities Research & Economics Group, World Financial Center, North Tower, 19th Floor, New York, NY 10281-1320; (212)449-1069.

Standard & Poor's Corporation, 25 Broadway, New York, NY 10004, (212)208-8000—Standard & Poor's *Compustat* and *Standard & Poor's Stock Reports.*

Tradeline, IDD Information Services, 100 Fifth Avenue, Waltham, MA 02154; (617)890-7227.

Value Line Investment Survey, 220 East 42nd St., 6th Floor, New York, NY 10017; (212)907-1500.

Wiltshire Associates Inc., 1299 Ocean Avenue, 7th Floor, Santa Monica, CA 90401-1085; (310)451-3051.

EARNINGS FORECASTS AND RELATED DATA

The information offered by providers listed here goes well beyond just earnings forecasts, because the providers also compile varying but almost intimidatingly vast amounts of other data and opinions about stocks, industries, and markets that can be helpful in estimating cost of capital. Four of the services listed herein compile data from hundreds of brokerage house analysts and one, *Value Line*, develops its prognostications in-house.

(The use of earnings forecasts in estimating cost of capital by the discounted cash flow (DCF) method is the subject of Chapter 12.)

Value Line Investment Survey

Value Line employs a staff of some 100 independent professional security analysts. Its basic *Value Line Investment Survey* covers 1,700 stocks, and the *Value Line Investment Survey—Expanded Edition* covers an additional 1,800 stocks.

In addition to historical financial data and betas, Value Line forecasts revenues, cash flow, earnings, dividends, capital expenditures, book value, shares outstanding, income tax rates, net profit margins, capital structure ratios, returns on both total capital and equity, and a three-to-five-year target price range for the stock.

For historical research, the *Value Line Investment Survey* is available on microfiche from 1980 and the *Expanded Edition* from March 1995. This organization has several other print services, including *The Value Line Mutual Fund Survey, The Value Line No-Load Fund Advisor, The Value Line OTC Special Situations Service, The Value Line Options Survey,* and *The Value Line Convertibles Survey.*

Value Line also has an array of electronic publications, starting with *Value Line Investment Survey for Windows.* The software includes 200 searchable data fields, more than 50 chart and graph options, and more than 100 screening options. An expanded version includes data on more than 5,000 stocks. In addition, there are several other electronic products.

The surveys are also available through CompuServe, and Value Line has an On-line bulletin board service updated weekly for subscribers.

There is a Value Line Data File with fundamental data on more than 5,000 companies. It has annual data since 1955, quarterly since 1963, and full 10-Q data since 1985. It includes balance sheet and income data, risk measures, rates of return, and analytic ratios.

Value Line is at 220 East 42nd Street, New York, NY 10017; (800)634-3583 for print services, (800)284-7607 for electronic services.

First Call

First Call Corporation is a source of earnings estimates, research, and corporate information.

First Call Real Time Earnings Estimates (RTEE), has more than 200 data items, including current and previous analysts' earnings estimates, operating data, expected reporting dates, footnotes, and the FIRST CALL consensus estimate. RTEE covers more than 17,500 companies, updated from more than 500 brokerage firms worldwide.

Other services include current research from 200 brokerage firms, more than 320,000 full-text research reports (including charts, graphs, color, and formatting), a Recommendations Database, and a Fundamentals Database on more than 7,000 companies updated weekly with balance sheet and income items, pricing and valuation data, and some financial ratios.

First Call has consensus earnings estimates updated weekly for about 6,500 companies via America Online and on the web at www.firstcall.com/individual.

All First Call products are available via flexible delivery options. They can be accessed through a dedicated First Call terminal, a local area network (LAN), via other third-party services, or through FIRST CALL On Call®, a dial-up method using a standard personal computer and modem. RTEE data are also available in various hard copy reports and fax products.

First Call is headquartered in Boston; phone (800)448-2348.

I/B/E/S

I/B/E/S covers 6,000 U.S. companies and 12,000 companies in 47 additional countries. It provides earnings estimates, recommendations, stock charts, current summaries and history, and analyst directories. The U.S. estimates come from a little more than 3,000 analysts in about 230 firms. In addition to earnings per share (EPS), I/B/E/S forecasts include cash flow per share, dividends per share, and pretax profits.

I/B/E/S has a U.S. History database that covers more than 20 years of U.S. earnings estimates and results for more than 10,000 companies. Data items include annual EPS projections and actual results since January 1976, long-term (five-year) growth projections since 1981, and quarterly data since 1984. The database is combined with I/B/E/S Rewind Software compatible with Windows.

I/B/E/S data are distributed through nearly every major source of electronic financial information. Although they emphasize electronic distribution, some products including earnings estimates are also available in print versions.

This summary of I/B/E/S products has focused largely on domestic earnings forecast information, but I/B/E/S also has a staggering array of other financial information available, especially that of a global nature.

In addition, I/B/E/S has supported academic research on earnings estimates for many years and has published an annotated bibliography, edited by Lawrence D. Brown, with abstracts of more than 400 articles and reports on such research.

I/B/E/S is at 345 Hudson Street, New York, NY 10014; (800) GET IBES. Its home page is at http://www.ibes.com.

Standard & Poor's ACE (Analysts' Consensus Estimates)

Standard & Poor's offers its Analysts' Consensus Estimates (ACE) through its Compustat distribution system. It provides EPS and five-year growth estimates for more than 5,200 of the 9,700 companies on the Compustat database. The EPS estimates for each company also include mean, median, high, low, and standard deviation. The estimates come from more than 2,300 analysts in more than 200 brokerage firms.

The data can be accessed through S&P's PC Plus Windows-based software. The S&P ACE file is available electronically for loading to the subscriber's computer system or through several COMPUSTAT® vendors distributing the file electronically.

Standard & Poor's Compustat group is at 7400 South Alton Court, Englewood, CO 80112; (800)525-8640.

Zacks Investment Research, Inc.

Zacks offers three quarterly print publications, *Zacks Earnings Forecaster, Zacks EPS Calendar,* and *Zacks Profit Guide.* They cover a total of just over 6,000 companies. Zacks material is also distributed electronically through several vendors.

Zacks is at 155 N. Wacker Drive, Chicago, IL 60606; (800)767-3771.

ARBITRAGE PRICING MODEL DATA

Two firms offer data to implement the Arbitrage Pricing Model (APT) cost of capital estimation.

The Alcar Group

Alcar offers APT!, updated quarterly or annually on disk.

APT offers a series of approaches for estimating the cost of debt and equity for both private and an estimated 9,000 public firms. A peer group performance comparison tool is included to allow you to analyze stock market returns over the previous quarter, year, or five years, and review key financial ratios.

The Alcar Group is at 5215 Old Orchard Road, Skokie, IL 60077; (888)802-5227.

BIRR Portfolio Analysis, Inc.

BIRR has a product called *BIRR Risks and Returns Analyzer®.* BIRR is an acronym for Burmeister (Ed), Ibbotson (Roger), Roll (Richard), and Ross (Stephen).

It provides APT multiregression factor inputs for companies and industries for five macroeconomic risk factors: confidence risk, time horizon risk, inflation risk, business cycle risk, and market timing risk. (Each of these factors is described in Exhibit 14-1 in the chapter on the Arbitrage Pricing Model.)

BIRR is at 2200 West Main Street, Suite 210, Durham, NC 27705; (919)687-7053. BIRR's homepage address is http://www.birr.com.

PUBLICLY TRADED STOCK DATA

Electronic Data Gathering and Retrieval (EDGAR) Service provides access to SEC filings for more than 15,000 companies through the Securities and Exchange Commission Internet home page: http://www.sec.gov/cgi-gin/srch-edgar, or the New York University Stern School of Business Internet home page: http://www.edgar.stern.nyu.edu. There is no charge for access through these channels.

Freeware that can be used to reformat EDGAR data to a more usable layout is available from these two sources, as well as from Business Valuation Resources, http://www.transport.com/~shannonp.

Moody's Investors Service provides a wide variety of publications on publicly traded companies, including *Moody's Industrial Manual, Moody's Bank & Financial Manual, Moody's OTC Industrial Manual, Moody's OTC Unlisted Manual, Moody's Public Utilities Manual, Moody's Transportation Manual, Moody's Company Data,* and *Moody's Industry Review.* These publications are available from Financial Information Services, 99 Church Street, New York, NY 10007; (800)342-5647.

Standard & Poor's Corporation provides a wide variety of publications, both print and electronic, on publicly traded companies, including *Compustat, Standard & Poor's Corporation Records, Standard & Poor's Industry Reports, Standard & Poor's Industry Survey, Standard & Poor's Stock Guide, Standard & Poor's Stock Reports, Standard & Poor's Earnings Guide, Standard & Poor's Analysts' Handbook,* and *Standard & Poor's Execucomp.* These are all available from Standard & Poor's Corporation, 7400 South Alton Court, Englewood, CO 80112; (800)525-8640.

LARGER COMPANY M&A TRANSACTION SOURCES

Mergerstat Review, published annually in March, with quarterly update reports, tracks mergers and acquisitions involving U.S. companies, including privately held, publicly traded, and cross-border transactions. Also tracks unit divestitures, management buy-outs, and certain asset sales. Includes industry analysis by size premium, and transaction multiples. Provides trend analysis by seller, type, deal size, and industry. Offers 25 years of summary merger and acquisition (M&A) statistics, including average premium and price/earnings ratio. For the most current and complete data, Mergerstat statistics are also available via Bloomberg and Lexis-Nexis. *Mergerstat* is available from Houlihan Lokey Howard & Zukin, 1930 Century Park West, Los Angeles, CA 90067; (800)455-8871. It is also available on the Internet at www.mergerstat@xls.com. Call Mergerstat to get a user I.D. and password.

Mergerstat Transaction Roster, published annually in March, tracks mergers and acquisitions involving U.S. companies, including privately held, publicly traded, and cross-border transaction synopses, Standard Industrial Classification (SIC) codes, announce and close dates, and deal values for thousands of transactions. Deals are sorted by target industry group. This publication is available from Houlihan Lokey Howard & Zukin, 1930 Century Park West, Los Angeles, CA 90067; (800)455-8871.

Mergerstat Health Care Review, published quarterly, tracks mergers and acquisitions involving U.S. companies in the health care industry, including privately held, publicly traded, and cross-border transactions. Also tracks unit divestitures, management buy-outs, and certain asset sales. Provides transaction synopses, SIC codes, announce and close dates, deal values, company financials, and sector overviews. Deals are sorted by seller into industry subgroups. This publication is available from Houlihan Lokey Howard & Zukin, 1930 Century Park West, Los Angeles, CA 90067; (800)455-8871.

Mergers & Acquisitions Journal, published bimonthly, covers terminology and techniques in the merger and acquisition field, analyzes specific transactions, and provides data on merger activity. Available from Investment Dealers' Digest, Two World Trade Center, 18th floor, New York, NY 10048; (212)227-1200.

Mergers & Acquisitions in Canada, published monthly, includes M&A data and analysis. Available from M&A Publishing, One First Canada Place, 9th floor, P.O. Box 116, Toronto, Ontario, Canada M5X 1A4; (416)362-0020.

Mergers & Acquisitions Sourcebook, published annually, is the most comprehensive source of M&A information (600 pages) available anywhere, with coverage of mergers and acquisitions, joint ventures, initial public offerings (IPOs), restructurings, and strategic minority stakes. Details on more than 3,000 transactions, including purchase price and three-year financial data on seller and buyer organized by seller's SIC code, special sections on leveraged buyouts (LBOs), buy-backs, and terminations; M&A and divestiture activity of company divisions, foreign M&A activity, and analysis of industry trends. This publication is available from Quality Services Company, 5290 Overpass Road, Suite 126, Santa Barbara, CA 93111; (800)266-3888.

Mergers & Acquisitions Quarterly is specifically designed to provide M&A sourcebook data on a quarterly basis. It offers purchase price data and ratios to seller's sales, earnings, and net worth data on more than 1,000 corporate growth transactions in all industries. In addition, it has detailed charts and graphs, book reviews, and M&A features not published elsewhere. This publication is available from Quality Services Company, 5290 Overpass Road, Suite 126, Santa Barbara, CA 93111; (800)266-3888.

The Weekly Corporate Growth Report, 50 issues per year, is a newsletter on corporate growth in the United States, with fast-breaking news of the M&A market, including acquisitions, mergers, divestitures, spin-offs, terminations, management buy-outs, restructurings, and methods of increasing shareholder value. This publication is available from Quality Services Company, 5290 Overpass Road, Suite 126, Santa Barbara, CA 93111; (800)266-3888.

The Merger Yearbook, published annually in March, provides information on tens of thousands of announced and completed deals, including total purchase price, price paid per share, form of payment, division/unit purchased, parent company, acquiring company, type of transaction, SIC number and industry section of target company and acquirer, price to earnings ratio, plus dozens of charts covering transactions by dollar amount and industry. This publication is available from Securities Data Publishing, 40 West 57th Street, New York, NY 10019; (800)455-5844.

PRIVATE COMPANY SALE TRANSACTION DATA

Done Deals Data, published quarterly in disk format. Data on more than 1,000 transactions with purchase prices from $1 million to $100 million, approximately 50% under $10 million. Available from World M&A Network, 717 D Street N.W., Washington, DC 20004; (800)809-0666.

Pratt's Stats, published quarterly—subscribers receive both print format and disk. Initial issue (September 1997) provided data on private company transactions, with detailed balance sheet, income statement, transaction terms, purchase price allocation, noncompete and employment agreement terms, and other data. Available from Business Valuation Resources, 4475 S.W. Scholls Ferry Road, Suite 101, Portland, OR 97225; (888) BUS-VALU.

PARTNERSHIP TRANSACTION DATA

Partnership Spectrum, a bimonthly, tracks the partnership industry, focusing especially on (but not limited to) real estate partnerships. The May-June issue each year is a compilation of empirical data concerning discounts on the net asset value at which partnerships trade in the informal resale market. Other issues are valuable to the partnership industry; however, they are not predominately data compilations. Detailed reports on approximately 90% of the limited partnerships included in the May-June issue are available for $120. Information for each partnership includes specific property holdings, cash distribution history, debt levels, key operating statistics, and more. Available from Partnership Profiles, Inc., P.O. Box 7938, Dallas, TX 75209; (800)634-4614.

PERIODICALS

Shannon Pratt's Business Valuation Update has a section titled "Cost of Capital" with 20 current debt and equity cost of capital indicators included in each monthly edition. The department often includes articles on new cost of capital developments. Subscription also includes the annually updated *Where to Find It—Business Valuation Data Directory*. Published by Business Valuation Resources, 4475 S.W. Scholls Ferry Road, Suite 101, Portland, OR 97225; (888) BUS-VALU.

Business Valuations Update Online includes all issues of *Shannon Pratt's Business Valuation Update*, plus full texts of professional conference presentation papers, court case opinions on business valuation issues, and Internal Revenue Service references on business valuation issues. Annual subscriptions are available to the online service only address http or at a discount price to *Shannon Pratt's Business Valuation Update* subscribers. Business Valuation Resources, 4475 S.W. Scholls Ferry Road, Suite 101, Portland, OR 97225; (888) BUS-VALU.

Developing Cost of Capital (Capitalization Rates and Discount Rates) Using ValuSource PRO Software

Z. Christopher Mercer, ASA, CFA

INTRODUCTION

Wiley ValuSource PRO was introduced in its present form in late 1996. Shannon Pratt asked me, as its developer, to prepare a short appendix regarding the development of cost of capital estimates, which could be helpful to users of the ValuSource PRO software. Although this appendix will discuss cost of capital in the context of the ValuSource PRO software, it may also be of broader interest for appraisers generally. The discussion is framed in the context of the development of capitalization rates in the "Appraisal" section of the software package.

COST OF CAPITAL, DISCOUNT RATES, AND CAPITALIZATION RATES

The term *cost of capital* is foreign to some business appraisers and many users of valuation reports who may have entered the business appraisal field via a route other than traditional finance. As indicated in the introduction of this book:

> The cost of capital estimate is the essential link that enables us to convert a stream of expected income into an estimate of present value.

In the *Business Valuation Standards* of the American Society of Appraisers, we find two similar definitions:[1]

> *Discount Rate.* A rate of return used to convert a monetary sum, payable or receivable in the future, into present value.
>
> *Capitalization Rate.* Any divisor (usually expressed as a percentage) that is used to convert income into value.

In the context of the typical business appraisal, appraisers are developing the cost of (equity) capital when they develop a capitalization rate (or factor) to *capitalize* an earnings estimate by converting an expected future stream of income into present value. As a result, the Wiley ValuSource PRO software provides a framework to develop discount rates and capitalization rates. That framework is based on the capital asset pricing model (CAPM) and, specifically, on what I have called the *adjusted capital asset pricing model* (ACAPM).[2]

This book has discussed several sources of cost of capital data:

- Ibbotson Associates publishes the *SBBI Yearbook* annually, as well as other publications, including *Cost of Capital Quarterly* and *Beta Book*.[3]
- Roger Grabowski and David King of Price Waterhouse have also done interesting work recently on the impact of size on historical rates of return in the public stock markets. This work has been published partially in *Business Valuation Review* and has been discussed in *Shannon Pratt's Business Valuation Update*.[4]
- Others, like Michael Julius, have analyzed the Ibbotson historical data to address the question of whether the arithmetic mean, the geometric mean, or some other statistic should be used as the basis for equity premiums.[5]

There is nothing magic about any of these studies. All are attempting to measure the historical returns generated in the public stock markets for differing groups of stocks. The *SBBI Yearbook*, portions of the *Cost of Capital Quarterly*, and the Grabowski/King studies have focused on market returns and stratified the public markets by various measures of size (sales, market capitalization, etc.). The major portion of the *Cost of Capital Quarterly* focuses on stratifying the public markets by industry (Standard Industrial Classification (SIC) codes).

Given the background of this book, we can focus briefly on the capital asset pricing model to derive some guidance on how to develop capitalization rates (i.e., cost of capital) using the Wiley ValuSource PRO software.

DATA FOR THE (ADJUSTED) CAPITAL ASSET PRICING MODEL

A number of chapters have developed the so-called *build-up method* for developing capitalization rates and the capital asset pricing model (CAPM). In my opinion, the basic build-up method is simply a variation of CAPM under the assumption that beta is equal to 1.0. In the absence of market evidence to the contrary, business appraisers sometimes assume that the appropriate assumption for beta is 1.0, or the expected volatility of the broader stock market, which forms the first building block of the "build-up" of an equity discount rate and reflects the long-run historical premium in returns of the broader market over long-term Treasuries. In years prior to 1994, this premium was referred to in the Ibbotson Associates *SBBI Yearbooks* as the *common stock premium*. Since then, it has been renamed the *large company stock premium*. Too often, some appraisers and writers try to make an arbitrary distinction between the build-up method and the CAPM. But, clearly, the former is a special instance of the latter with beta equal to 1.0.

So first of all, users of ValuSource PRO have to be aware of this assumption each time a decision is made to use the build-up method.

Many business appraisers and other financial analysts have used the historical premium return analysis presented in each year's *SBBI Yearbook*. In recent years, that information has come from Table 2.1 in each *SBBI Yearbook*. Appraisers have typically used the current year's analysis (e.g., the *SBBI 1997 Yearbook*, which covers Ibbotson's analysis of historical return information from 1926 to 1996). Historical appraisals typically reference the cumulative premium data from the then-current *SBBI Yearbook*. The actual historical geometric and arithmetic mean returns for the cumulative periods are provided for large company stocks, small company stocks, and long-term government bonds, and the actual premiums are calculated:

- The large company stock premium returns in excess of long-term government bond returns
- The small company stock premium returns in excess of large stock returns
- The small company stock premium in excess of long-term government bond returns

The current numbers for the appropriate premiums are often used by appraisers in building up discount rates. Users selecting the capital asset pricing model in ValuSource PRO find a screen providing the various components of a capitalization rate (or factor). An illustrative example is shown in Exhibit D.1. The figures for the arithmetic mean and the geometric mean returns come from the *SBBI 1997 Yearbook*, and the figures labeled "Julius Multi-Year Holding Period Analysis" are derived from the article referenced in Note 5.

The CAPM components above are called ACAPM components for the adjusted capital asset pricing model. I have referred to this model as the *adjusted* CAPM because the basic CAPM stops at the net cash flow or net earnings discount rate and, in the process, assumes that company-specific (nonsystematic) factors are "diversified away." The ACAPM incorporates company-specific risk factors.

Any user of ValuSource PRO should recognize from Exhibit D.1 that neither software nor any single publication will enable the appraiser to develop an appropriate net equity discount rate or capitalization rate without the exercise of considerable judgment and the review and understanding of numerous sources of direct or indirect market evidence. With all assumptions remaining the same in Exhibit D.1 except the selection of the arithmetic mean or geometric mean returns, a spread in implied base capitalization rates (CR) is developed, ranging from 12.0% to 17.0%. To put this in perspective by converting these capitalization rates into price/earnings multiples (P/E = 1/CR), the arithmetic mean selection developed a net earnings multiple of 5.88× and the geometric mean selection developed a multiple of 8.33×, or some 42% greater. The use of the Julius multiyear holding period analysis produces a price/earnings multiple of 6.67×, which is higher than that developed using the arithmetic mean, but closer to that result than to the multiple derived using the geometric mean.

My best advice to any appraiser, whether using ValuSource PRO or not, is to be very clear at each of the numbered decision points (noted in Exhibit D.1) as to what market data are being used and why. Furthermore, appraisers should be clear about the assumptions made regarding the lettered decision points in Exhibit D.1, as well.

Appraisers referring to the *SBBI Yearbooks* will develop components for the common stock equity premium, the appropriate beta, if applicable, and the small stock premium. Those referring to the Grabowski/King analyses may have to calculate the implied size premium in relationship to the base equity premiums initially used. The point is that at numbered decision 4, the net size adjustment is developed by subtracting a total premium over Treasuries implied by Grabowski/King from the common stock premium used in the analysis. In addition, appraisers may make a judgmental adjustment for size in addition to any developed by Ibbotson, Grabowski/King, or anyone else — if their subject companies are substantially smaller than the public companies used as reference points.

In the ValuSource PRO software, size premiums are best considered in the "Risk Adjustment for Size" line. Appraisers using other than a so-called standard small stock premium from Ibbotson should explain in their reports exactly how their size premiums were developed.

Note that some appraisers have considered very small size as a company-specific risk factor. There is nothing conceptually wrong with this treatment; however, before doing so, they should be familiar with current research on size premiums or run the possible risk of being viewed as arbitrary.

The *company-specific premium* is an integral part of the development of the cost of equity capital. A breakout of several possible factors to consider in developing this premium is provided in the software. There is no market evidence to help the appraiser deal with most of these factors, and appraiser judgment must be carefully exercised.[6]

ValuSource PRO provides a line called "Cash Flow to Earnings Conversion." Shannon Pratt has indicated that he believes that the CAPM (or ACAPM) discount rate is applicable to the net cash flow of a business enterprise. I have suggested that it may be applicable to the net income of the enterprise. In *Valuing Financial Institutions,* I prepared an analysis indicating a methodology for developing a conversion of a net cash flow discount rate to a net income discount rate, and suggested that for many private companies the differential might not be large.[7] Certainly in the

Exhibit D.1 Calculating Build-up or CAPM Discount and Capitalization Rates

| | | Appraiser Decision Letters | | |
| | | A | B | C |
Appraiser Decision Numbers	ACAPM Component	SBBI 1997 Yearbook Arithmetic Mean	SBBI 1997 Yearbook Geometric Mean	Julius Multi-Year Holding Period Analysis
1	**Risk-free rate of return**	6.5%	6.5%	6.5%
2	**Equity risk premium**	7.3%	5.6%	6.5%
3	**× Industry beta**	1.0	1.0	1.0
Calc	= Beta-adjusted common stock premium	7.3%	5.6%	6.5%
4	**+ Risk adjustment for size**	5.0%	1.9%	3.5%
Calc	= Base equity discount rate	18.8%	14.0%	16.5%
5	*+ Company-specific premium*	3.0%	3.0%	3.0%
6	*+ Cash flow to earnings conversion*	0.0%	0.0%	0.0%
Calc	= Net earnings discount rate *(cost of equity capital)*	21.8%	17.0%	19.5%
7	*− Sustainable growth*	5.0%	5.0%	5.0%
Calc	= Base capitalization rate for next year*	17.0%	12.0%	15.0%
Calc	Base capitalization rate for current year*	16.2%	11.4%	14.3%
Calc	Base capitalization factor*	5.88	8.33	6.67

* User Options.
User selects desired factor
Boldfaced items require market evidence and appraiser judgments.
Italicized items require specific appraiser judgments.
Calc = calculated by software.
Source: From *Business Valuation Review*, June 1996, pp. 57–71. Article by Michael J. Julius, "Market Returns in Rolling Multi-Year Holding Periods, An Alternative Interpretation of the Ibbotson Data." Reprinted with permission.

very long run, the net cash flow of an enterprise will approximate its net income. In any event, appraisers should be clear in their own minds what they believe on this issue and why, and then develop their remaining judgments consistently from this vantage point.

At this point, we have conceptually developed a net cash flow or net earnings discount rate. This discount rate is the *equity cost of capital*. This discount rate would be applicable to projected net earnings in a discounted future earnings analysis (or, properly styled or adjusted, to the projected net cash flows in a discounted cash flow analysis).

However, many appraisals are prepared without specific projections. To develop a single-period capitalization rate, expected future earnings growth must be subtracted from the discount rate (for all the reasons explained earlier in this book).

THE EARNINGS STREAM TO BE CAPITALIZED

It should be fairly obvious that the discount rate or capitalization rate applied to any measure of earnings should be appropriately developed for that measure, whether net income, pretax income, debt-free pretax income, or another level of the income statement. The CAPM discount rate discussed here and elsewhere in this book is generally considered as applicable to either the net income or the net cash flow of a business enterprise. In application in actual appraisals, however, a legitimate question can be raised: To what net income or cash flow does the discount rate apply?

There has been considerable discussion in recent years regarding whether discounted future earnings (DFE) or discounted cash flow (DCF) valuation methods develop minority interest or controlling interest indications of value. A detailed discussion of the concept of levels of value is beyond the scope of this appendix; however, the question deserves some treatment.[8]

The two major trains of thought are as follows:

- Since the CAPM discount rate is applicable to the net income of a business enterprise, and since this discount rate is generally believed to develop value indications at the marketable minority interest level of value, the value indication from a discounted future cash flow or earnings valuation is a minority interest (marketable) conclusion. As a result, it would be proper to apply a control premium to this value indication if a controlling interest conclusion is called for in the appraisal.[9]
- Since appraisers make so-called controlling interest adjustments in developing their projections for DFE or DCF methods, the income stream is said to be control-adjusted, and the resulting valuation indication is at the controlling interest level.[10]

According to the former argument, buyers of companies might appear to have different discount rates than hypothetical investors at the marketable minority interest level. According to the latter argument, there is only one discount rate, and it is the same for appraisers at the marketable minority interest level and for acquirers at the controlling interest level.

According to the former argument, one would add an appropriate control premium to a DCF/DFE valuation method to arrive at a controlling interest level of value. According to the latter argument, a control premium might not be appropriate.

As is often the case, the truth may lie somewhere in between. To begin to resolve the controversy, we can divide the so-called controlling interest adjustments into their two primary component parts:

- *Normalizing Adjustments.* In developing capitalization rates using data from Ibbotson Associates, Grabowski/King, or any other source of market return information, there are implicit "market baskets" of publicly traded companies that constitute the basis of comparison with subject private companies. We know that the typical public company in a group is larger than many of the closely held businesses that appraisers value, and this size differential gives rise to premium required returns. We also know, generally, that public companies must pay competitive salaries to senior management, or else run the risk of being penalized in their market capitalizations. Likewise, related party transactions, to the extent they exist, must be conducted on an arm's-length basis, and nonworking members of the president's family are not normally found on the payroll of public companies. The point is that a significant portion of the controlling interest adjustments made in many appraisals are, in reality, adjustments to normalize the earnings of the subject company with the group of public companies with which it is implicitly being compared.

- *Acquirer's Potential Economic (Control) Adjustments.* Logically, an acquirer would make the normalizing adjustments noted earlier in the context of an acquisition of a private company. Clearly, an owner is not going to be paid for the capitalized value of excess salary and then continue to receive that salary. However, acquirers look at acquisition prospects differently than public market securities investors. Acquirers often have an opportunity to generate economic benefits from acquisitions that go beyond the normalizing adjustments noted earlier. For example, an acquirer in a similar business may be able to generate significant economies by stripping out general and administrative or selling expenses from the acquired entity. Alternatively, an acquirer may be able to generate economic benefits that are not readily visible on a private company's financial statements. For example, an acquirer may be willing to pay a premium for a business because of planned increased sales of existing products through the acquired company's sales force. These types of potential economic benefits (adjustments) may generate the willingness to pay an apparent control premium for a company that otherwise might not be immediately justified.

The example in Exhibit D.2 illustrates a delineation of potential valuation adjustments into those categorized as normalizing (Line 2) and those noted as economic (control) adjustments made by a potential acquirer of control (Line 3).

In most appraisals, the adjustments made normally fall into the category of *normalizing adjustments*. The analysis in Exhibit D.2 indicates that it is not at all inconsistent to suggest that the discount rates are the same for the potential buyer of a company as for the hypothetical willing buyer of a marketable minority interest. (See Line 7, where the same price/earnings multiple and, implicitly, discount rate, is applied to differing perceptions of a subject company's earnings.) This would suggest, however, that the economic benefits of control have not yet been factored into the appraisal process at the marketable minority interest level, and that a control premium may be necessary to reach a proper conclusion of value on a controlling interest basis (see Line 10, where the implied control premium is 20%).

In the alternative, the appraiser would estimate these economic benefits specifically and capitalize them to develop a controlling interest conclusion. In the example in Exhibit D.2, the control premium provides a vehicle to estimate the magnitude of the benefit of potential economic (control) adjustments and to reflect them in the appraisal.

For users of ValuSource PRO software, the message is clear. Be sure to understand what adjustments have been made in an appraisal. To the extent that the normalizing adjustments of an appraisal do not consider the potential economic benefits available to potential acquirers, a judgmental control premium may be required. The software makes this option readily available. That control premium, however, should be justified by a separate analysis or discussion of the potential factors leading to the apparent additional value attributable to control relative to the initially derived discount rate.

APPLICATION OF MARKETABILITY DISCOUNTS

Earlier in this book a suggestion was made that the marketability discount can be considered as a premium to the equity cost of capital. Conceptually, this is correct; however, such a consideration would make the implicit assumption that the cash flows from which the initial marketable minority interest value indication is derived are the same as available to the prospective holder of nonmarketable minority interests of private companies, which is clearly not the case in many closely held businesses.

Exhibit D.2   Calculating Indicated Values

Line	Item	As Reported	Appraiser's Normalizing Adjustments	Acquirer's Economic (Control) Adjustments
1	Reported pretax earnings	$1,000	$1,000	$1,000
2	+ Normalizing adjustment (owner compensation)	—	200	200
3	+ Acquirer's economic adjustments	—	—	240
4	= Adjusted pretax income	1,000	1,200	1,440
5	– Taxes @ assumed rate of 40%	(400)	(480)	(576)
6	= Adjusted net income	600	720	864
7	× Net income capitalization factor (1/cap rate=P/E)		7	7
8	= Indicated value		$4,802	$5,763
9	Indicated level of value		Marketable, minority	Control
10	Implied control premium over marketable minority value indication			20%
11	Apparent net multiple without economic adjustments			8

For this reason, among others, we have developed a Quantitative Marketability Discount Model, which develops appropriate marketability discounts based on the facts and circumstances facing hypothetical willing buyers of a company's minority interests.[11] Unless the expected cash flows available to a hypothetical minority investor are the same as those that formed the basis for developing the marketable minority interest value indication (a very rare circumstance), it is preferable to develop a marketability discount analysis separate from the initial development of the equity cost of capital (i.e., the capitalization factor). There is no separate analysis section in ValuSource PRO for this development at the present time.

Notes

1. *ASA Business Valuation Standards and Portions of Uniform Standards of Professional Appraisal Practice (USPAP)* (Herndon, VA: American Society of Appraisers, revised January 1994), 18.
2. Z. Christopher Mercer, "The Adjusted Capital Asset Pricing Model for Developing Capitalization Rates: An Extension of Previous 'Build-Up' Methodologies Based upon the Capital Asset Pricing Model," *Business Valuation Review* (December 1989): 147–156. Also see Chapter 13 in Z. Christopher Mercer, *Valuing Financial Institutions* (Burr Ridge, IL: McGraw-Hill, 1992), and Exhibit 8.2 in Z. Christopher Mercer, *Quantifying Marketability Discounts* (Memphis, TN: Peabody Publishing, 1997). *Quantifying Marketability Discounts* is available from the publisher at 800-769-0967.
3. *Stocks, Bonds, Bills and Inflation*, published annually; *Cost of Capital Quarterly*, published annually with quarterly updates; and *Beta Book*, published semi-annually. Chicago: Ibbotson Associates.
4. Roger Grabowski and David King, "Size Effects and Equity Returns, An Update," *Business Valuation Review*, March 1997, pp. 22–26. Discussed in Shannon Pratt's *Business Valuation Update*, August 1997, p. 1.
5. J. Michael Julius, "Market Returns in Rolling Multi-Year Holding Periods: An Alternative Interpretation of the Ibbotson Data," *Business Valuation Review* (June 1996): 57–71. There has been something of a controversy over whether the more appropriate average statistic from Ibbotson's *SBBI Yearbook* is the arithmetic mean or the geometric mean. At its simplest, the Julius analysis recognizes that the arithmetic mean of the Ibbotson return data from 1926 to 1997 is the arithmetic mean (average) of 71 annual returns. The annual returns are the geometric means of the annual observations. So the arithmetic mean advanced by Ibbotson Associates is the arithmetic mean of 71 annual (geometric) returns, reflecting 71 one-year holding periods. The geometric mean advanced by others is simply the compound growth rate in total return from 1926 to 1997, or the geometric mean return for the period, which represents a single, 71-year holding period. From a practical viewpoint, neither extreme makes logical sense (and I am oversimplifying complex logical arguments to be practical). The Julius analysis examines the arithmetic mean of geometric returns for multiyear holding periods that have occurred from 1926 to 1995 (in the cited article). The effect of this averaging process over many multiyear holding periods is to develop a series of average returns for more reasonable holding periods such as, say five or ten years. The result, incidentally, is effectively to split the difference between the arithmetic mean and the geometric mean as calculated by Ibbotson. We have used this

analysis for years as a basis for determining the appropriate common stock and small stock premium return measures.

6. As the appraisal profession matures, various appraisers are creatively examining the public stock markets for guidance on fundamental issues like developing company-specific risk premiums. A recent article typifies these efforts: Steven Bolten and Yan Wang, "The Impact of Management Depth on Valuation," *Business Valuation Review* (September 1997): 143–146.

7. See Mercer, *Valuing Financial Institutions*, Exhibit 14.7, pp. 262–266.

8. See Mercer, *Quantifying Marketability Discounts,* Chapter 1.

9. See *Estate of Jung* for a discussion of this argument, 101 T.C. 412 (1993).

10. See Chapter 13 of this book, written by Michael Annin and Dominic Falaschetti of Ibbotson Associates, for elements of this argument.

11. See Mercer, *Quantifying Marketability Discounts*, Chapter 8.

Index